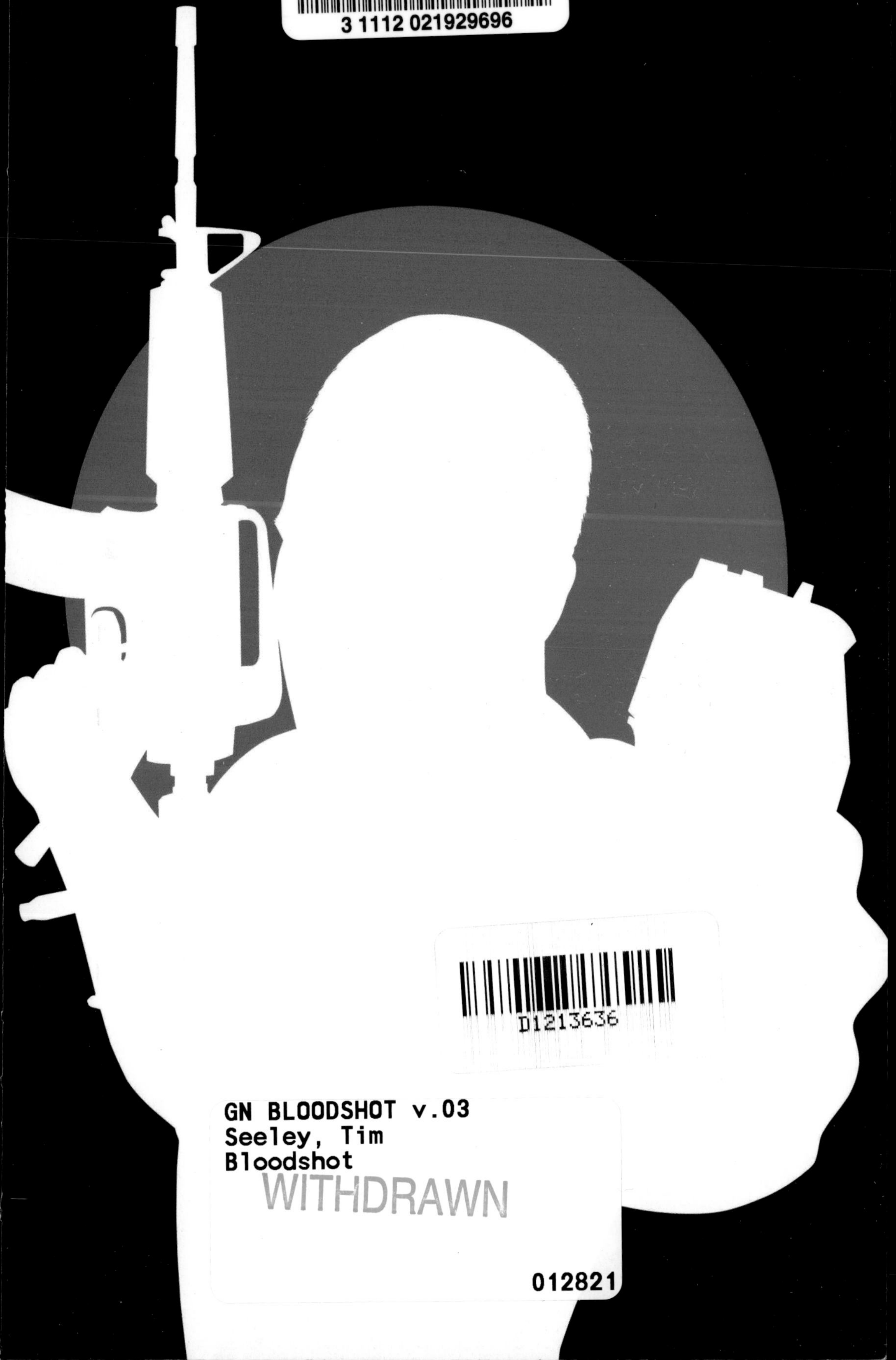

BLOODSHOT

WRITER
TIM SEELEY

ARTISTS
MARC LAMING
JASON MASTERS
PEDRO ANDREO

COLORIST
ANDREW DALHOUSE

LETTERER
DAVE SHARPE

COVERS BY
ROBERTO DE LA TORRE
TYLER KIRKHAM

ASSISTANT EDITOR
DREW BAUMGARTNER

SENIOR EDITOR
LYSA HAWKINS

GALLERY
BRETT BOOTH
CRYSSY CHEUNG
ADELSO CORONA
ANDREW DALHOUSE
JUAN DOE
MARC LAMING
JASON MASTERS
KAEL NGU
FRANCIS PORTELA
NIK VIRELLA

COLLECTION COVER ART
KAEL NGU

COLLECTION BACK COVER ART
TYLER KIRKHAM

COLLECTION FRONT ART
CRYSSY CHEUNG
TYLER KIRKHAM
KAEL NGU

COLLECTION EDITOR
IVAN COHEN

COLLECTION DESIGNER
STEVE BLACKWELL

VALIANT®

DAN MINTZ Chairman **FRED PIERCE** Publisher **WALTER BLACK** VP Operations **MATTHEW KLEIN** VP Sales & Marketing
TRAVIS ESCARFULLERY Director of Design & Production **PETER STERN** Director of International Publishing & Merchandising
LYSA HAWKINS, HEATHER ANTOS & DAVID WOHL Senior Editors **JEFF WALKER** Production & Design Manager
JOHN PETRIE Senior Manager - Sales & Merchandising **DANIELLE WARD** Sales Manager **GREGG KATZMAN** Marketing & Publicity Manager

RUSS BROWN President, Consumer Products, Promotions & Ad Sales

Bloodshot® Book Three. Published by Valiant Entertainment LLC. Office of Publication: 350 Seventh Avenue, New York, NY 10001. Compilation copyright © 2020 Valiant Entertainment LLC. All rights reserved. Contains materials originally published in single magazine form as Bloodshot #0 and Bloodshot #7-9. Copyright © 2020 Valiant Entertainment LLC. All rights reserved. All characters, their distinctive likeness and related indicia featured in this publication are trademarks of Valiant Entertainment LLC. The stories, characters, and incidents featured in this publication are entirely fictional. Valiant Entertainment does not read or accept unsolicited submissions of ideas, stories, or artwork. Printed in Korea. First Printing. ISBN: 9781682153666.

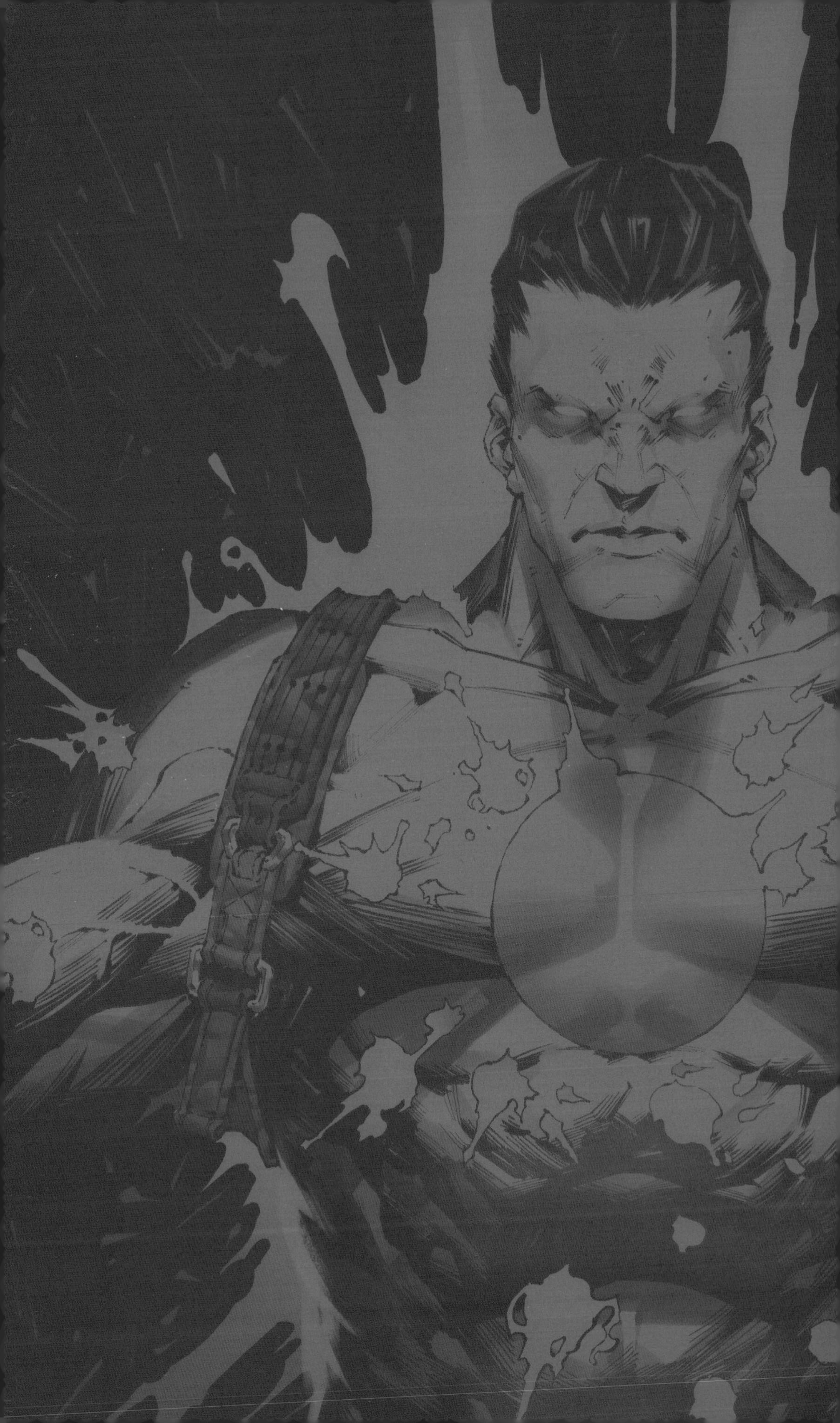

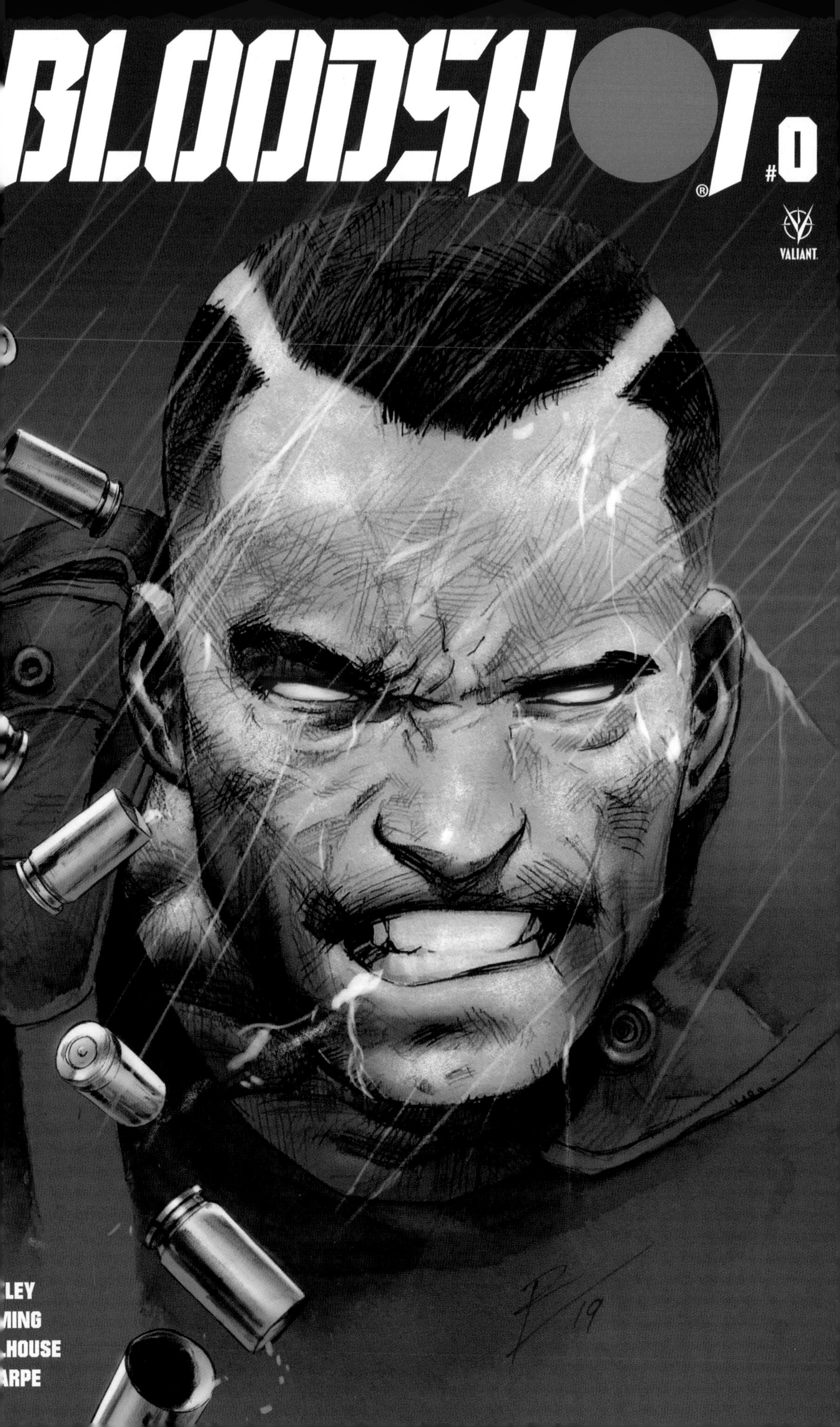
BLOODSHOT®
#0
VALIANT
LEY
MING
HOUSE
ARPE

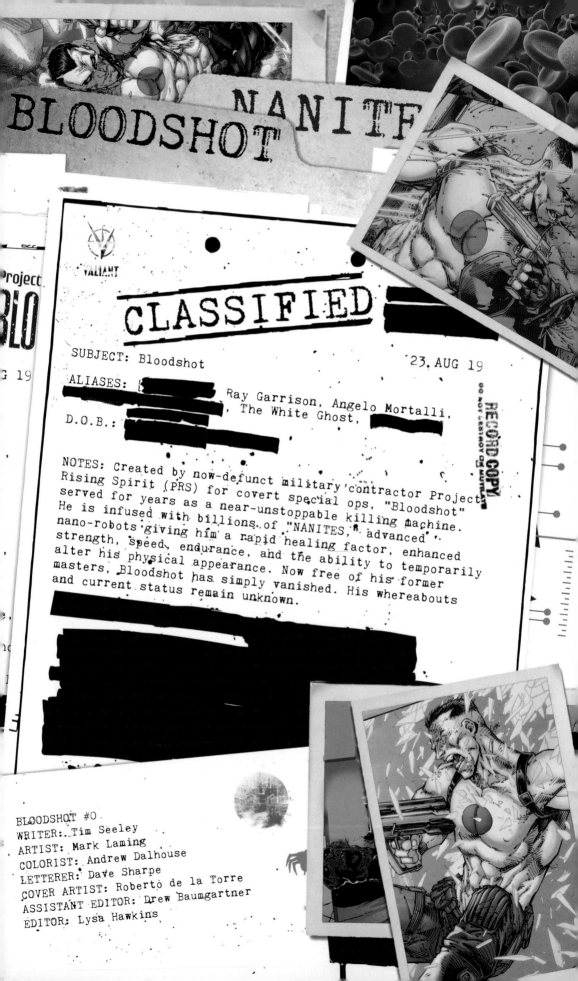

BLOODSHOT

NANITE

CLASSIFIED

SUBJECT: Bloodshot 23 AUG 19

ALIASES: [redacted] Ray Garrison, Angelo Mortalli, [redacted], The White Ghost, [redacted]

D.O.B.: [redacted]

RECORD COPY
DO NOT DESTROY OR MUTILATE

NOTES: Created by now-defunct military contractor Project Rising Spirit (PRS) for covert special ops, "Bloodshot" served for years as a near-unstoppable killing machine. He is infused with billions of "NANITES," advanced nano-robots giving him a rapid healing factor, enhanced strength, speed, endurance, and the ability to temporarily alter his physical appearance. Now free of his former masters, Bloodshot has simply vanished. His whereabouts and current status remain unknown.

[redacted]

BLOODSHOT #0
WRITER: Tim Seeley
ARTIST: Mark Laming
COLORIST: Andrew Dalhouse
LETTERER: Dave Sharpe
COVER ARTIST: Roberto de la Torre
ASSISTANT EDITOR: Drew Baumgartner
EDITOR: Lysa Hawkins

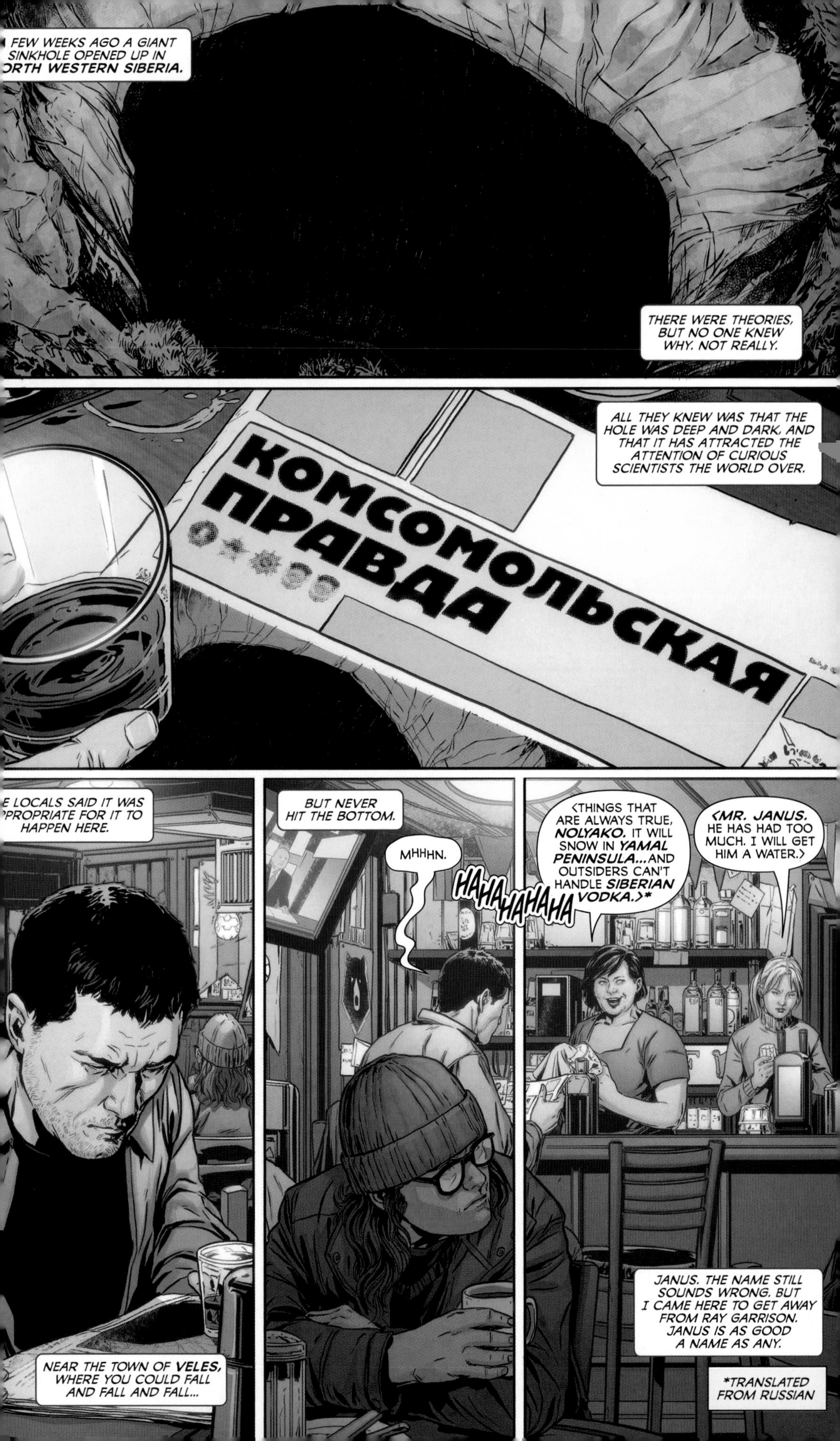

A FEW WEEKS AGO A GIANT SINKHOLE OPENED UP IN NORTH WESTERN SIBERIA.
THERE WERE THEORIES, BUT NO ONE KNEW WHY. NOT REALLY.
ALL THEY KNEW WAS THAT THE HOLE WAS DEEP AND DARK, AND THAT IT HAS ATTRACTED THE ATTENTION OF CURIOUS SCIENTISTS THE WORLD OVER.
КОМСОМОЛЬСКАЯ ПРАВДА
THE LOCALS SAID IT WAS APPROPRIATE FOR IT TO HAPPEN HERE.
NEAR THE TOWN OF VELES, WHERE YOU COULD FALL AND FALL AND FALL...
BUT NEVER HIT THE BOTTOM.
MHHHN.
HAHAHAHAHA
<THINGS THAT ARE ALWAYS TRUE, NOLYAKO. IT WILL SNOW IN YAMAL PENINSULA...AND OUTSIDERS CAN'T HANDLE SIBERIAN VODKA.>*
<MR. JANUS. HE HAS HAD TOO MUCH. I WILL GET HIM A WATER.>
JANUS. THE NAME STILL SOUNDS WRONG. BUT I CAME HERE TO GET AWAY FROM RAY GARRISON. JANUS IS AS GOOD A NAME AS ANY.
*TRANSLATED FROM RUSSIAN

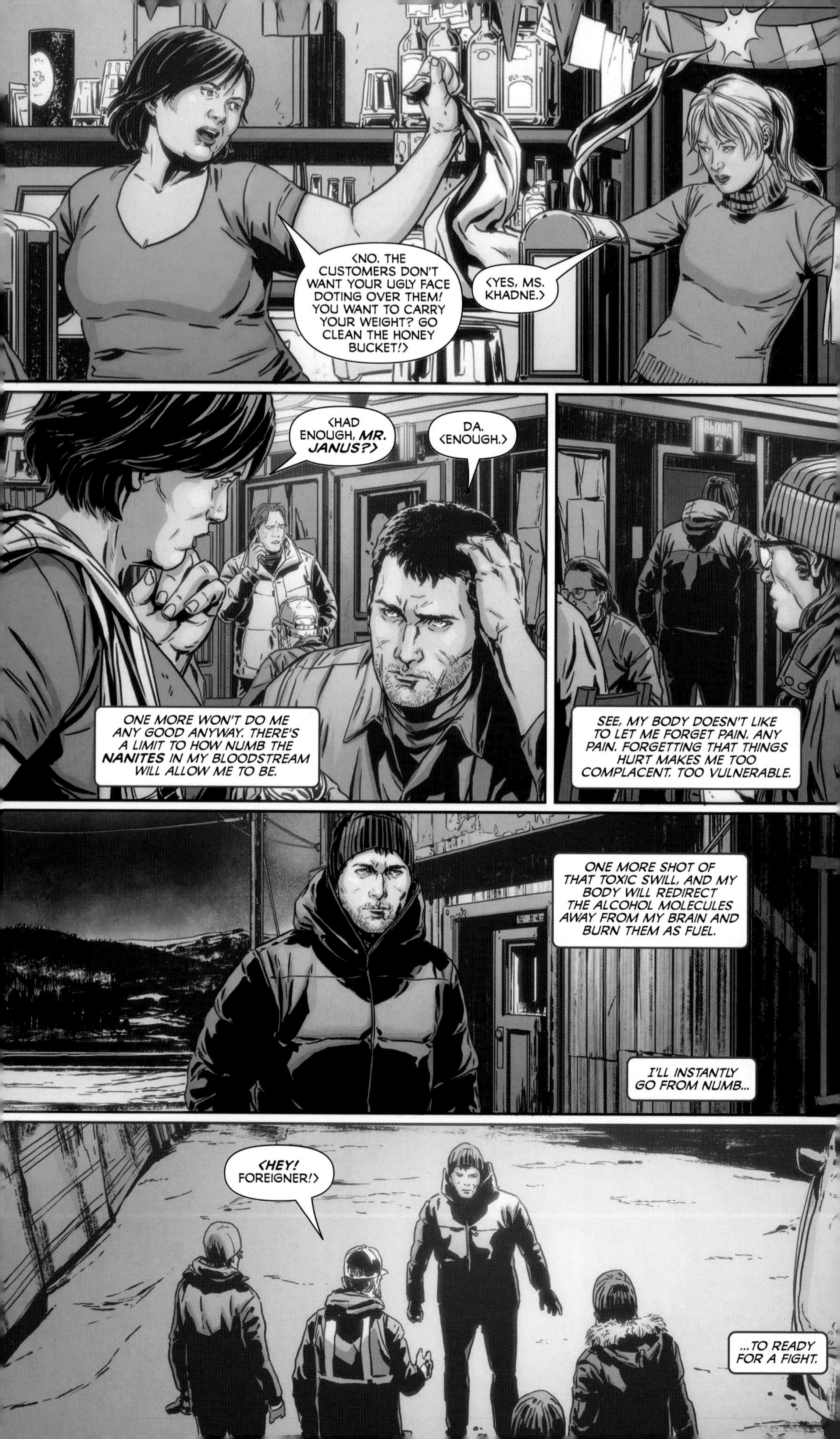
<NO. THE CUSTOMERS DON'T WANT YOUR UGLY FACE DOTING OVER THEM! YOU WANT TO CARRY YOUR WEIGHT? GO CLEAN THE HONEY BUCKET!>
<YES, MS. KHADNE.>
<HAD ENOUGH, MR. JANUS?>
DA. <ENOUGH.>
ONE MORE WON'T DO ME ANY GOOD ANYWAY. THERE'S A LIMIT TO HOW NUMB THE NANITES IN MY BLOODSTREAM WILL ALLOW ME TO BE.
SEE, MY BODY DOESN'T LIKE TO LET ME FORGET PAIN. ANY PAIN. FORGETTING THAT THINGS HURT MAKES ME TOO COMPLACENT. TOO VULNERABLE.
ONE MORE SHOT OF THAT TOXIC SWILL, AND MY BODY WILL REDIRECT THE ALCOHOL MOLECULES AWAY FROM MY BRAIN AND BURN THEM AS FUEL.
I'LL INSTANTLY GO FROM NUMB...
<HEY! FOREIGNER!>
...TO READY FOR A FIGHT.

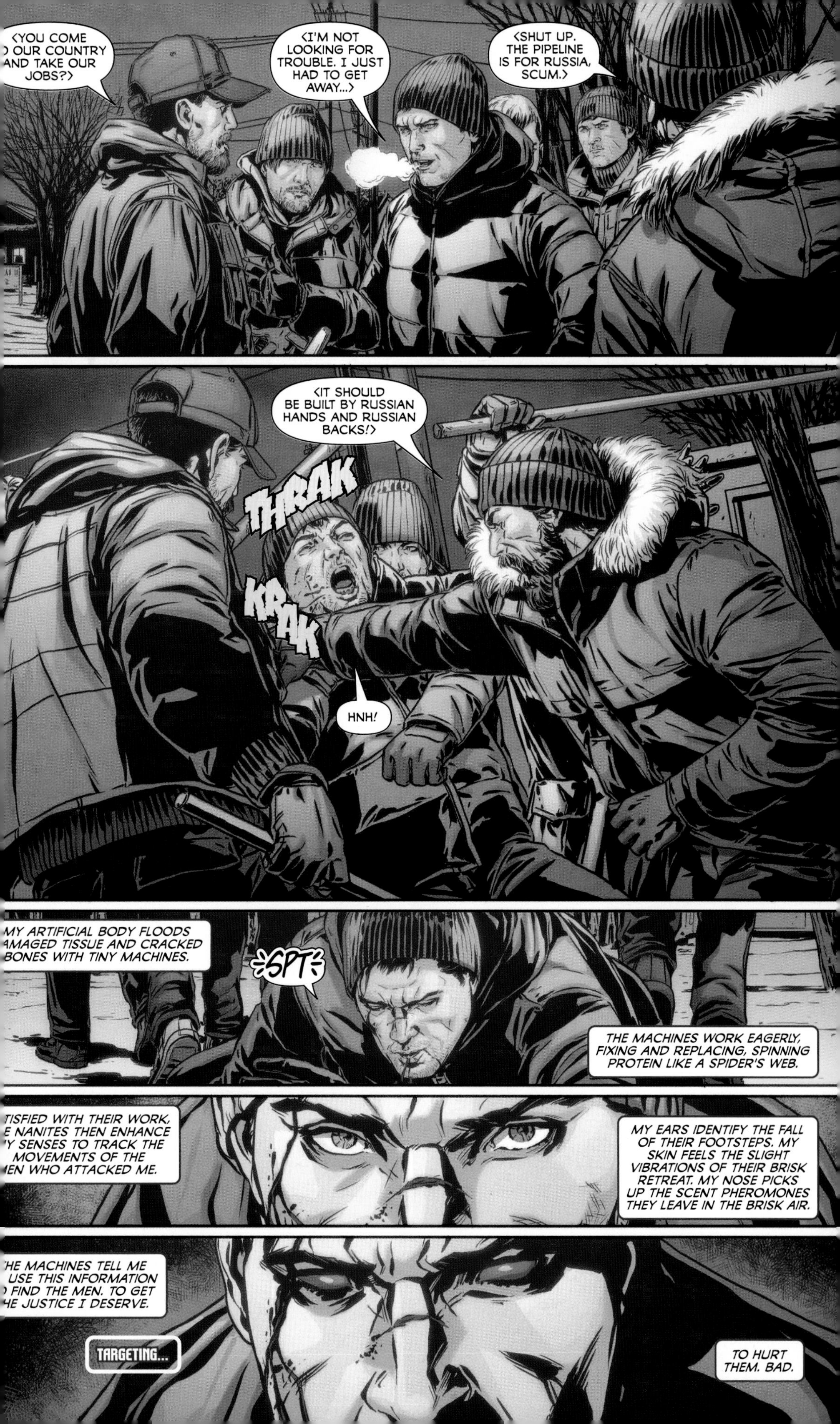
<YOU COME
O OUR COUNTRY
AND TAKE OUR
JOBS?>
<I'M NOT LOOKING FOR TROUBLE. I JUST HAD TO GET AWAY...>
<SHUT UP. THE PIPELINE IS FOR RUSSIA, SCUM.>
<IT SHOULD BE BUILT BY RUSSIAN HANDS AND RUSSIAN BACKS!>
THRAK
KRAK
HNH!
MY ARTIFICIAL BODY FLOODS
AMAGED TISSUE AND CRACKED
BONES WITH TINY MACHINES.
SPT
THE MACHINES WORK EAGERLY, FIXING AND REPLACING, SPINNING PROTEIN LIKE A SPIDER'S WEB.
TISFIED WITH THEIR WORK,
E NANITES THEN ENHANCE
Y SENSES TO TRACK THE
MOVEMENTS OF THE
IEN WHO ATTACKED ME.
MY EARS IDENTIFY THE FALL OF THEIR FOOTSTEPS. MY SKIN FEELS THE SLIGHT VIBRATIONS OF THEIR BRISK RETREAT. MY NOSE PICKS UP THE SCENT PHEROMONES THEY LEAVE IN THE BRISK AIR.
HE MACHINES TELL ME
USE THIS INFORMATION
FIND THE MEN. TO GET
HE JUSTICE I DESERVE.
TARGETING...
TO HURT THEM. BAD.

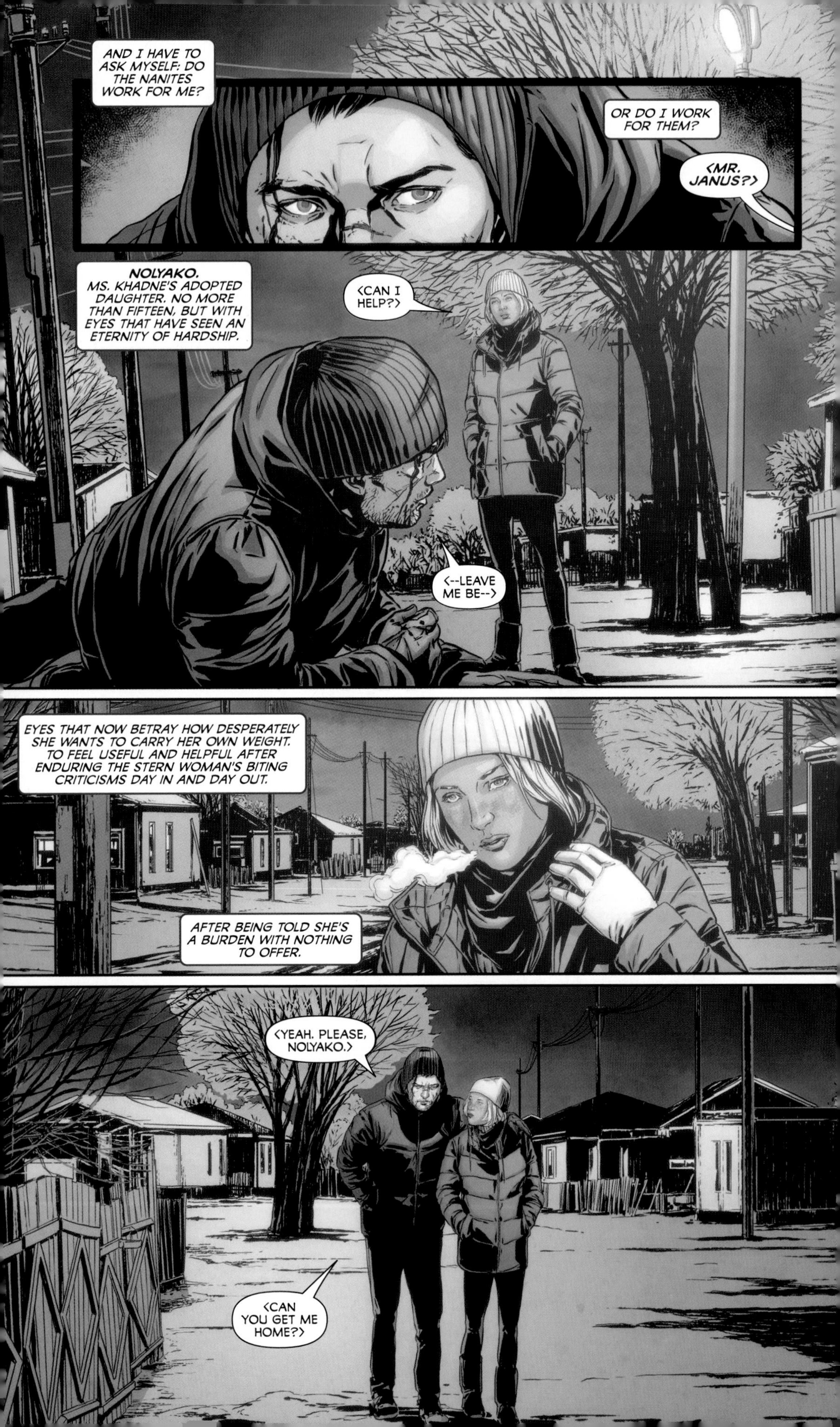
AND I HAVE TO ASK MYSELF: DO THE NANITES WORK FOR ME?
OR DO I WORK FOR THEM?
<MR. JANUS?>
NOLYAKO. MS. KHADNE'S ADOPTED DAUGHTER. NO MORE THAN FIFTEEN, BUT WITH EYES THAT HAVE SEEN AN ETERNITY OF HARDSHIP.
<CAN I HELP?>
<--LEAVE ME BE-->
EYES THAT NOW BETRAY HOW DESPERATELY SHE WANTS TO CARRY HER OWN WEIGHT. TO FEEL USEFUL AND HELPFUL AFTER ENDURING THE STERN WOMAN'S BITING CRITICISMS DAY IN AND DAY OUT.
AFTER BEING TOLD SHE'S A BURDEN WITH NOTHING TO OFFER.
<YEAH. PLEASE, NOLYAKO.>
<CAN YOU GET ME HOME?>

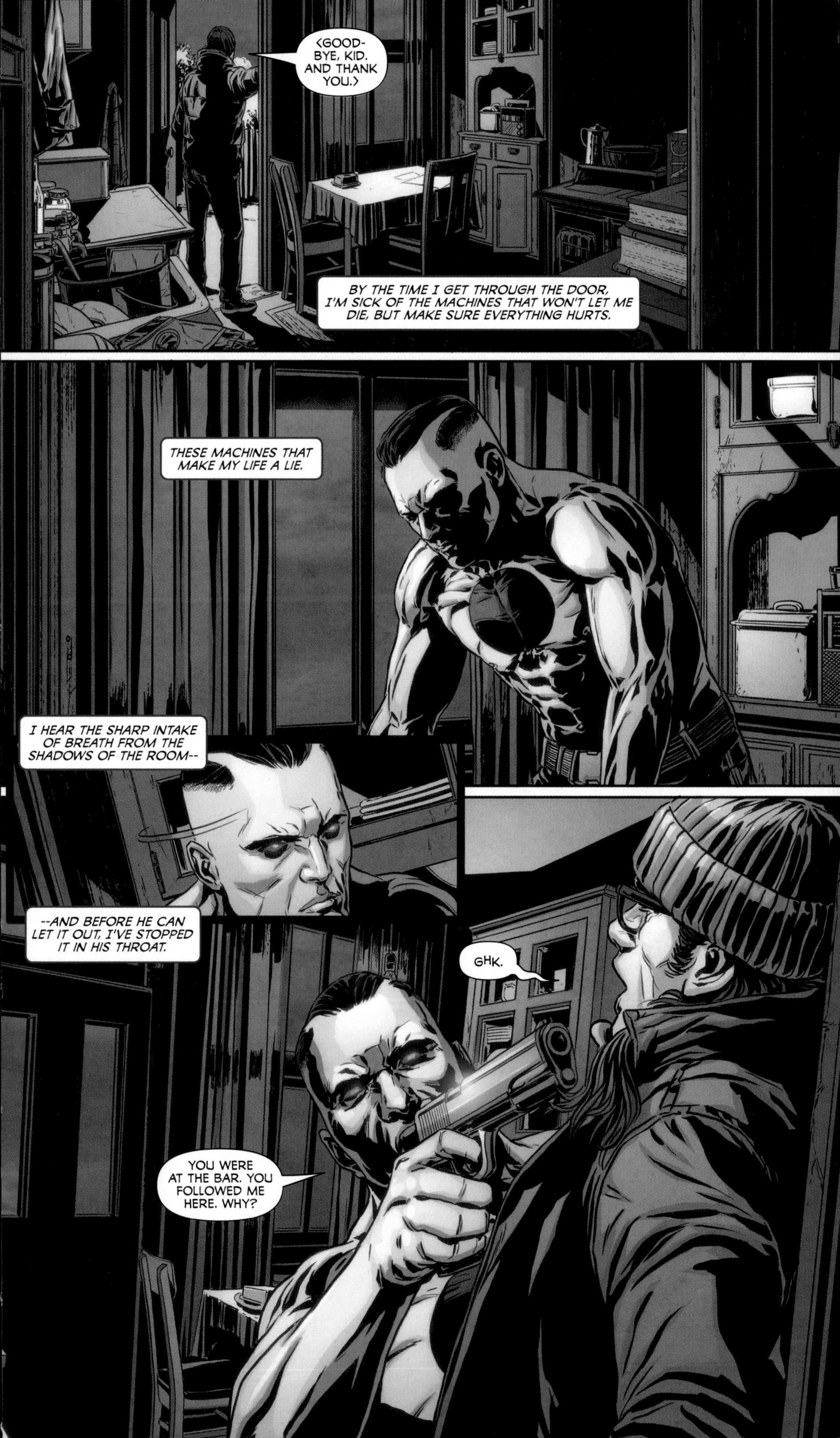

<GOOD-BYE, KID. AND THANK YOU.>
BY THE TIME I GET THROUGH THE DOOR, I'M SICK OF THE MACHINES THAT WON'T LET ME DIE, BUT MAKE SURE EVERYTHING HURTS.
THESE MACHINES THAT MAKE MY LIFE A LIE.
I HEAR THE SHARP INTAKE OF BREATH FROM THE SHADOWS OF THE ROOM--
--AND BEFORE HE CAN LET IT OUT, I'VE STOPPED IT IN HIS THROAT.
GHK.
YOU WERE AT THE BAR. YOU FOLLOWED ME HERE. WHY?

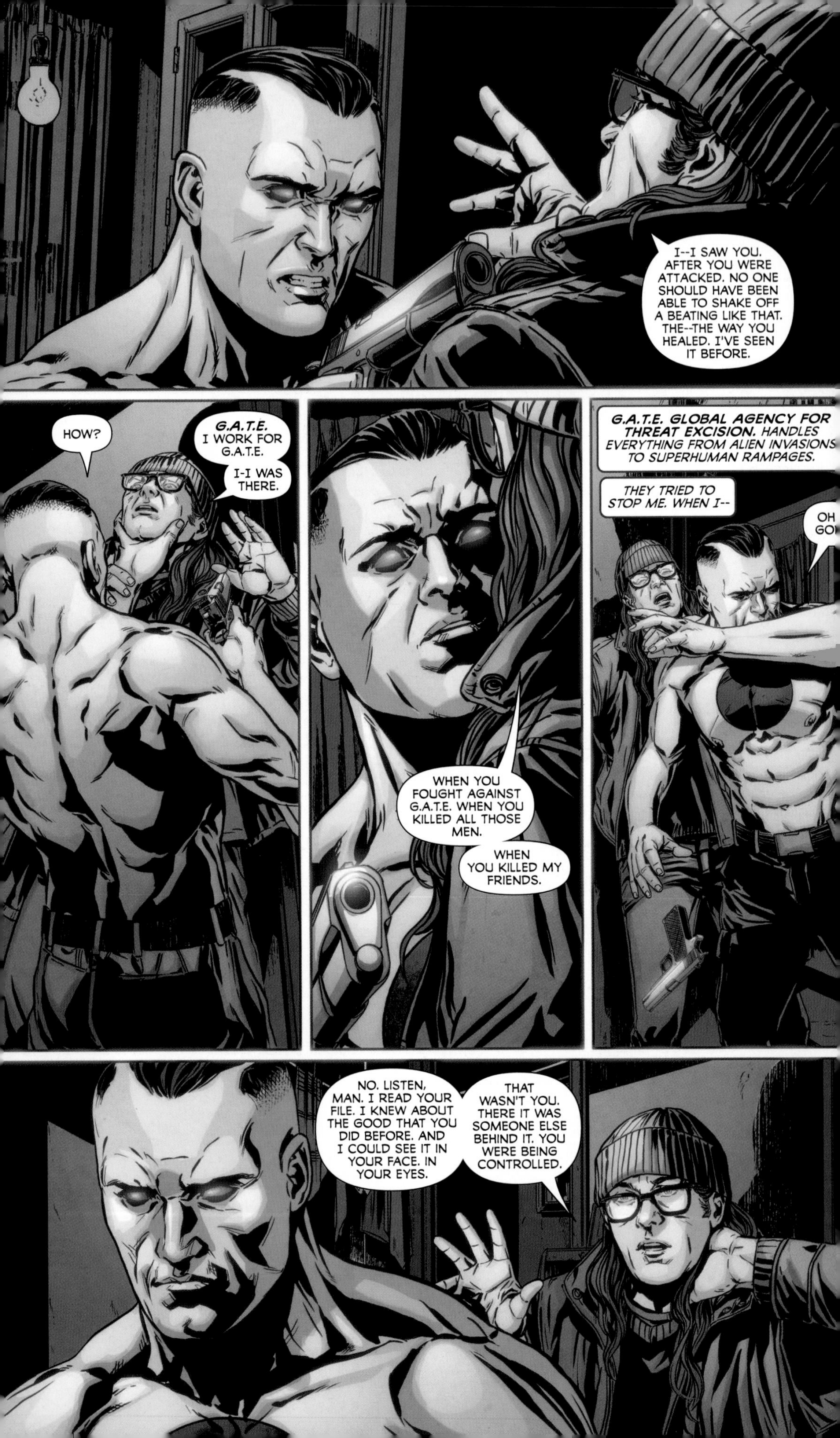

I--I SAW YOU. AFTER YOU WERE ATTACKED. NO ONE SHOULD HAVE BEEN ABLE TO SHAKE OFF A BEATING LIKE THAT. THE--THE WAY YOU HEALED. I'VE SEEN IT BEFORE.
HOW?
G.A.T.E. I WORK FOR G.A.T.E.
I-I WAS THERE.
WHEN YOU FOUGHT AGAINST G.A.T.E. WHEN YOU KILLED ALL THOSE MEN.
WHEN YOU KILLED MY FRIENDS.
G.A.T.E. GLOBAL AGENCY FOR THREAT EXCISION. HANDLES EVERYTHING FROM ALIEN INVASIONS TO SUPERHUMAN RAMPAGES.
THEY TRIED TO STOP ME. WHEN I--
NO. LISTEN, MAN. I READ YOUR FILE. I KNEW ABOUT THE GOOD THAT YOU DID BEFORE. AND I COULD SEE IT IN YOUR FACE. IN YOUR EYES.
THAT WASN'T YOU. THERE IT WAS SOMEONE ELSE BEHIND IT. YOU WERE BEING CONTROLLED.

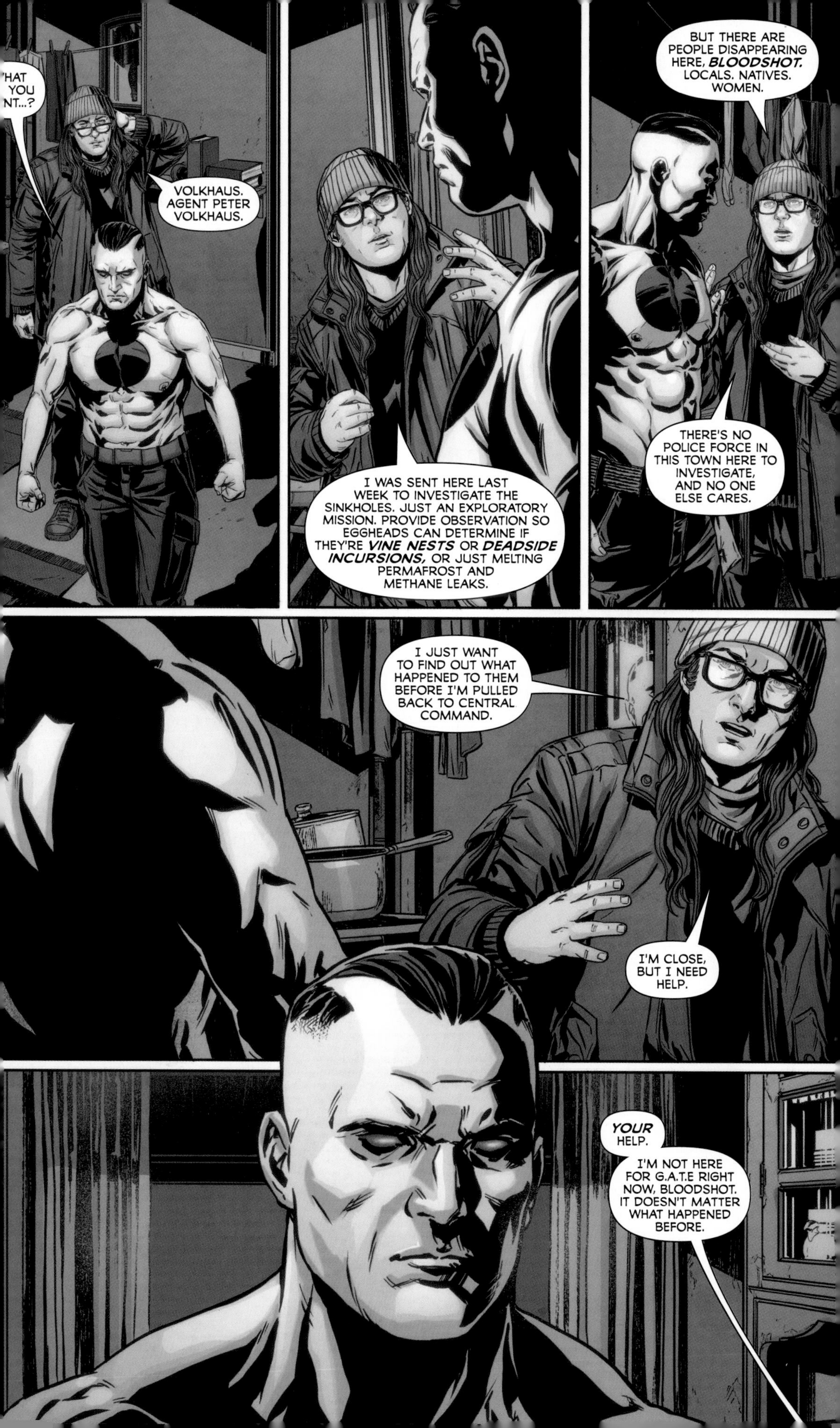
'HAT YOU NT...?
VOLKHAUS. AGENT PETER VOLKHAUS.
I WAS SENT HERE LAST WEEK TO INVESTIGATE THE SINKHOLES. JUST AN EXPLORATORY MISSION. PROVIDE OBSERVATION SO EGGHEADS CAN DETERMINE IF THEY'RE ***VINE NESTS*** OR ***DEADSIDE INCURSIONS,*** OR JUST MELTING PERMAFROST AND METHANE LEAKS.
BUT THERE ARE PEOPLE DISAPPEARING HERE, ***BLOODSHOT.*** LOCALS. NATIVES. WOMEN.
THERE'S NO POLICE FORCE IN THIS TOWN HERE TO INVESTIGATE, AND NO ONE ELSE CARES.
I JUST WANT TO FIND OUT WHAT HAPPENED TO THEM BEFORE I'M PULLED BACK TO CENTRAL COMMAND.
I'M CLOSE, BUT I NEED HELP.
YOUR HELP.
I'M NOT HERE FOR G.A.T.E RIGHT NOW, BLOODSHOT. IT DOESN'T MATTER WHAT HAPPENED BEFORE.

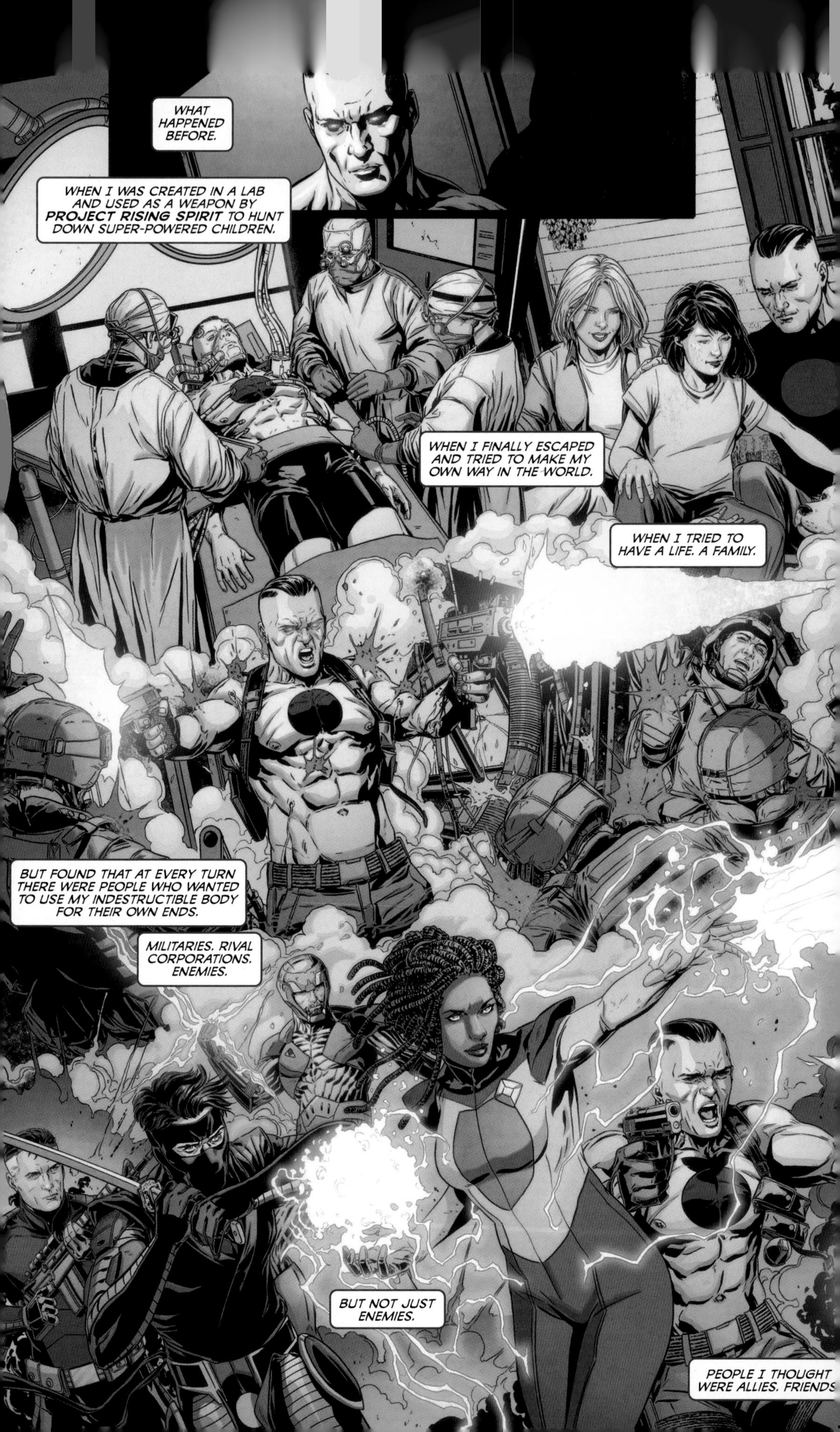
WHAT HAPPENED BEFORE.
WHEN I WAS CREATED IN A LAB AND USED AS A WEAPON BY **PROJECT RISING SPIRIT** TO HUNT DOWN SUPER-POWERED CHILDREN.
WHEN I FINALLY ESCAPED AND TRIED TO MAKE MY OWN WAY IN THE WORLD.
WHEN I TRIED TO HAVE A LIFE. A FAMILY.
BUT FOUND THAT AT EVERY TURN THERE WERE PEOPLE WHO WANTED TO USE MY INDESTRUCTIBLE BODY FOR THEIR OWN ENDS.
MILITARIES. RIVAL CORPORATIONS. ENEMIES.
BUT NOT JUST ENEMIES.
PEOPLE I THOUGHT WERE ALLIES. FRIENDS

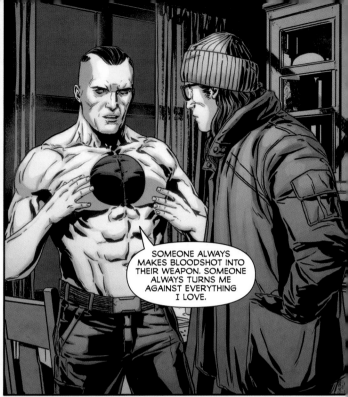

WHAT HAPPENED BEFORE IS WHY I CAME HERE TO THE END OF THE WORLD.

BECAUSE IT DOESN'T MATTER HOW MUCH GOOD I TRY TO DO, I ALWAYS END UP DOING BAD.

SOMEONE ALWAYS MAKES BLOODSHOT INTO THEIR WEAPON. SOMEONE ALWAYS TURNS ME AGAINST EVERYTHING I LOVE.

SO NOW BLOODSHOT IS DEAD.

HE'S BURIED. DROPPED INTO A BOTTOMLESS HOLE THAT THERE'S NO COMING OUT OF.

GOOD LUCK, AGENT. NOW FORGET I'M HERE. BECAUSE PRETTY SOON, I WON'T BE.

PLEASE, MAN. TRUST ME--

NO. I CAN'T TRUST ANYONE.

LEAST OF ALL MYSELF.

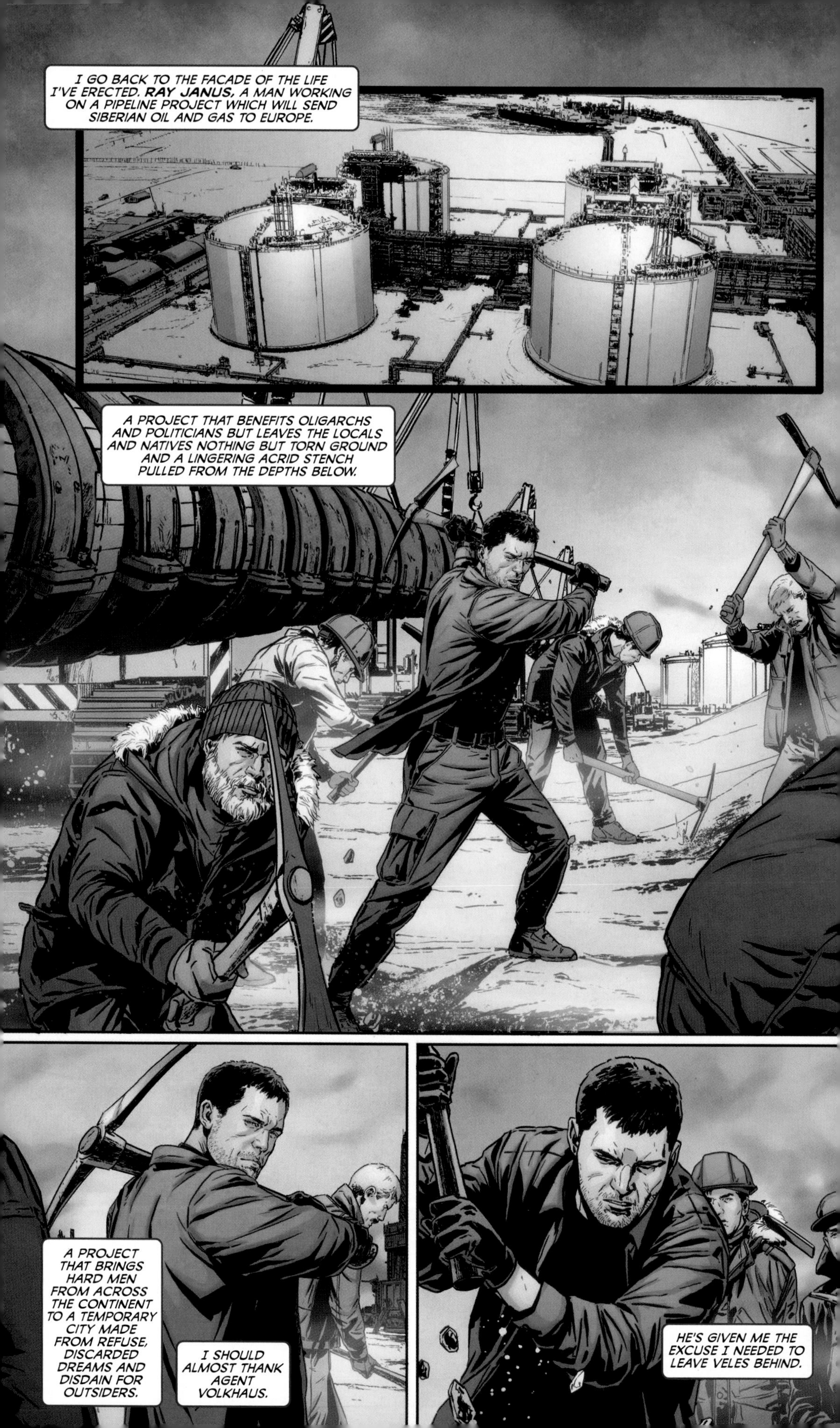
I GO BACK TO THE FACADE OF THE LIFE I'VE ERECTED. RAY JANUS, A MAN WORKING ON A PIPELINE PROJECT WHICH WILL SEND SIBERIAN OIL AND GAS TO EUROPE.
A PROJECT THAT BENEFITS OLIGARCHS AND POLITICIANS BUT LEAVES THE LOCALS AND NATIVES NOTHING BUT TORN GROUND AND A LINGERING ACRID STENCH PULLED FROM THE DEPTHS BELOW.
A PROJECT THAT BRINGS HARD MEN FROM ACROSS THE CONTINENT TO A TEMPORARY CITY MADE FROM REFUSE, DISCARDED DREAMS AND DISDAIN FOR OUTSIDERS.
I SHOULD ALMOST THANK AGENT VOLKHAUS.
HE'S GIVEN ME THE EXCUSE I NEEDED TO LEAVE VELES BEHIND.

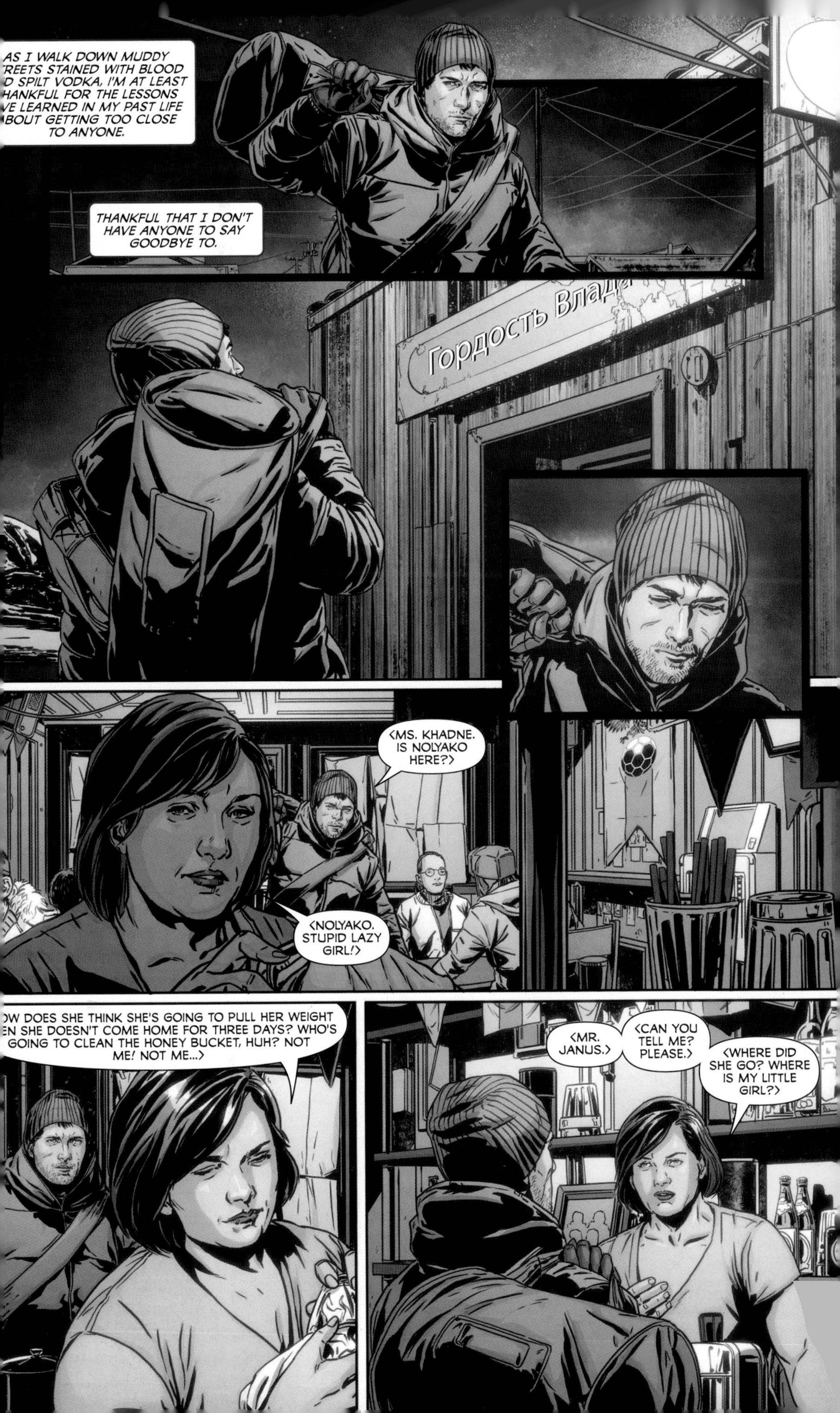
AS I WALK DOWN MUDDY
REETS STAINED WITH BLOOD
D SPILT VODKA, I'M AT LEAST
HANKFUL FOR THE LESSONS
VE LEARNED IN MY PAST LIFE
BOUT GETTING TOO CLOSE
TO ANYONE.
THANKFUL THAT I DON'T HAVE ANYONE TO SAY GOODBYE TO.
Гордость Влад
‹MS. KHADNE. IS NOLYAKO HERE?›
‹NOLYAKO. STUPID LAZY GIRL!›
OW DOES SHE THINK SHE'S GOING TO PULL HER WEIGHT
EN SHE DOESN'T COME HOME FOR THREE DAYS? WHO'S
GOING TO CLEAN THE HONEY BUCKET, HUH? NOT
ME! NOT ME...›
‹MR. JANUS.›
‹CAN YOU TELL ME? PLEASE.›
‹WHERE DID SHE GO? WHERE IS MY LITTLE GIRL?›

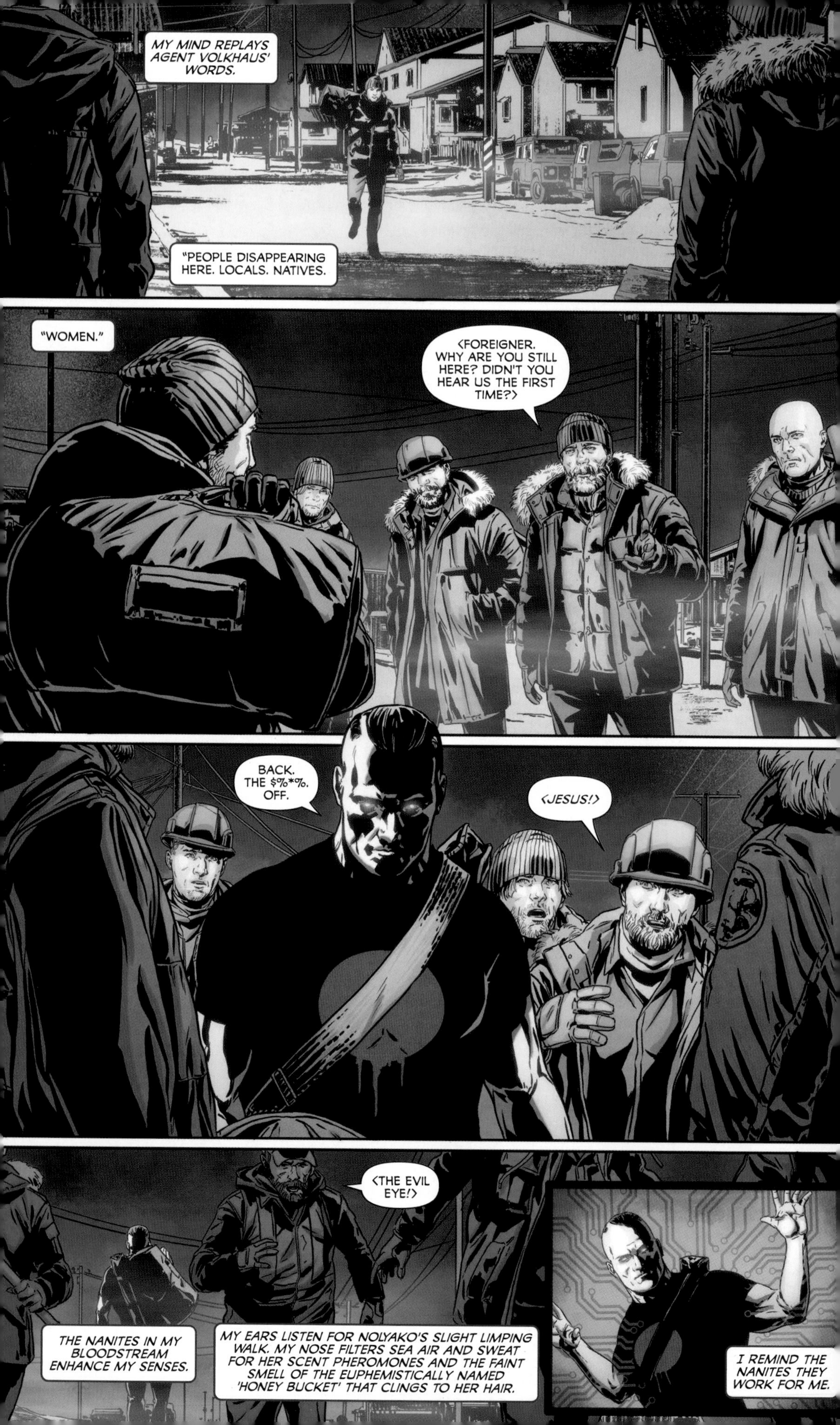
MY MIND REPLAYS AGENT VOLKHAUS' WORDS.
"PEOPLE DISAPPEARING HERE. LOCALS. NATIVES.
"WOMEN."
<FOREIGNER. WHY ARE YOU STILL HERE? DIDN'T YOU HEAR US THE FIRST TIME?>
BACK. THE $%*%. OFF.
<JESUS!>
<THE EVIL EYE!>
THE NANITES IN MY BLOODSTREAM ENHANCE MY SENSES.
MY EARS LISTEN FOR NOLYAKO'S SLIGHT LIMPING WALK. MY NOSE FILTERS SEA AIR AND SWEAT FOR HER SCENT PHEROMONES AND THE FAINT SMELL OF THE EUPHEMISTICALLY NAMED 'HONEY BUCKET' THAT CLINGS TO HER HAIR.
I REMIND THE NANITES THEY WORK FOR ME.

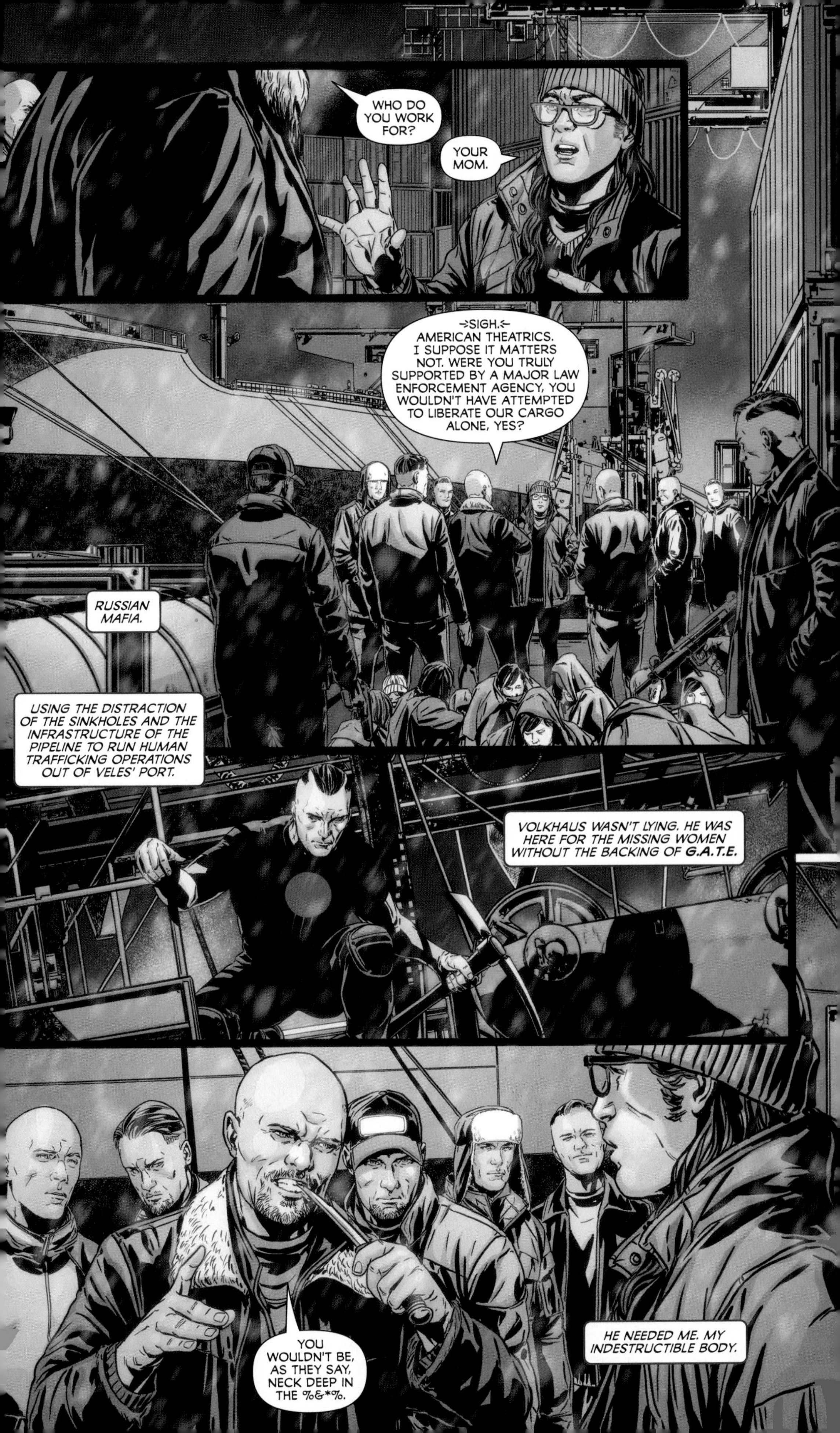

WHO DO YOU WORK FOR?
YOUR MOM.
>SIGH.< AMERICAN THEATRICS. I SUPPOSE IT MATTERS NOT. WERE YOU TRULY SUPPORTED BY A MAJOR LAW ENFORCEMENT AGENCY, YOU WOULDN'T HAVE ATTEMPTED TO LIBERATE OUR CARGO ALONE, YES?
RUSSIAN MAFIA.
USING THE DISTRACTION OF THE SINKHOLES AND THE INFRASTRUCTURE OF THE PIPELINE TO RUN HUMAN TRAFFICKING OPERATIONS OUT OF VELES' PORT.
VOLKHAUS WASN'T LYING. HE WAS HERE FOR THE MISSING WOMEN WITHOUT THE BACKING OF G.A.T.E.
YOU WOULDN'T BE, AS THEY SAY, NECK DEEP IN THE %&*%.
HE NEEDED ME. MY INDESTRUCTIBLE BODY.

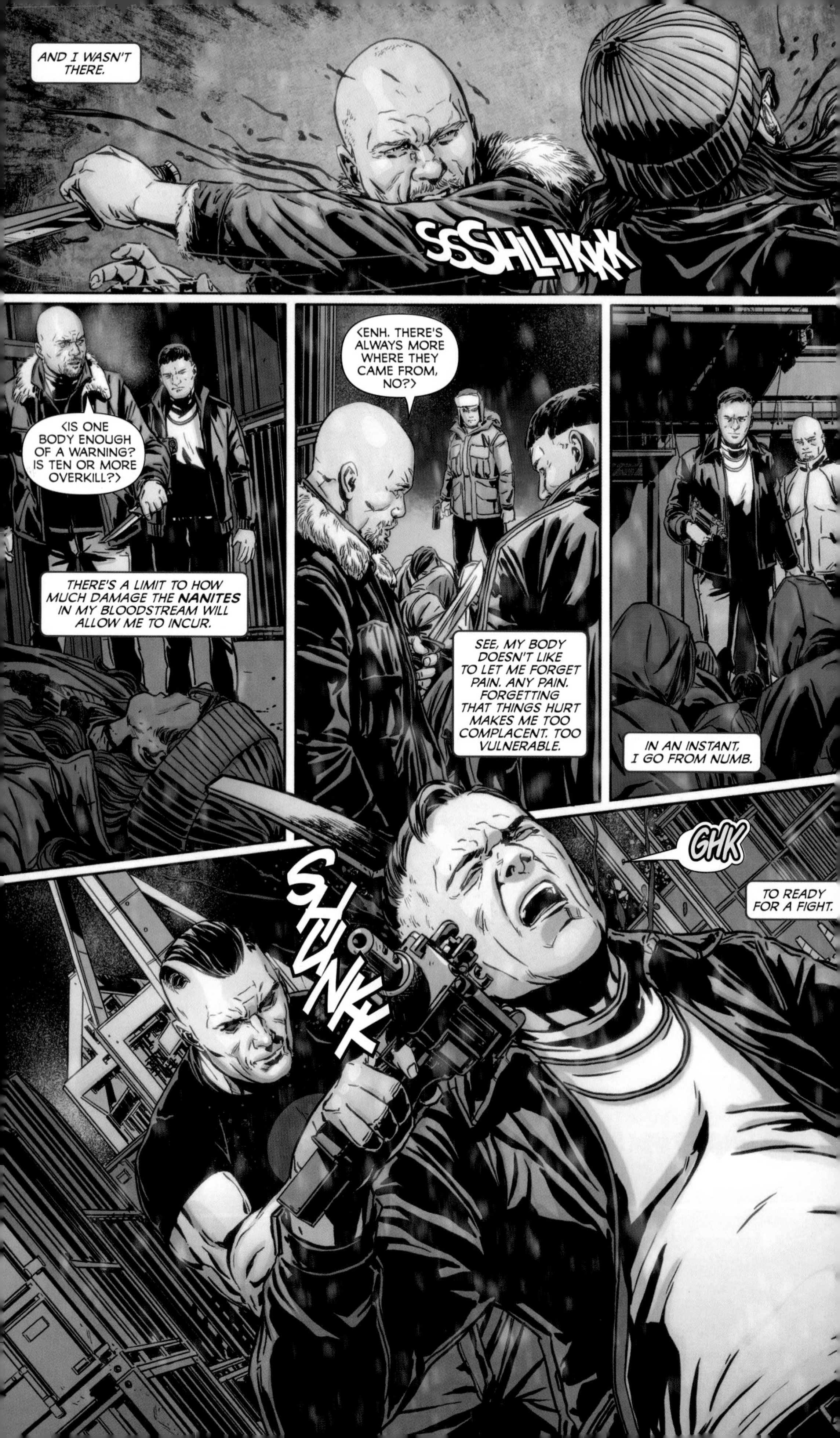
AND I WASN'T THERE.
SSSHILLIKKK
<IS ONE BODY ENOUGH OF A WARNING? IS TEN OR MORE OVERKILL?>
THERE'S A LIMIT TO HOW MUCH DAMAGE THE **NANITES** IN MY BLOODSTREAM WILL ALLOW ME TO INCUR.
<ENH. THERE'S ALWAYS MORE WHERE THEY CAME FROM, NO?>
SEE, MY BODY DOESN'T LIKE TO LET ME FORGET PAIN. ANY PAIN. FORGETTING THAT THINGS HURT MAKES ME TOO COMPLACENT. TOO VULNERABLE.
IN AN INSTANT, I GO FROM NUMB.
GHK
TO READY FOR A FIGHT.
SHUNKK

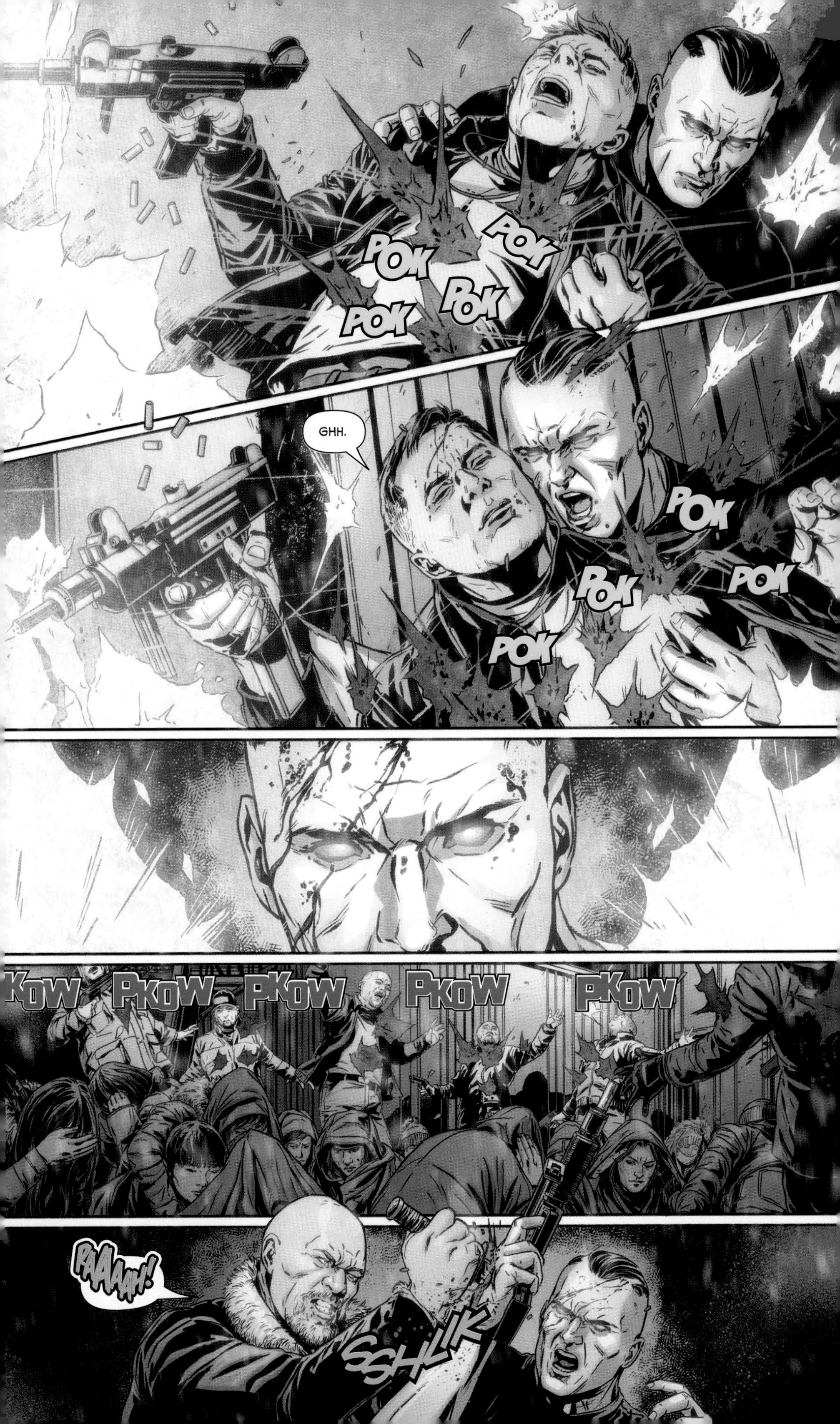

POK
POK
POK
POK
GHH.
POK
POK
POK
POK
KOW
PKOW
PKOW
PKOW
PKOW
RAAAAH!
SSHLIK

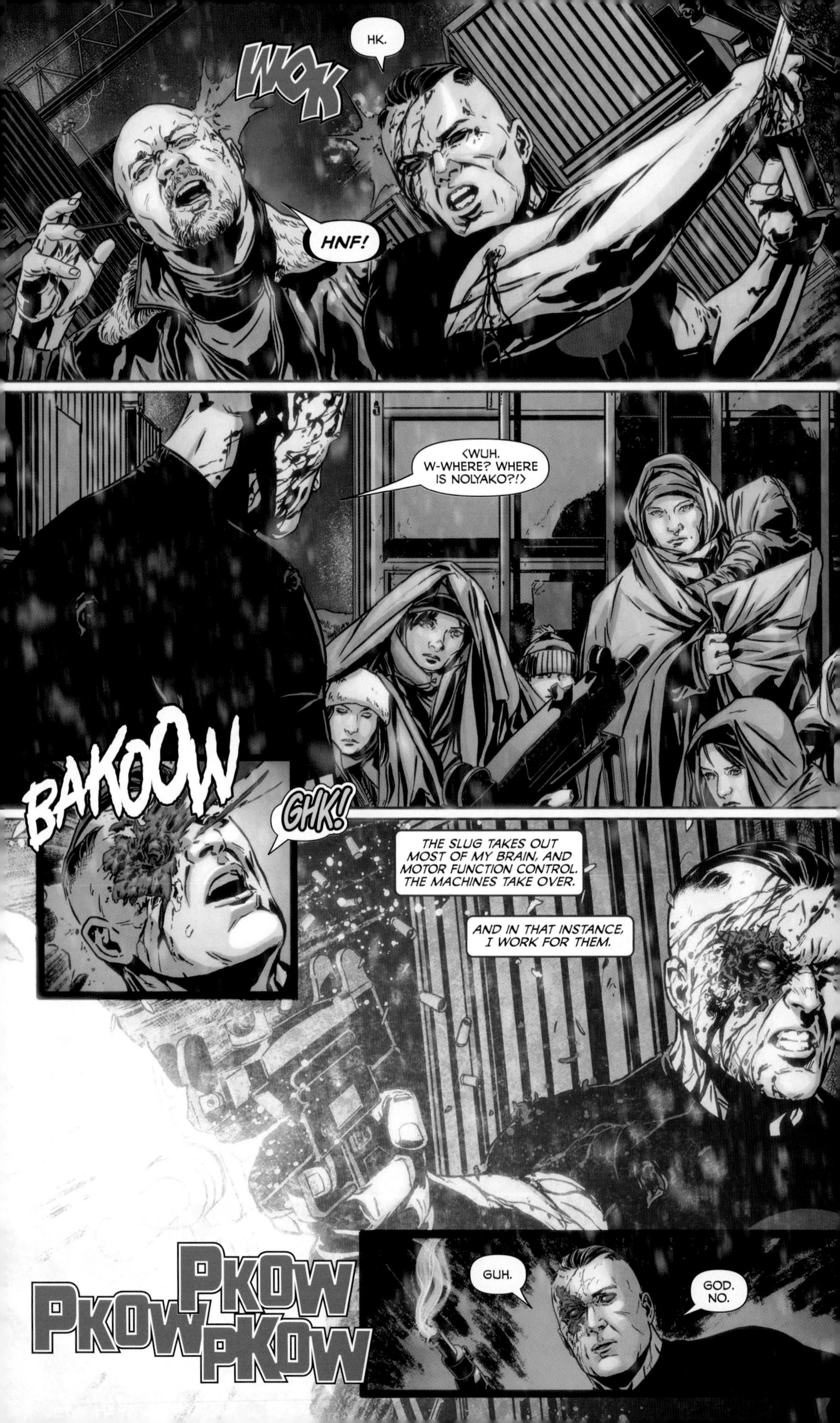
HK.
WOK
HNF!
<WUH. W-WHERE? WHERE IS NOLYAKO?!>
BAKOOW
GHK!
THE SLUG TAKES OUT MOST OF MY BRAIN, AND MOTOR FUNCTION CONTROL. THE MACHINES TAKE OVER.
AND IN THAT INSTANCE, I WORK FOR THEM.
PKOW PKOW PKOW PKOW
GUH.
GOD. NO.

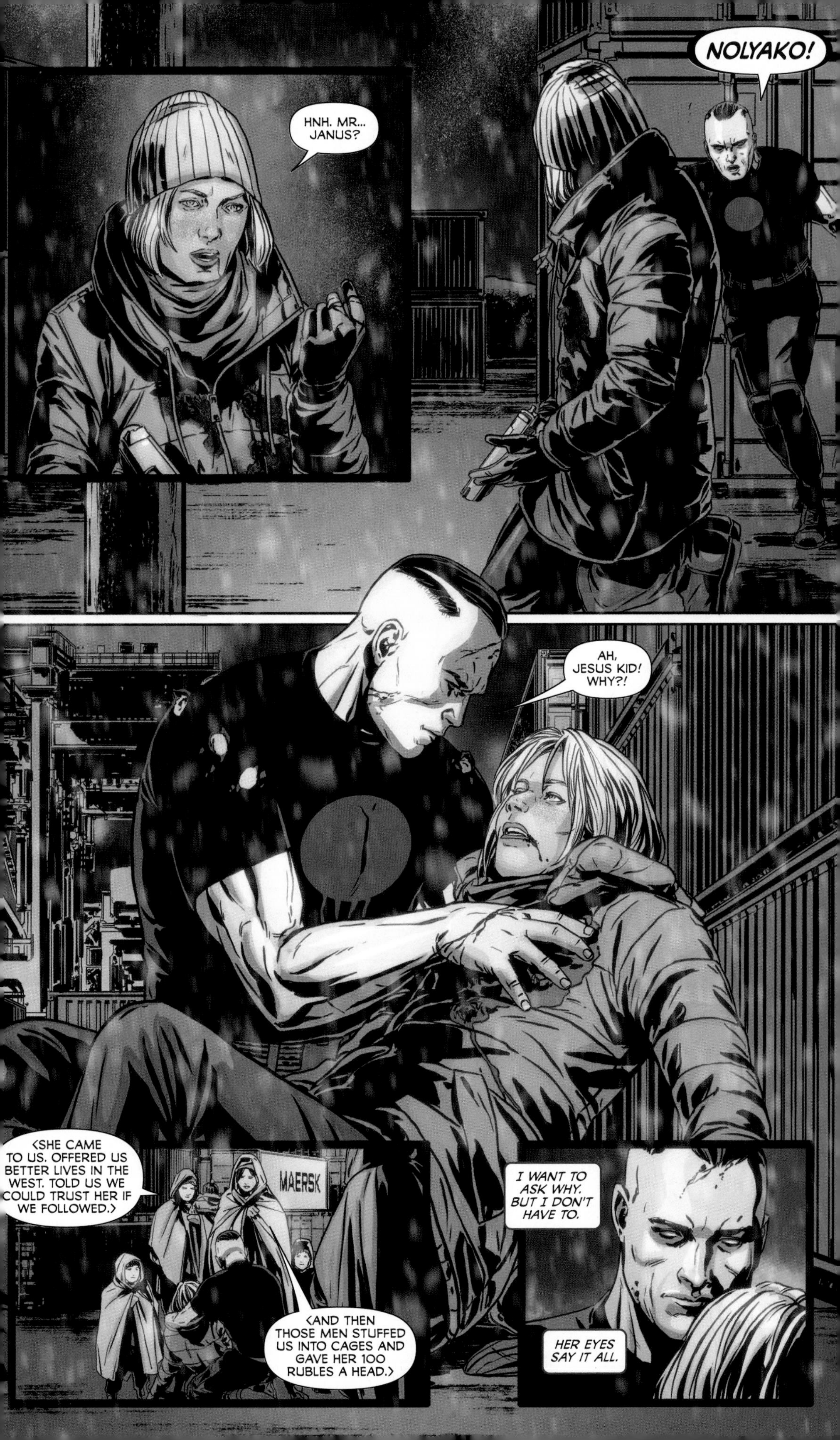
HNH. MR... JANUS?
NOLYAKO!
AH, JESUS KID! WHY?!
<SHE CAME TO US. OFFERED US BETTER LIVES IN THE WEST. TOLD US WE COULD TRUST HER IF WE FOLLOWED.>
MAERSK
<AND THEN THOSE MEN STUFFED US INTO CAGES AND GAVE HER 100 RUBLES A HEAD.>
I WANT TO ASK WHY. BUT I DON'T HAVE TO.
HER EYES SAY IT ALL.

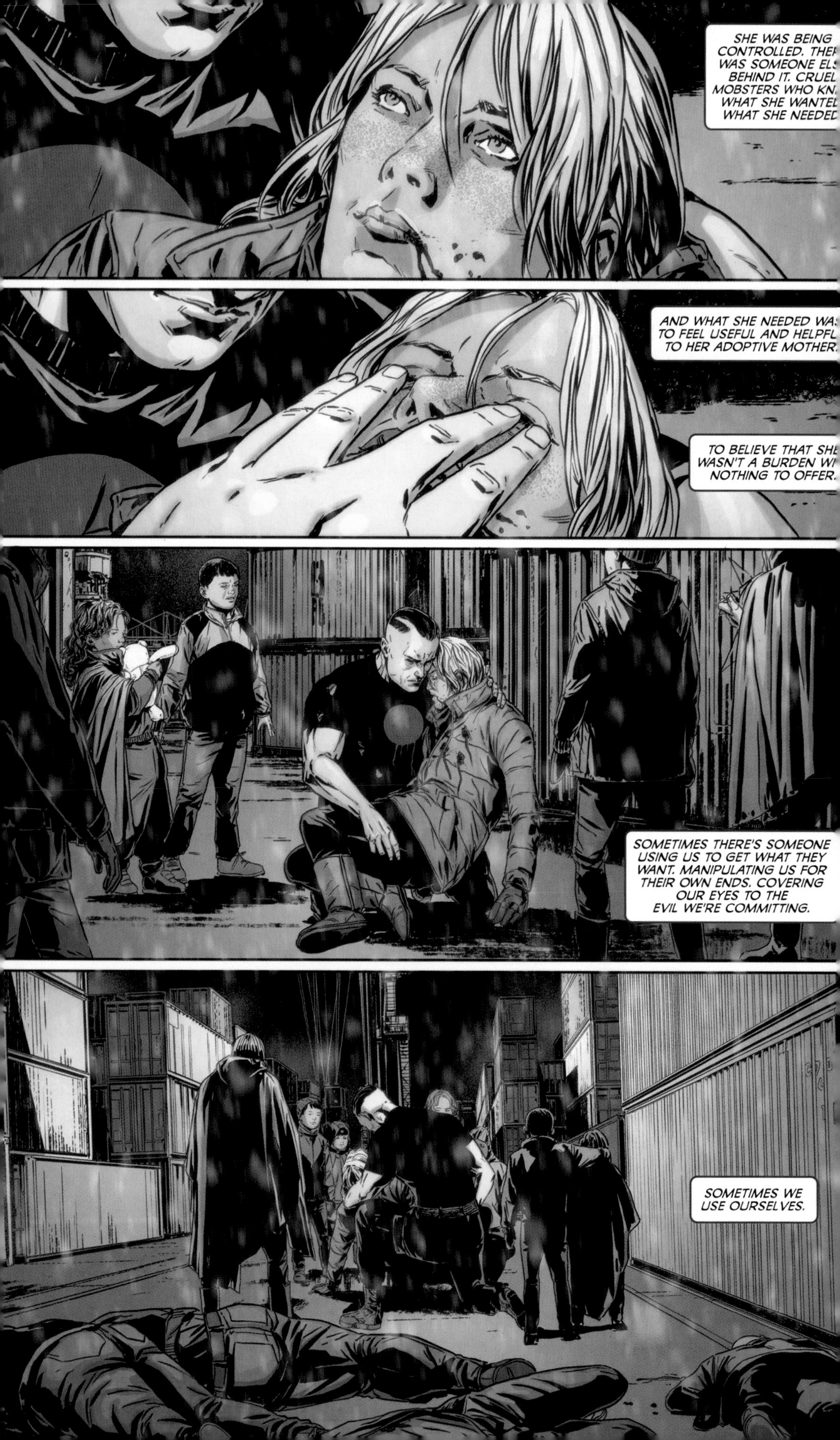
SHE WAS BEING
CONTROLLED. THE
WAS SOMEONE ELS
BEHIND IT. CRUEL
MOBSTERS WHO KN
WHAT SHE WANTE
WHAT SHE NEEDED
AND WHAT SHE NEEDED WA
TO FEEL USEFUL AND HELPF
TO HER ADOPTIVE MOTHER.
TO BELIEVE THAT SH
WASN'T A BURDEN W
NOTHING TO OFFER.
SOMETIMES THERE'S SOMEONE USING US TO GET WHAT THEY WANT. MANIPULATING US FOR THEIR OWN ENDS. COVERING OUR EYES TO THE EVIL WE'RE COMMITTING.
SOMETIMES WE USE OURSELVES.

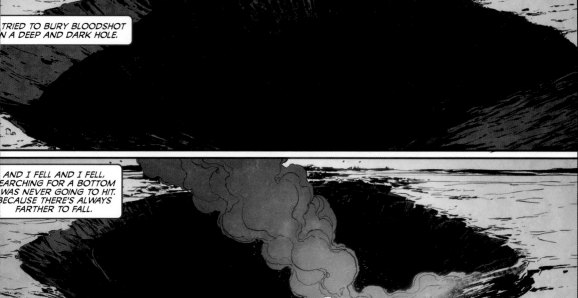

TRIED TO BURY BLOODSHOT IN A DEEP AND DARK HOLE.

AND I FELL AND I FELL, SEARCHING FOR A BOTTOM I WAS NEVER GOING TO HIT. BECAUSE THERE'S ALWAYS FARTHER TO FALL.

I'VE BEEN USED. MANIPULATED. TURNED INTO A WEAPON OVER AND OVER AGAIN.

AND THE FEAR OF IT HAPPENING AGAIN MADE ME BLIND TO THE NEEDS OF OTHERS. LED THEM DOWN DARK PATHS LIKE NOLYAKO. LED THEM TO THEIR DEATHS LIKE AGENT VOLKHAUS.

<PLEASE... I--I HAVE A CHILD...>

IT HURTS. HURTS BAD.

BUT I SEE NOW THAT THE KEY IS NOT IN FORGETTING IT, OR GOING NUMB. IT'S USING THE PAIN AS FUEL.

<COMMANDER. THE AIRSTRIKE HAS LEFT CIVILIAN CASUALTIES.>

<UNFORTUNATE. LEAVE NO WITNESSES.>

I CAN MAKE UP FOR WHAT I'VE DONE BY PUTTING THE NANITES IN MY BLOOD TO WORK FOR ME.

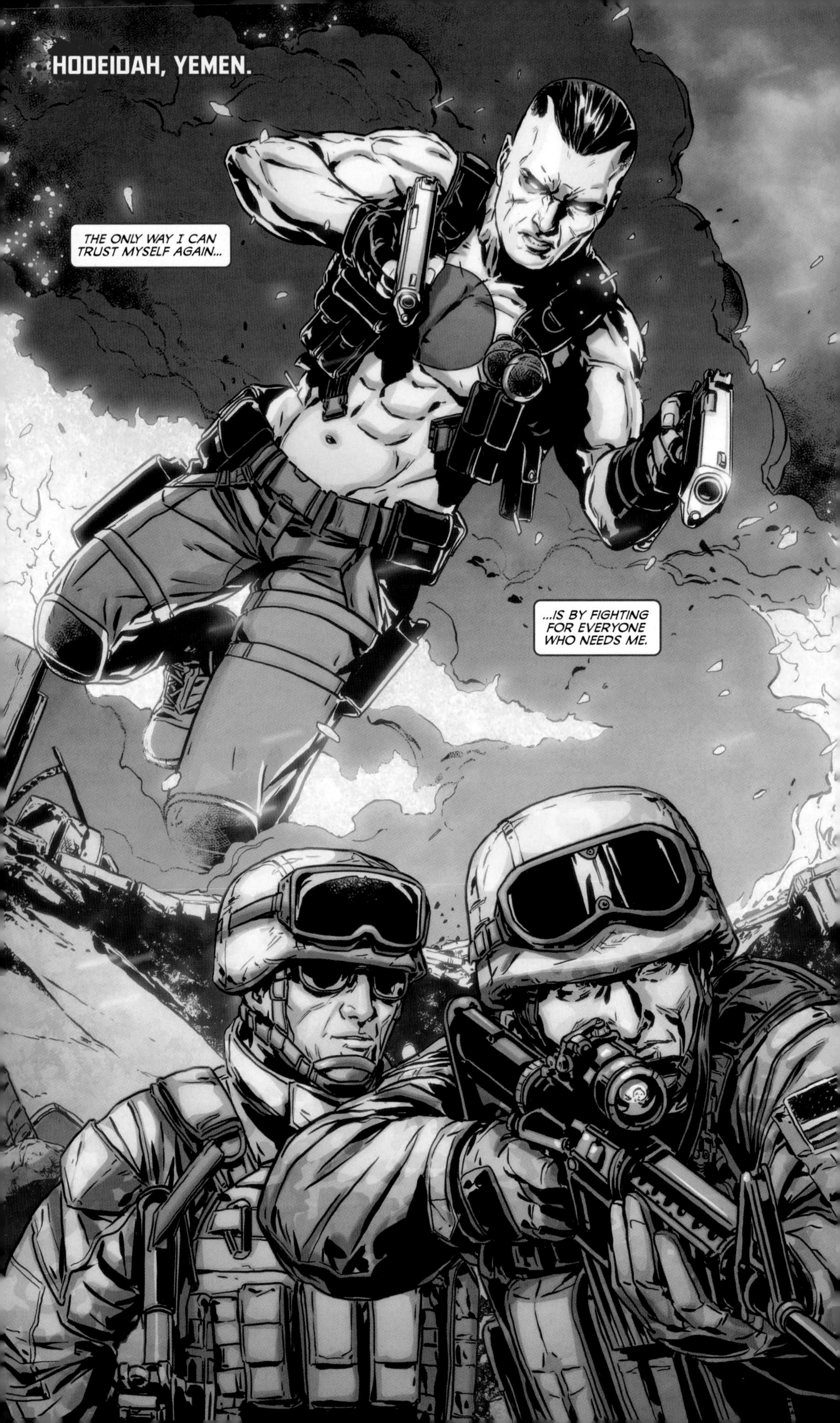
HODEIDAH, YEMEN.
THE ONLY WAY I CAN TRUST MYSELF AGAIN...
...IS BY FIGHTING FOR EVERYONE WHO NEEDS ME.

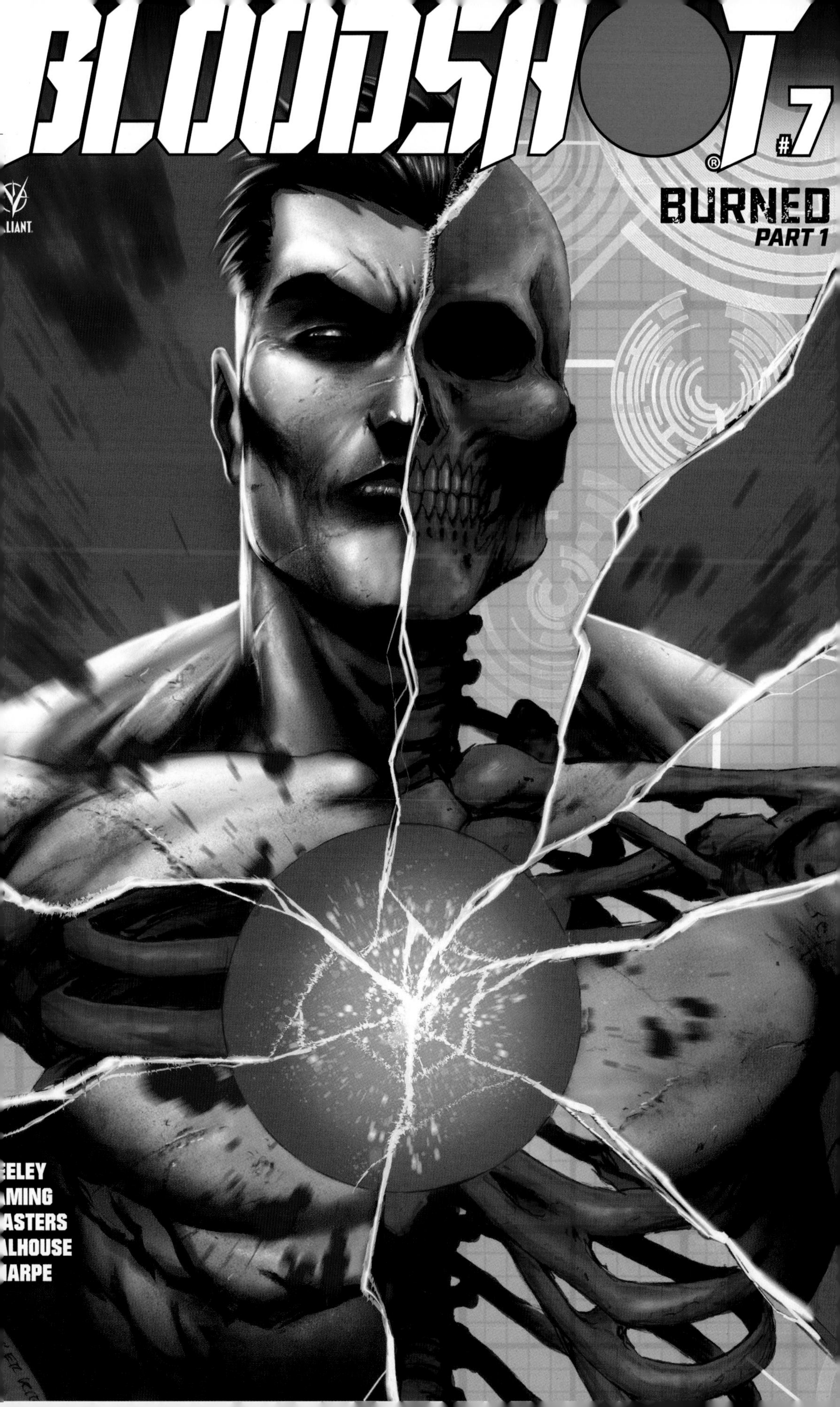
BLOODSHOT®
#7
BURNED
PART 1
LIANT
EELEY
MING
ASTERS
LHOUSE
ARPE

"Burned, Part 1"

BLOODSHOT #7

WRITER: Tim Seeley
ARTISTS: Mark Laming and Jason Masters
COLORIST: Andrew Dalhouse
LETTERER: Dave Sharpe
COVER ARTIST: Tyler Kirkham
ASSISTANT EDITOR: Drew Baumgartner
EDITOR: Lysa Hawkins

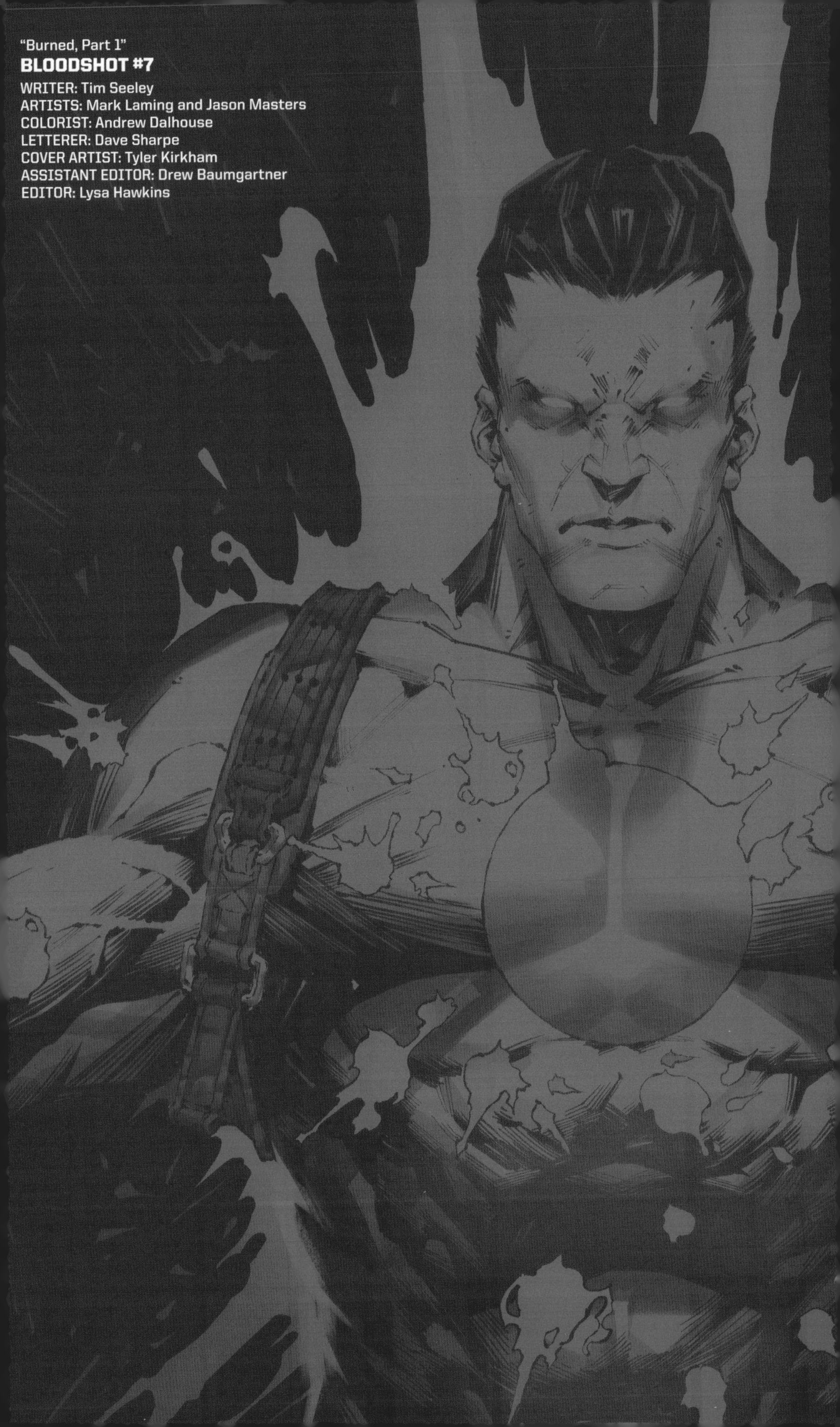

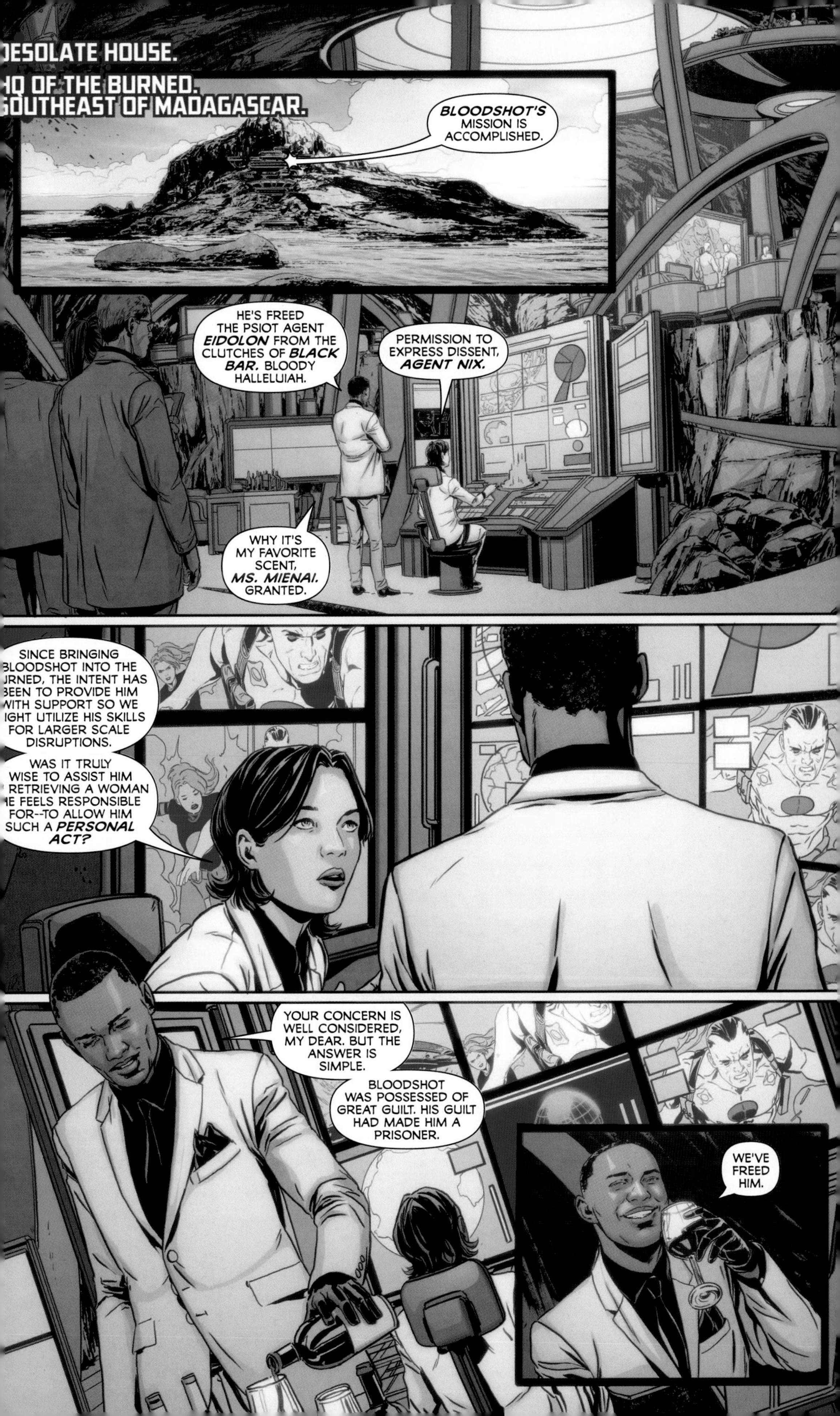

ESOLATE HOUSE.
Q OF THE BURNED. OUTHEAST OF MADAGASCAR.
BLOODSHOT'S MISSION IS ACCOMPLISHED.
HE'S FREED THE PSIOT AGENT EIDOLON FROM THE CLUTCHES OF BLACK BAR. BLOODY HALLELUIAH.
PERMISSION TO EXPRESS DISSENT, AGENT NIX.
WHY IT'S MY FAVORITE SCENT, MS. MIENAI. GRANTED.
SINCE BRINGING LOODSHOT INTO THE RNED, THE INTENT HAS EEN TO PROVIDE HIM WITH SUPPORT SO WE IGHT UTILIZE HIS SKILLS FOR LARGER SCALE DISRUPTIONS.
WAS IT TRULY WISE TO ASSIST HIM RETRIEVING A WOMAN E FEELS RESPONSIBLE FOR--TO ALLOW HIM SUCH A PERSONAL ACT?
YOUR CONCERN IS WELL CONSIDERED, MY DEAR. BUT THE ANSWER IS SIMPLE.
BLOODSHOT WAS POSSESSED OF GREAT GUILT. HIS GUILT HAD MADE HIM A PRISONER.
WE'VE FREED HIM.

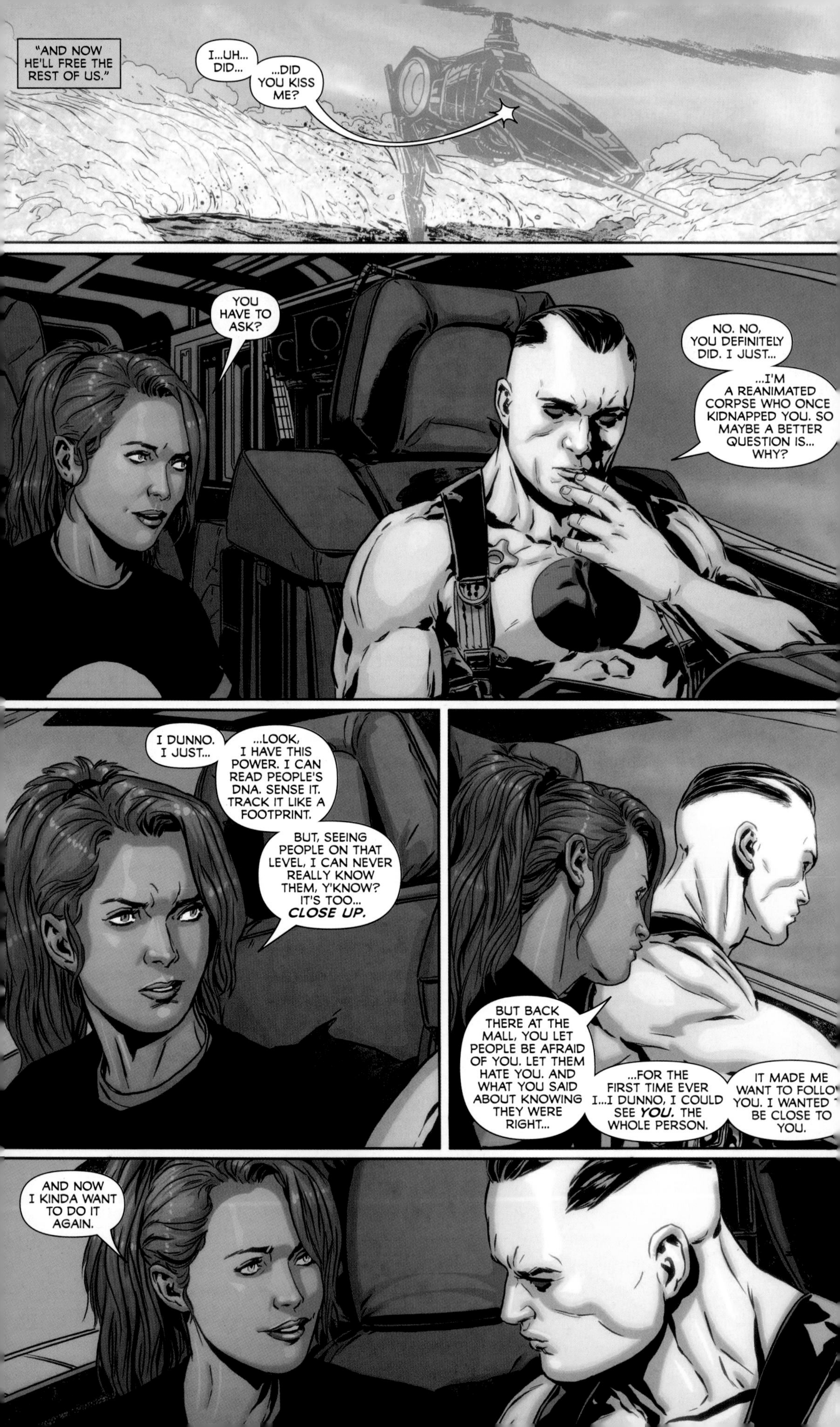

"AND NOW HE'LL FREE THE REST OF US."
I...UH... DID...
...DID YOU KISS ME?
YOU HAVE TO ASK?
NO. NO, YOU DEFINITELY DID. I JUST...
...I'M A REANIMATED CORPSE WHO ONCE KIDNAPPED YOU. SO MAYBE A BETTER QUESTION IS... WHY?
I DUNNO. I JUST...
...LOOK, I HAVE THIS POWER. I CAN READ PEOPLE'S DNA. SENSE IT. TRACK IT LIKE A FOOTPRINT.
BUT, SEEING PEOPLE ON THAT LEVEL, I CAN NEVER REALLY KNOW THEM, Y'KNOW? IT'S TOO... CLOSE UP.
BUT BACK THERE AT THE MALL, YOU LET PEOPLE BE AFRAID OF YOU. LET THEM HATE YOU. AND WHAT YOU SAID ABOUT KNOWING THEY WERE RIGHT...
...FOR THE FIRST TIME EVER I...I DUNNO, I COULD SEE YOU. THE WHOLE PERSON.
IT MADE ME WANT TO FOLLO YOU. I WANTED BE CLOSE TO YOU.
AND NOW I KINDA WANT TO DO IT AGAIN.

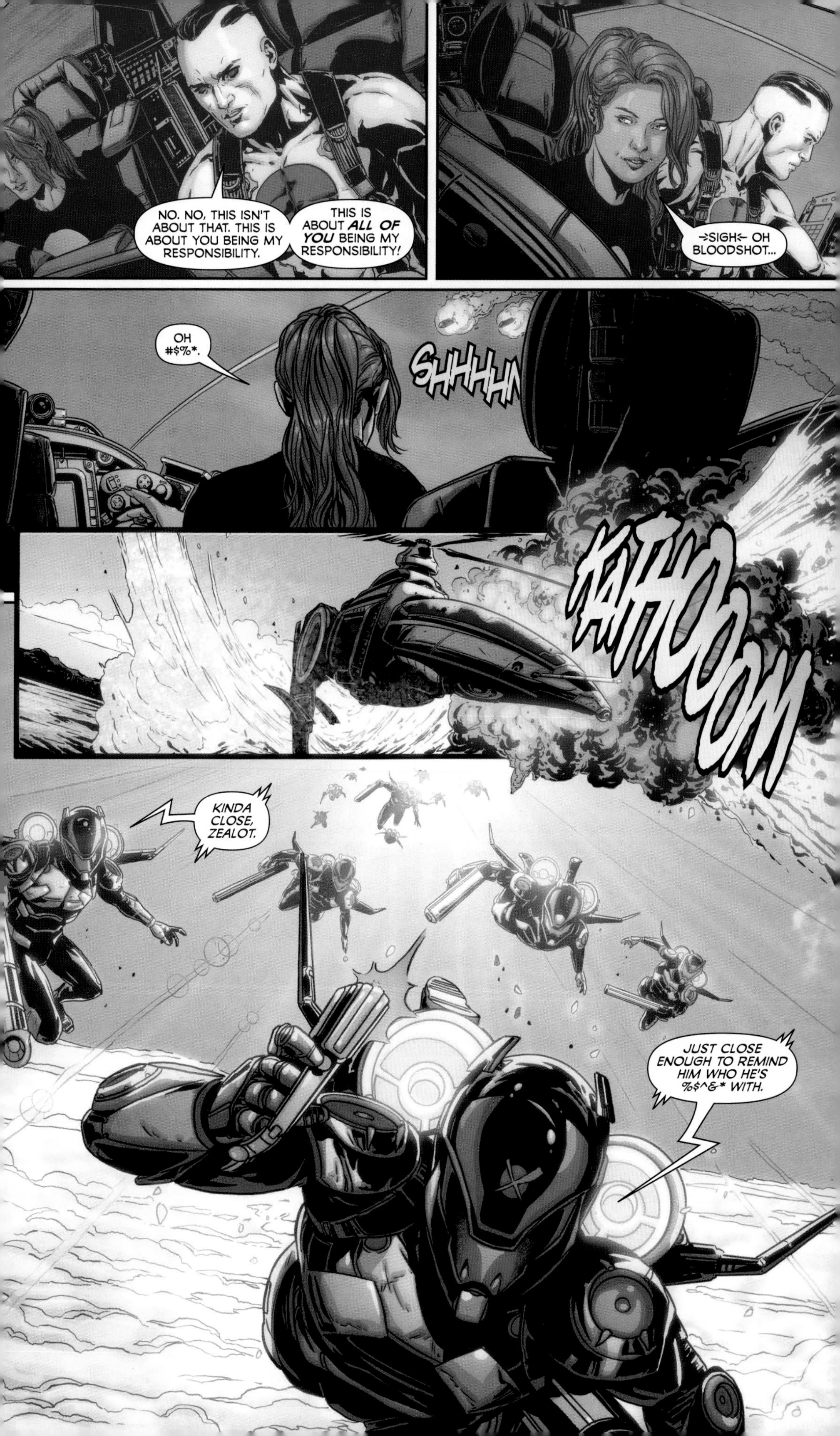
NO. NO, THIS ISN'T ABOUT THAT. THIS IS ABOUT YOU BEING MY RESPONSIBILITY.
THIS IS ABOUT ***ALL OF YOU*** BEING MY RESPONSIBILITY!
>SIGH< OH BLOODSHOT...
OH #$%*.
SHHHHN
KATHOOOOM
KINDA CLOSE, ZEALOT.
JUST CLOSE ENOUGH TO REMIND HIM WHO HE'S %$^&* WITH.

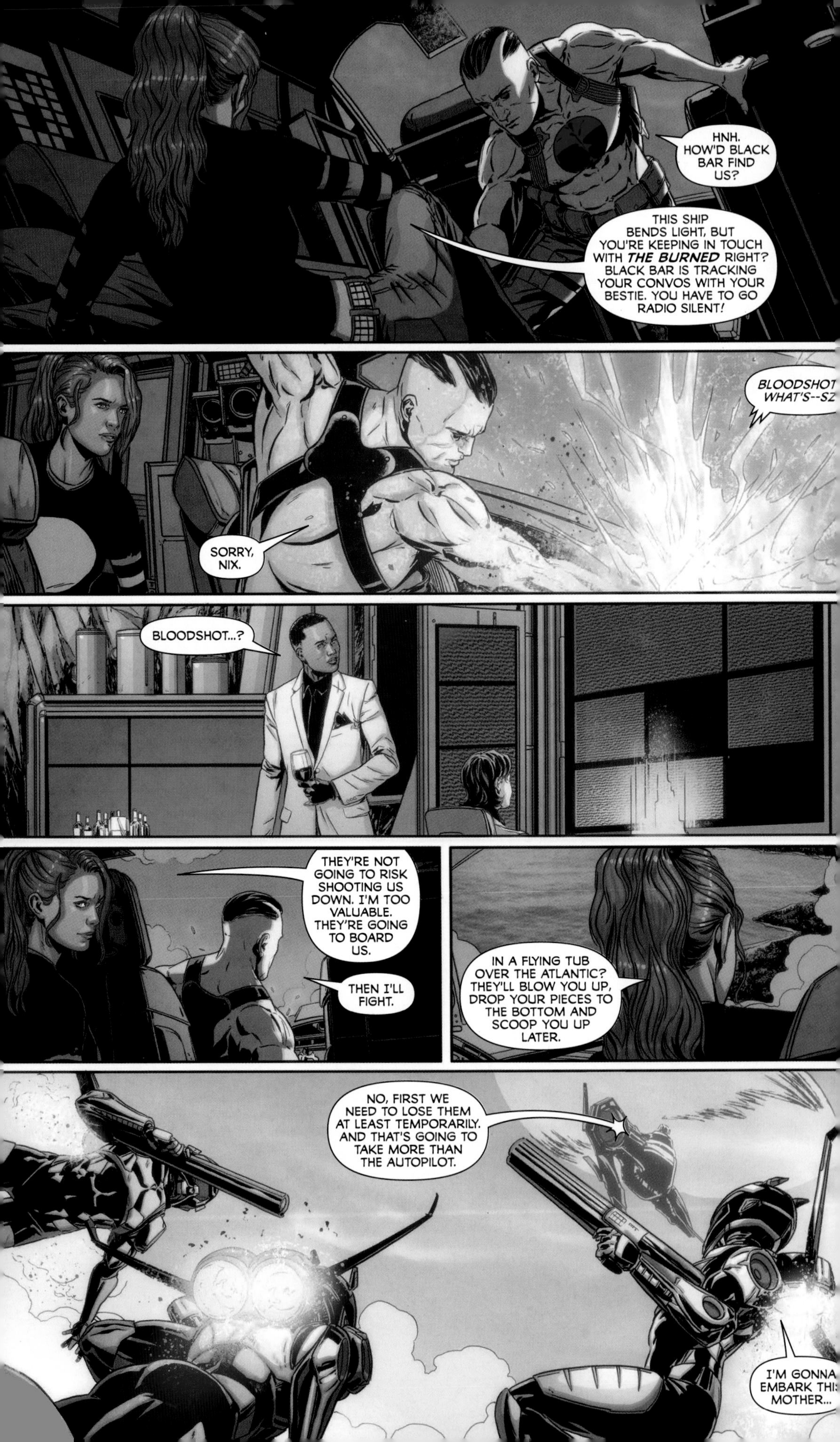
HNH. HOW'D BLACK BAR FIND US?
THIS SHIP BENDS LIGHT, BUT YOU'RE KEEPING IN TOUCH WITH ***THE BURNED*** RIGHT? BLACK BAR IS TRACKING YOUR CONVOS WITH YOUR BESTIE. YOU HAVE TO GO RADIO SILENT*!*
BLOODSHOT WHAT'S--SZ
SORRY, NIX.
BLOODSHOT...?
THEY'RE NOT GOING TO RISK SHOOTING US DOWN. I'M TOO VALUABLE. THEY'RE GOING TO BOARD US.
THEN I'LL FIGHT.
IN A FLYING TUB OVER THE ATLANTIC? THEY'LL BLOW YOU UP, DROP YOUR PIECES TO THE BOTTOM AND SCOOP YOU UP LATER.
NO, FIRST WE NEED TO LOSE THEM AT LEAST TEMPORARILY. AND THAT'S GOING TO TAKE MORE THAN THE AUTOPILOT.
I'M GONNA EMBARK THIS MOTHER...

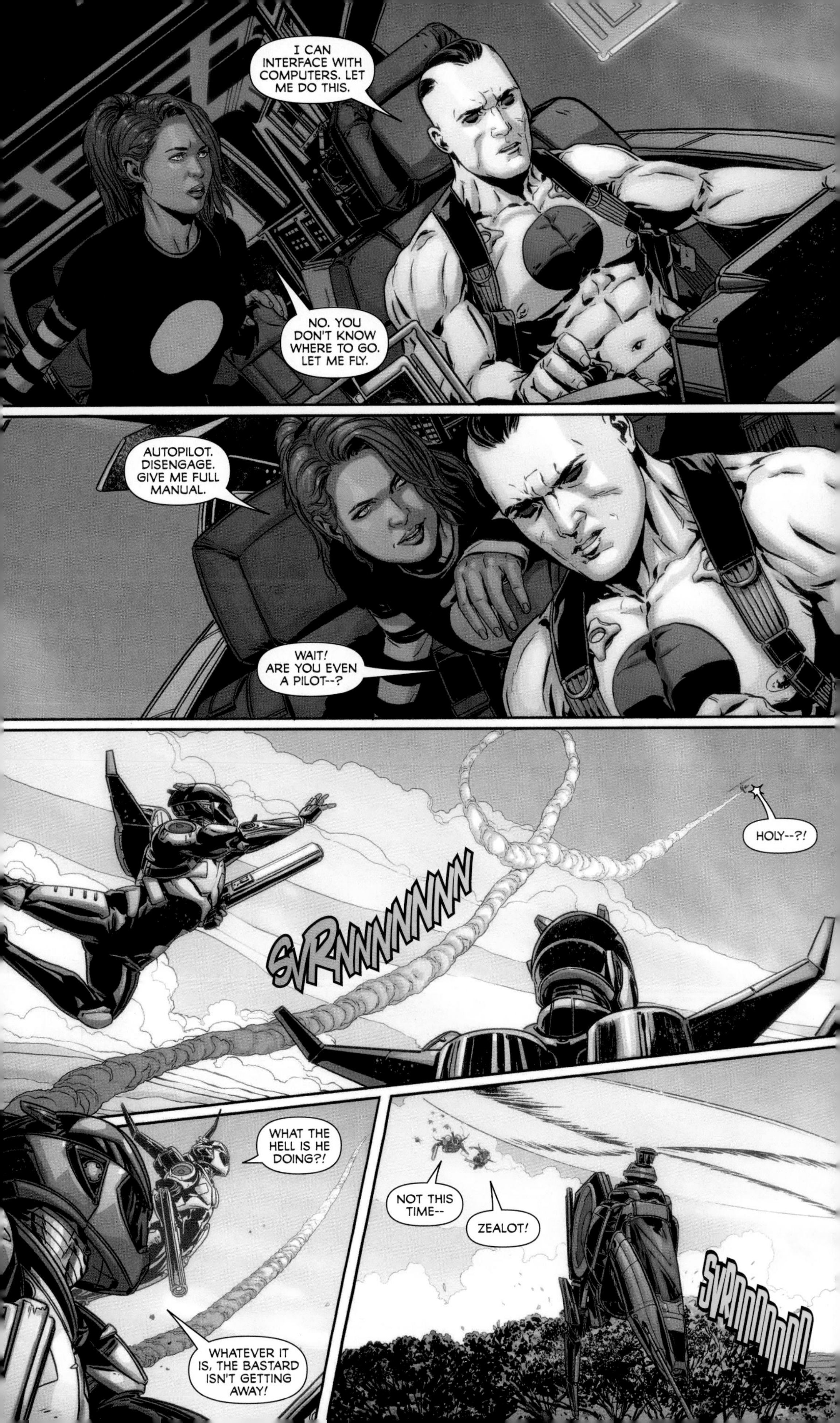
I CAN INTERFACE WITH COMPUTERS. LET ME DO THIS.
NO. YOU DON'T KNOW WHERE TO GO. LET ME FLY.
AUTOPILOT. DISENGAGE. GIVE ME FULL MANUAL.
WAIT! ARE YOU EVEN A PILOT--?
HOLY--?!
SVRNNNNNNN
WHAT THE HELL IS HE DOING?!
WHATEVER IT IS, THE BASTARD ISN'T GETTING AWAY!
NOT THIS TIME--
ZEALOT!
SVRNNNNN

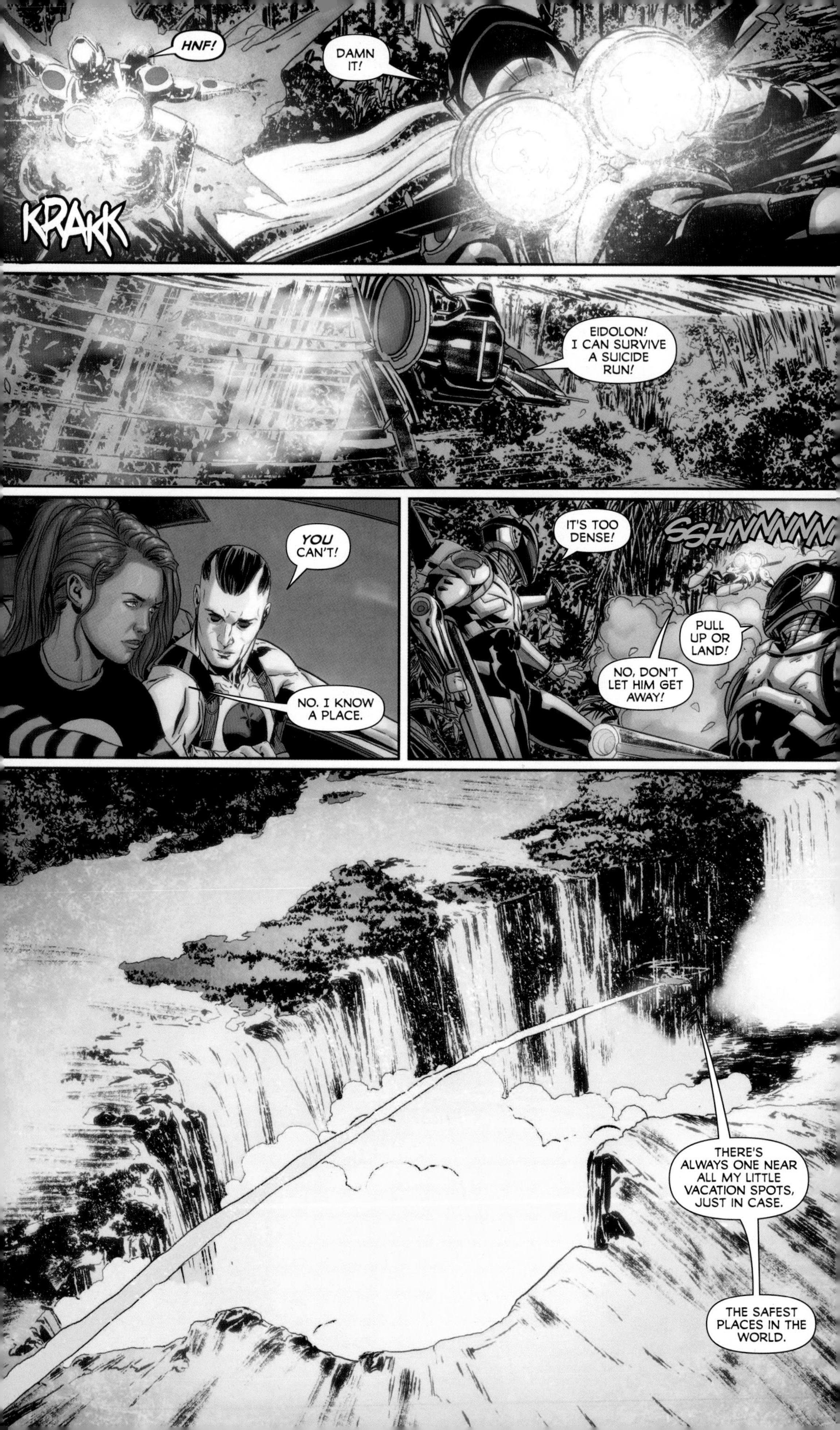

HNF!
DAMN IT!
KRAKK
EIDOLON! I CAN SURVIVE A SUICIDE RUN!
YOU CAN'T!
NO. I KNOW A PLACE.
IT'S TOO DENSE!
SSHNNNNNN
PULL UP OR LAND!
NO, DON'T LET HIM GET AWAY!
THERE'S ALWAYS ONE NEAR ALL MY LITTLE VACATION SPOTS, JUST IN CASE.
THE SAFEST PLACES IN THE WORLD.

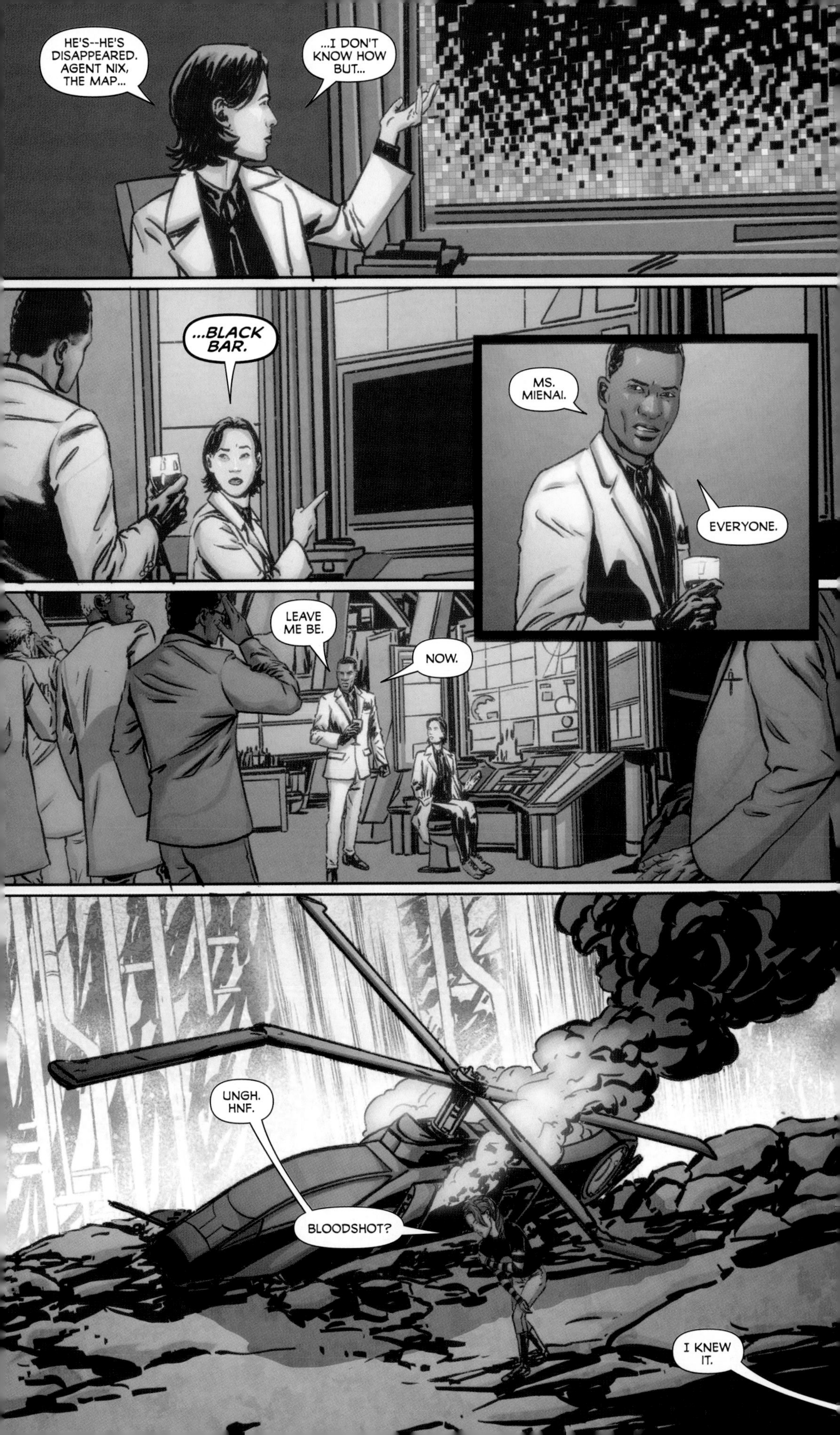

HE'S--HE'S DISAPPEARED. AGENT NIX, THE MAP...
...I DON'T KNOW HOW BUT...
...BLACK BAR.
MS. MIENAI.
EVERYONE.
LEAVE ME BE.
NOW.
UNGH. HNF.
BLOODSHOT?
I KNEW IT.

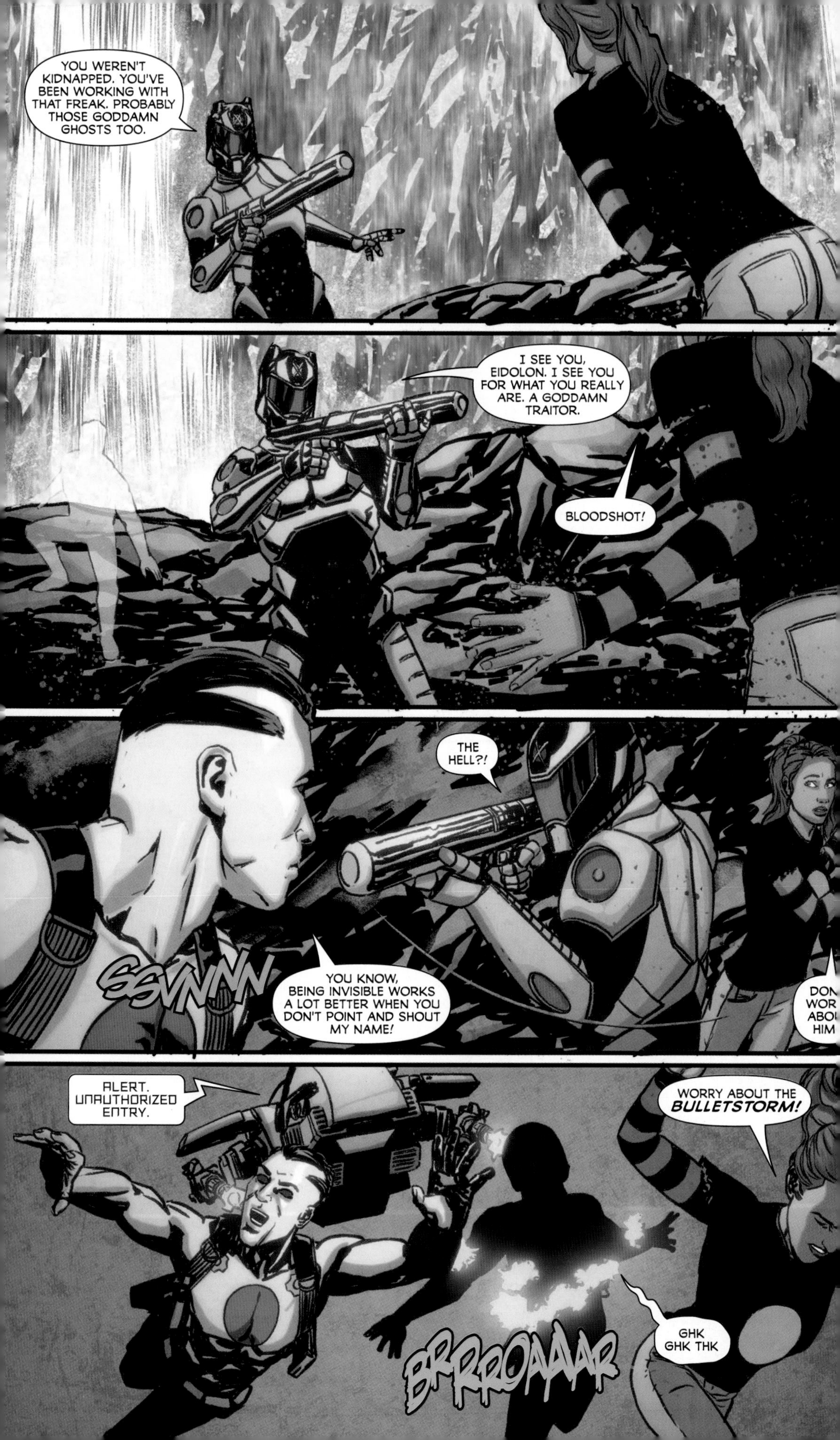

YOU WEREN'T KIDNAPPED. YOU'VE BEEN WORKING WITH THAT FREAK. PROBABLY THOSE GODDAMN GHOSTS TOO.
I SEE YOU, EIDOLON. I SEE YOU FOR WHAT YOU REALLY ARE. A GODDAMN TRAITOR.
BLOODSHOT!
THE HELL?!
SSVNNN
YOU KNOW, BEING INVISIBLE WORKS A LOT BETTER WHEN YOU DON'T POINT AND SHOUT MY NAME!
ALERT. UNAUTHORIZED ENTRY.
WORRY ABOUT THE *BULLETSTORM!*
GHK GHK THK
BRRROAAAR

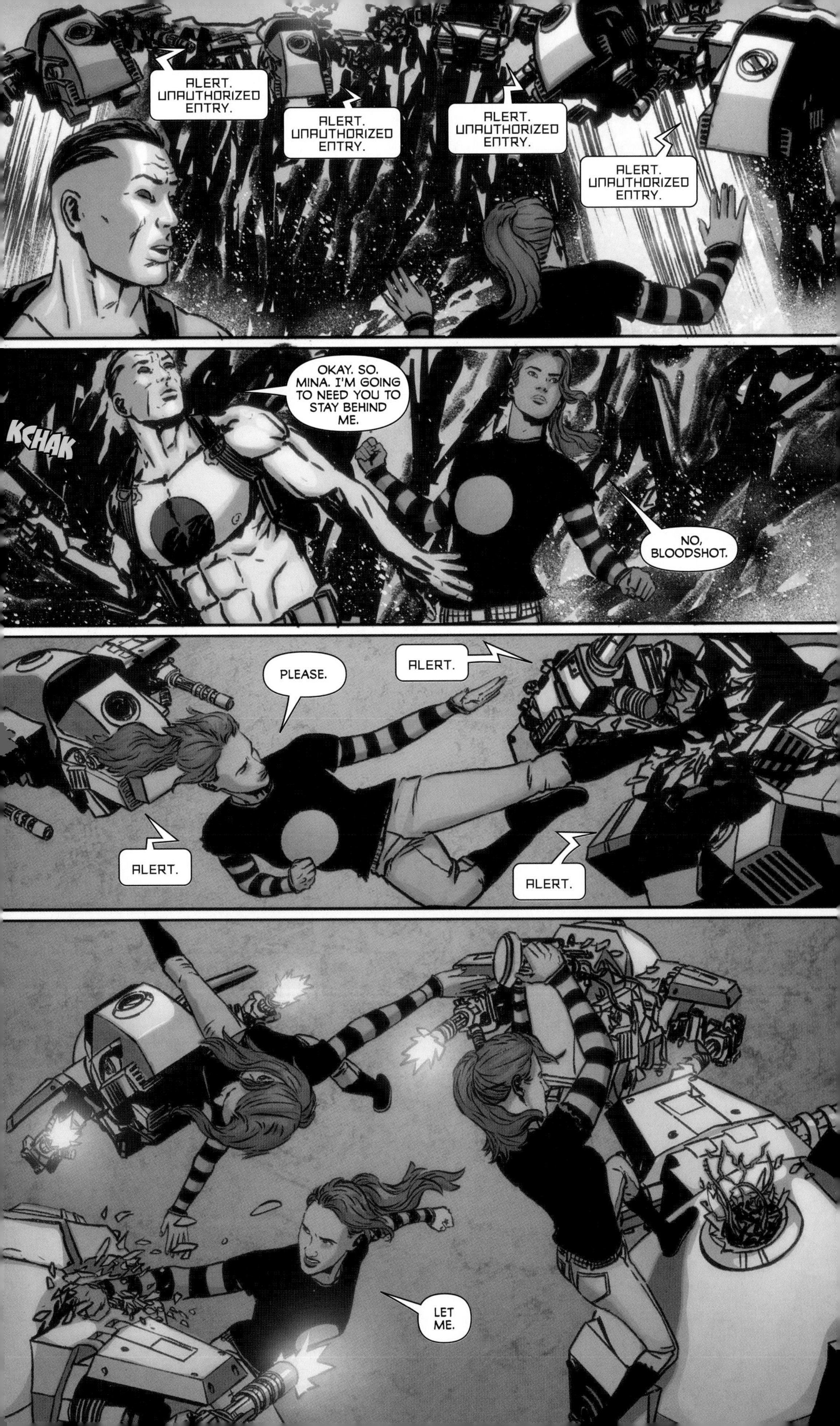
ALERT. UNAUTHORIZED ENTRY.
ALERT. UNAUTHORIZED ENTRY.
ALERT. UNAUTHORIZED ENTRY.
ALERT. UNAUTHORIZED ENTRY.
KCHAK
OKAY. SO. MINA. I'M GOING TO NEED YOU TO STAY BEHIND ME.
NO, BLOODSHOT.
PLEASE.
ALERT.
ALERT.
ALERT.
LET ME.

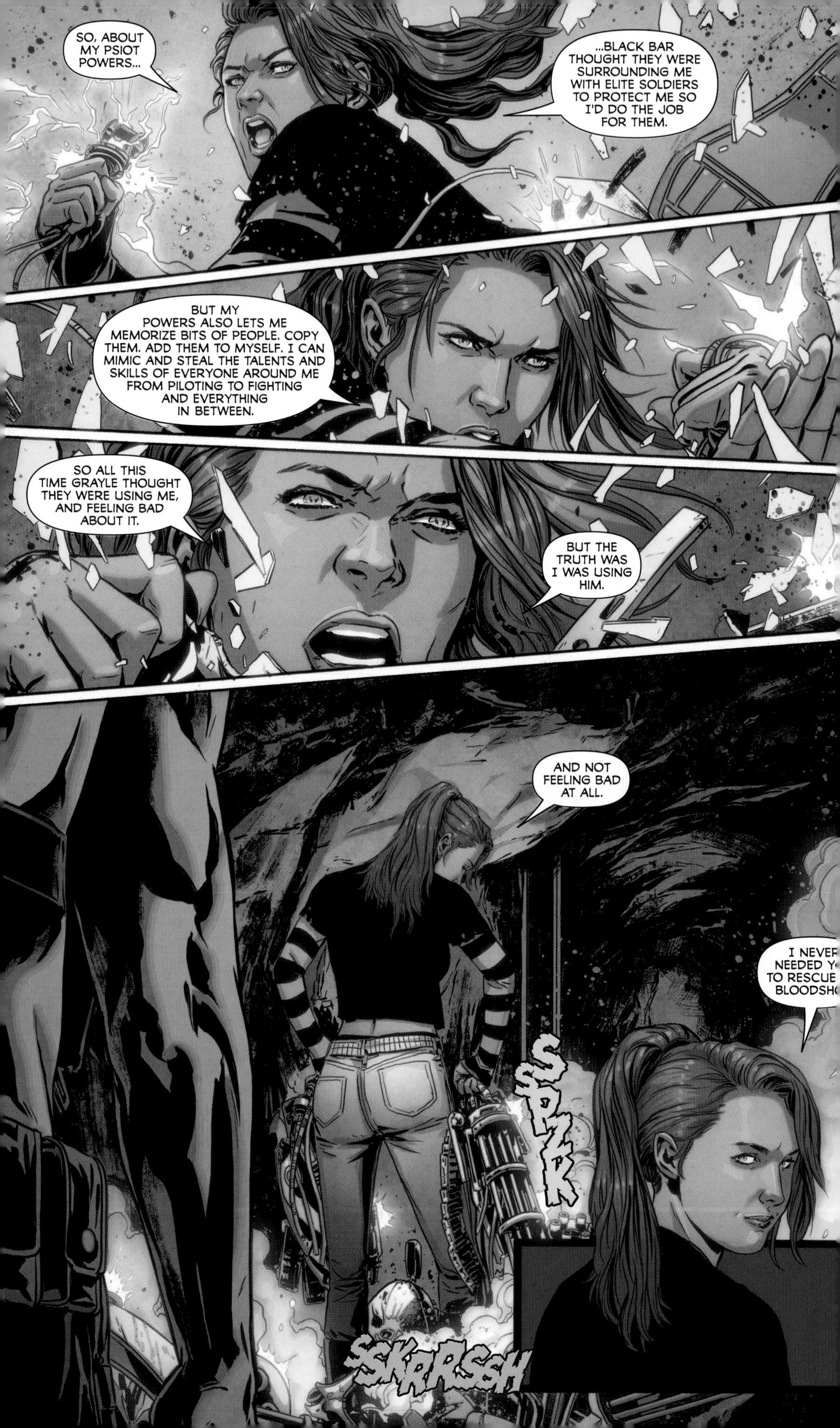
SO, ABOUT MY PSIOT POWERS...
...BLACK BAR THOUGHT THEY WERE SURROUNDING ME WITH ELITE SOLDIERS TO PROTECT ME SO I'D DO THE JOB FOR THEM.
BUT MY POWERS ALSO LETS ME MEMORIZE BITS OF PEOPLE. COPY THEM. ADD THEM TO MYSELF. I CAN MIMIC AND STEAL THE TALENTS AND SKILLS OF EVERYONE AROUND ME FROM PILOTING TO FIGHTING AND EVERYTHING IN BETWEEN.
SO ALL THIS TIME GRAYLE THOUGHT THEY WERE USING ME, AND FEELING BAD ABOUT IT.
BUT THE TRUTH WAS I WAS USING HIM.
AND NOT FEELING BAD AT ALL.
I NEVER NEEDED Y TO RESCUE BLOODSH
SPZK
SSKRRSSH

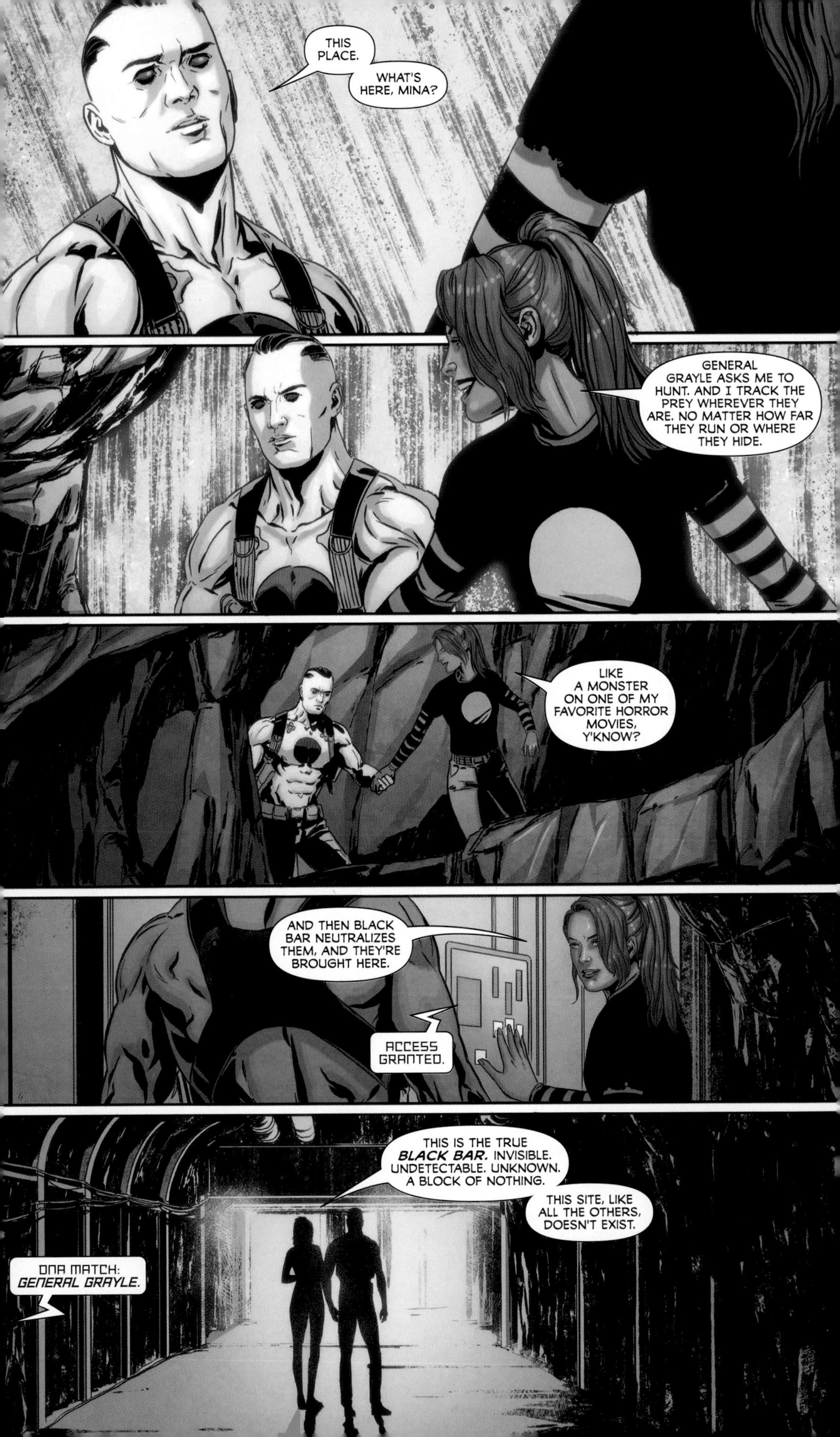
THIS PLACE.
WHAT'S HERE, MINA?
GENERAL GRAYLE ASKS ME TO HUNT. AND I TRACK THE PREY WHEREVER THEY ARE. NO MATTER HOW FAR THEY RUN OR WHERE THEY HIDE.
LIKE A MONSTER ON ONE OF MY FAVORITE HORROR MOVIES, Y'KNOW?
AND THEN BLACK BAR NEUTRALIZES THEM, AND THEY'RE BROUGHT HERE.
ACCESS GRANTED.
THIS IS THE TRUE *BLACK BAR.* INVISIBLE. UNDETECTABLE. UNKNOWN. A BLOCK OF NOTHING.
THIS SITE, LIKE ALL THE OTHERS, DOESN'T EXIST.
DNA MATCH: *GENERAL GRAYLE.*

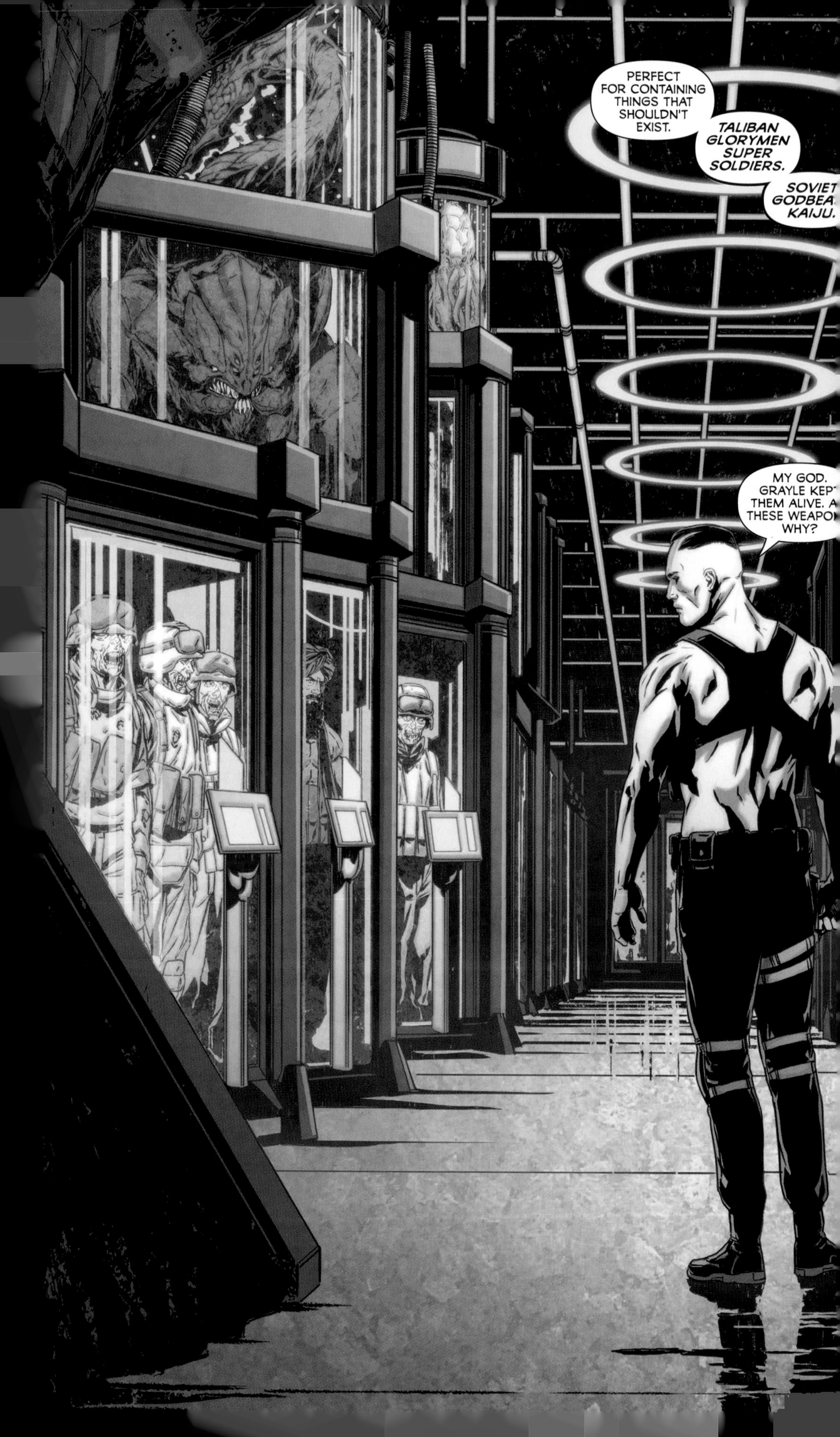
PERFECT FOR CONTAINING THINGS THAT SHOULDN'T EXIST.
TALIBAN GLORYMEN SUPER SOLDIERS.
SOVIET GODBEA KAIJU.
MY GOD. GRAYLE KEP THEM ALIVE. A THESE WEAPO WHY?

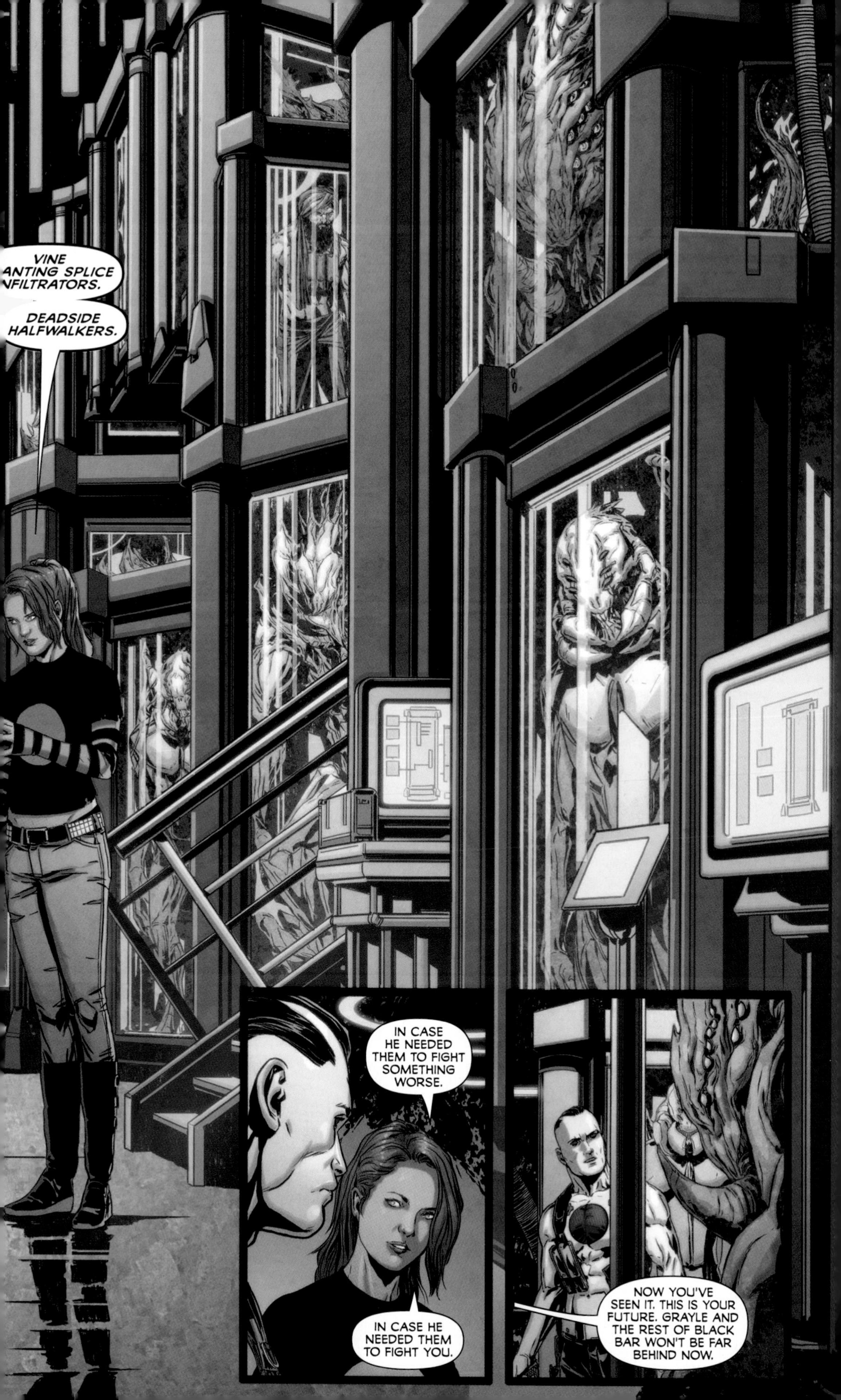

VINE
ANTING SPLICE
NFILTRATORS.
DEADSIDE
HALFWALKERS.
IN CASE HE NEEDED THEM TO FIGHT SOMETHING WORSE.
IN CASE HE NEEDED THEM TO FIGHT YOU.
NOW YOU'VE SEEN IT. THIS IS YOUR FUTURE. GRAYLE AND THE REST OF BLACK BAR WON'T BE FAR BEHIND NOW.

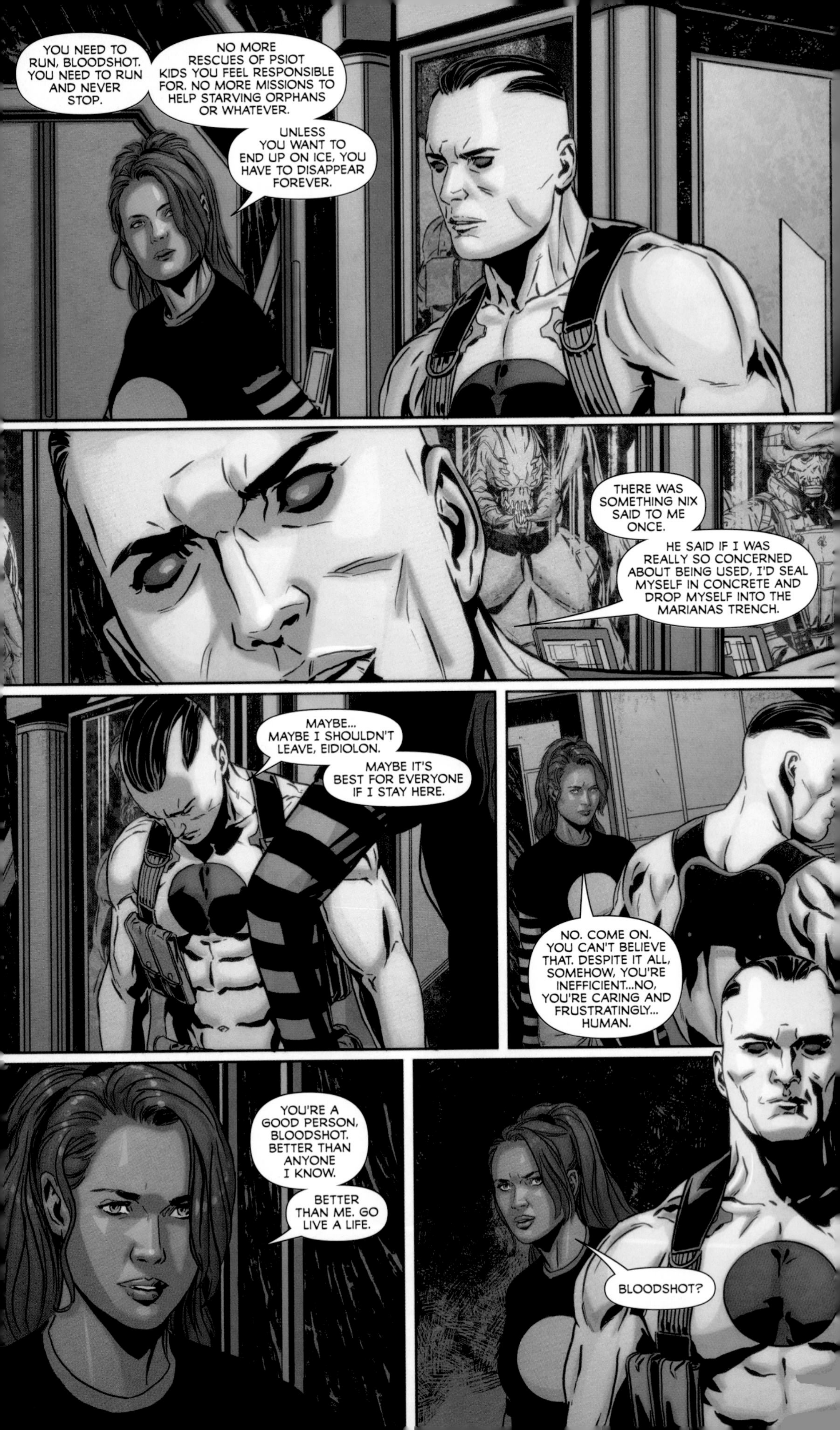
YOU NEED TO RUN, BLOODSHOT. YOU NEED TO RUN AND NEVER STOP.
NO MORE RESCUES OF PSIOT KIDS YOU FEEL RESPONSIBLE FOR. NO MORE MISSIONS TO HELP STARVING ORPHANS OR WHATEVER.
UNLESS YOU WANT TO END UP ON ICE, YOU HAVE TO DISAPPEAR FOREVER.
THERE WAS SOMETHING NIX SAID TO ME ONCE.
HE SAID IF I WAS REALLY SO CONCERNED ABOUT BEING USED, I'D SEAL MYSELF IN CONCRETE AND DROP MYSELF INTO THE MARIANAS TRENCH.
MAYBE... MAYBE I SHOULDN'T LEAVE, EIDIOLON.
MAYBE IT'S BEST FOR EVERYONE IF I STAY HERE.
NO. COME ON. YOU CAN'T BELIEVE THAT. DESPITE IT ALL, SOMEHOW, YOU'RE INEFFICIENT...NO, YOU'RE CARING AND FRUSTRATINGLY... HUMAN.
YOU'RE A GOOD PERSON, BLOODSHOT. BETTER THAN ANYONE I KNOW.
BETTER THAN ME. GO LIVE A LIFE.
BLOODSHOT?

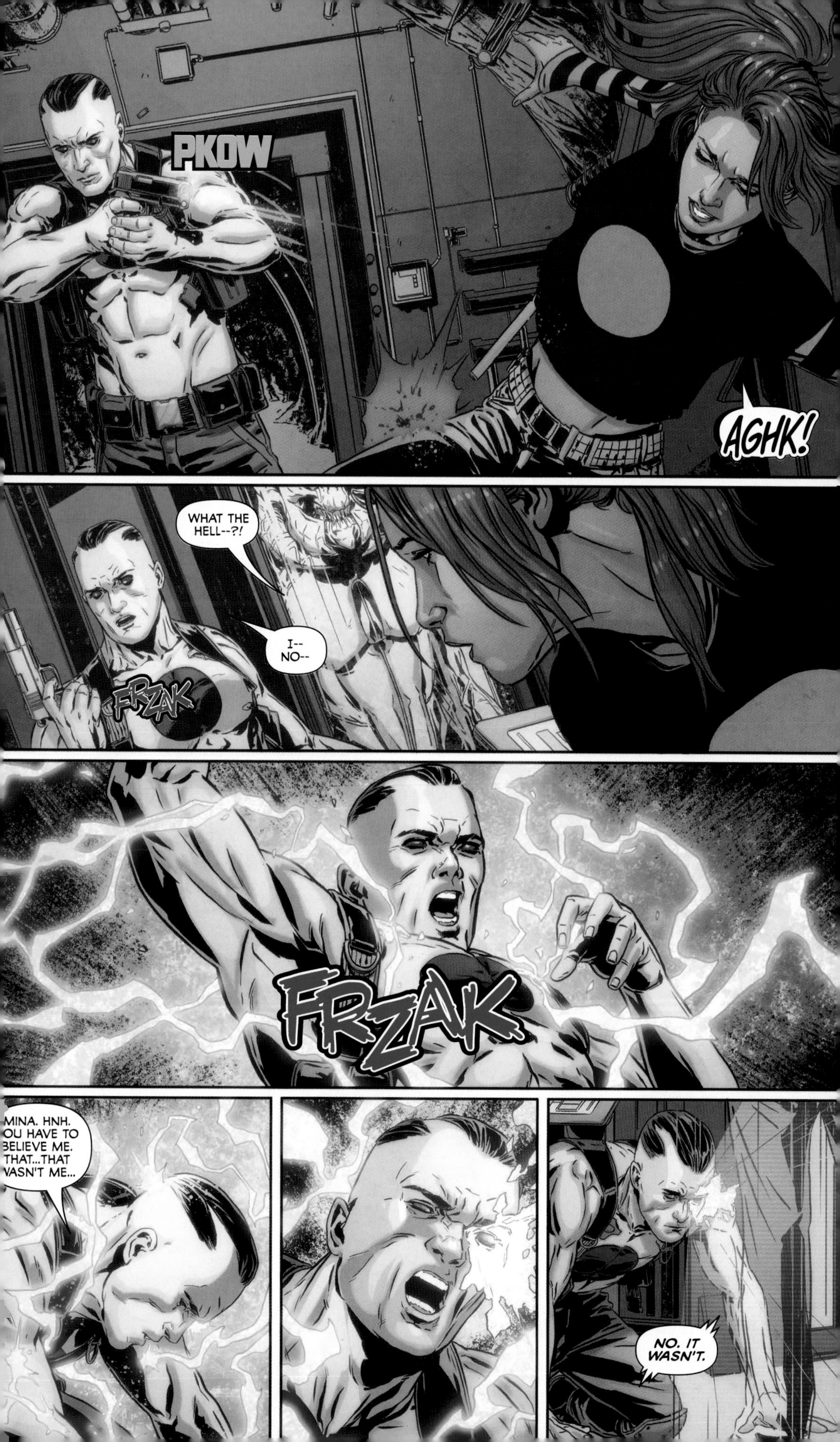
PKOW
AGHK!
WHAT THE HELL--?!
I-- NO--
FRZAK
FRZAK
MINA. HNH. OU HAVE TO BELIEVE ME. THAT...THAT WASN'T ME...
NO. IT WASN'T.

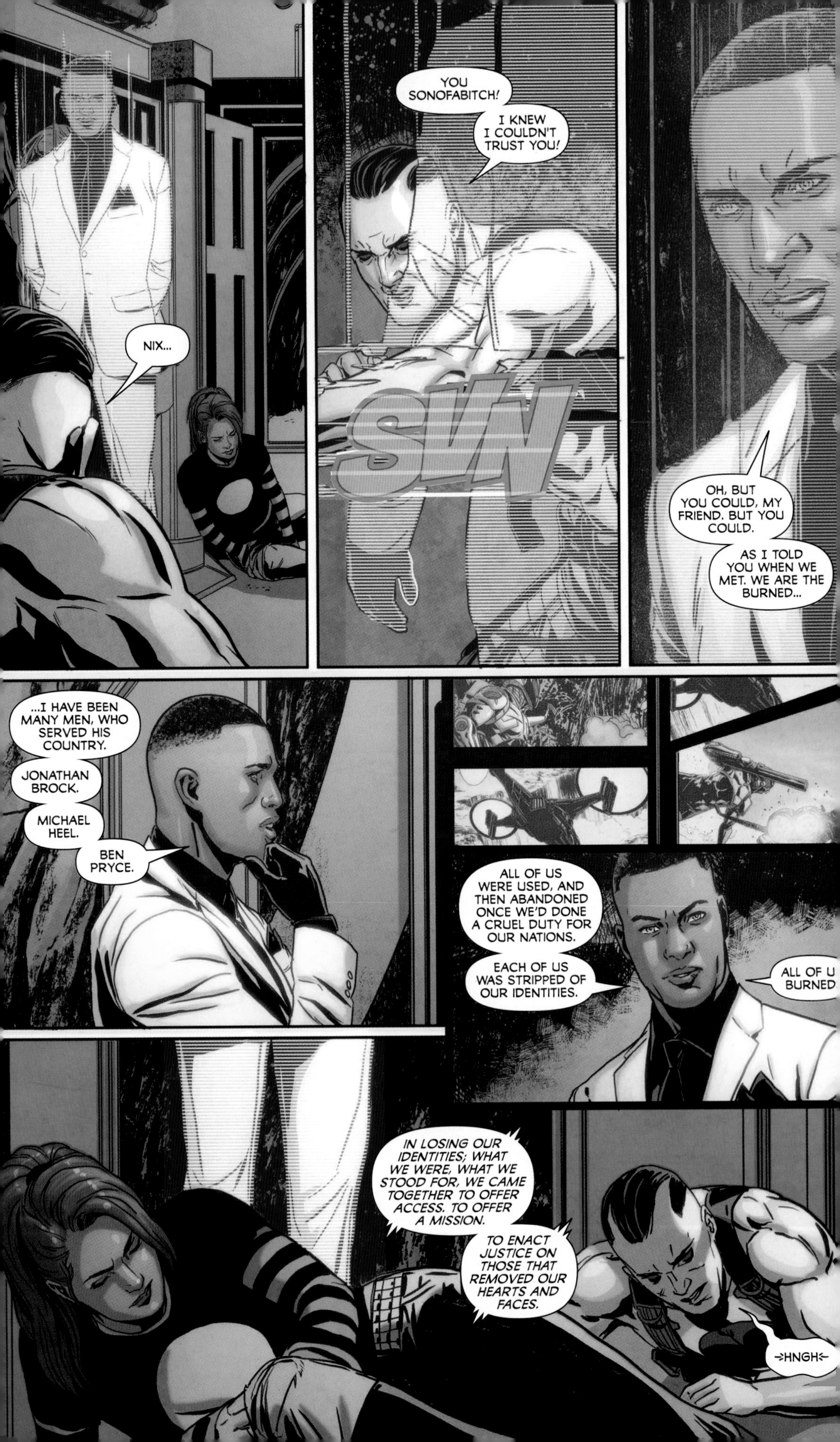

NIX...
YOU SONOFABITCH!
I KNEW I COULDN'T TRUST YOU!
SWN
OH, BUT YOU COULD, MY FRIEND. BUT YOU COULD.
AS I TOLD YOU WHEN WE MET. WE ARE THE BURNED...
...I HAVE BEEN MANY MEN, WHO SERVED HIS COUNTRY.
JONATHAN BROCK.
MICHAEL HEEL.
BEN PRYCE.
ALL OF US WERE USED, AND THEN ABANDONED ONCE WE'D DONE A CRUEL DUTY FOR OUR NATIONS.
EACH OF US WAS STRIPPED OF OUR IDENTITIES.
ALL OF U BURNED
IN LOSING OUR IDENTITIES; WHAT WE WERE, WHAT WE STOOD FOR, WE CAME TOGETHER TO OFFER ACCESS. TO OFFER A MISSION.
TO ENACT JUSTICE ON THOSE THAT REMOVED OUR HEARTS AND FACES.
HNGH

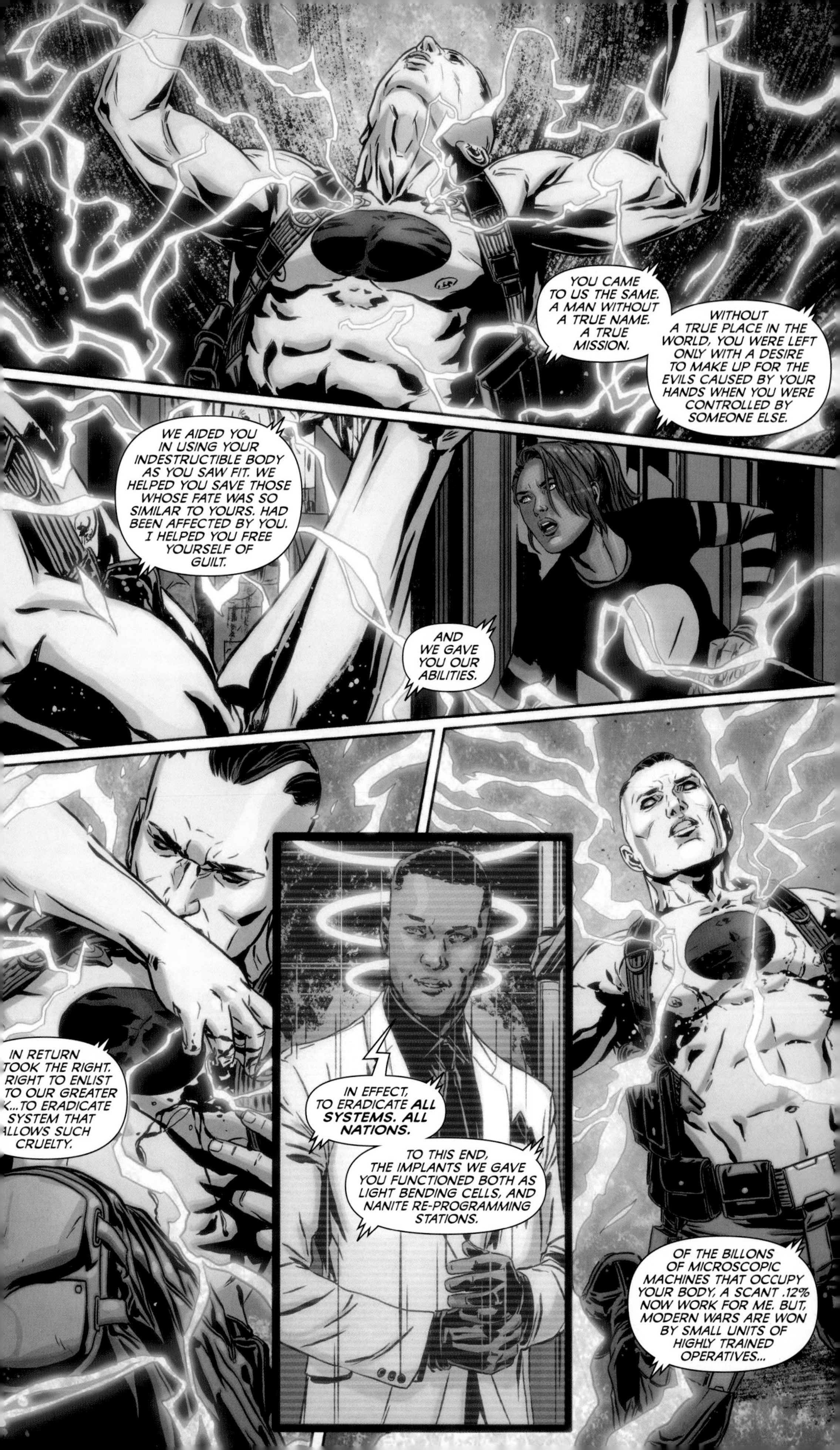

YOU CAME TO US THE SAME. A MAN WITHOUT A TRUE NAME. A TRUE MISSION.
WITHOUT A TRUE PLACE IN THE WORLD, YOU WERE LEFT ONLY WITH A DESIRE TO MAKE UP FOR THE EVILS CAUSED BY YOUR HANDS WHEN YOU WERE CONTROLLED BY SOMEONE ELSE.
WE AIDED YOU IN USING YOUR INDESTRUCTIBLE BODY AS YOU SAW FIT. WE HELPED YOU SAVE THOSE WHOSE FATE WAS SO SIMILAR TO YOURS. HAD BEEN AFFECTED BY YOU. I HELPED YOU FREE YOURSELF OF GUILT.
AND WE GAVE YOU OUR ABILITIES.
IN RETURN TOOK THE RIGHT. RIGHT TO ENLIST TO OUR GREATER ...TO ERADICATE SYSTEM THAT ALLOWS SUCH CRUELTY.
IN EFFECT, TO ERADICATE **ALL SYSTEMS. ALL NATIONS.**
TO THIS END, THE IMPLANTS WE GAVE YOU FUNCTIONED BOTH AS LIGHT BENDING CELLS, AND NANITE RE-PROGRAMMING STATIONS.
OF THE BILLONS OF MICROSCOPIC MACHINES THAT OCCUPY YOUR BODY, A SCANT .12% NOW WORK FOR ME. BUT, MODERN WARS ARE WON BY SMALL UNITS OF HIGHLY TRAINED OPERATIVES...

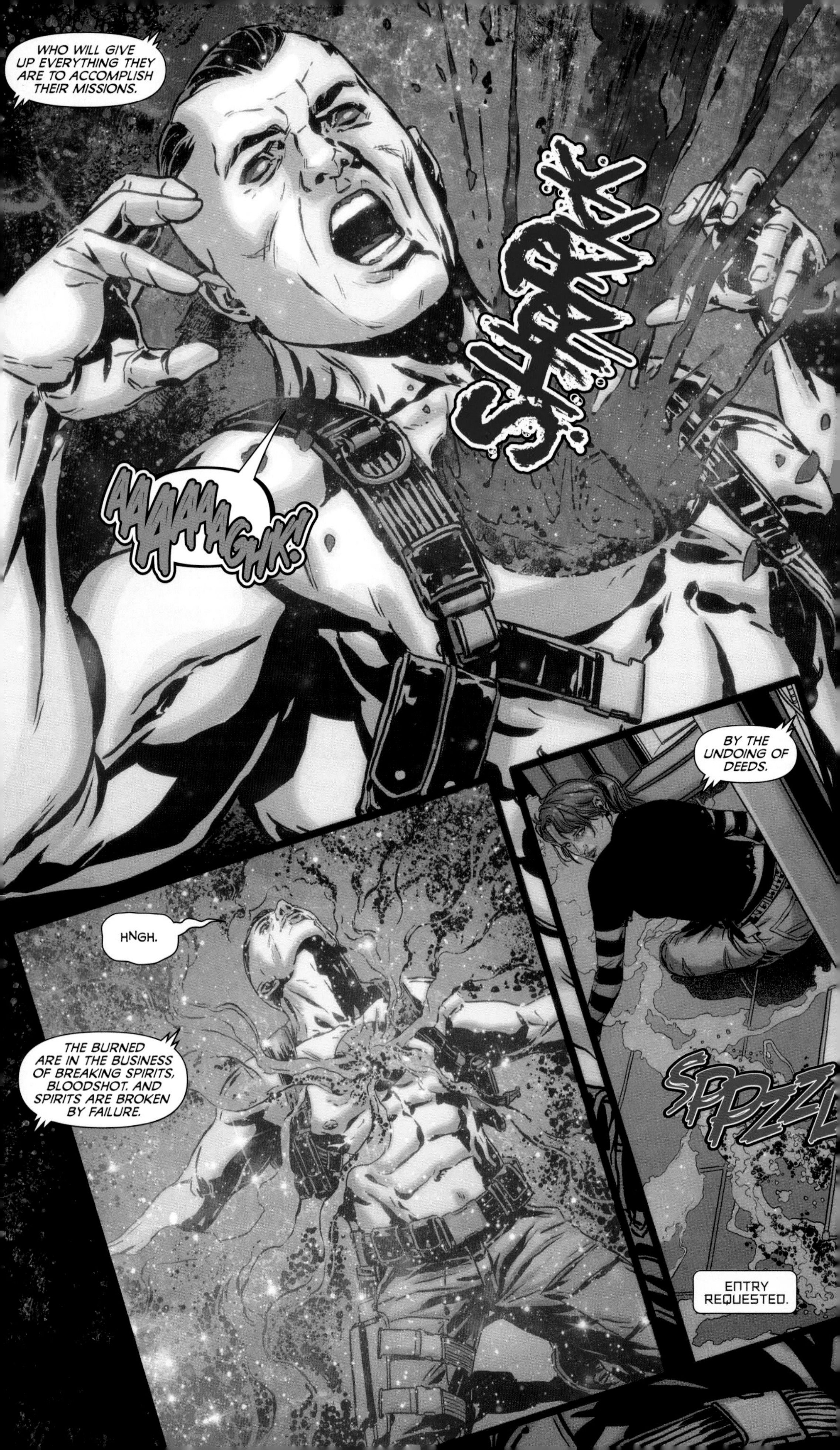
WHO WILL GIVE UP EVERYTHING THEY ARE TO ACCOMPLISH THEIR MISSIONS.
AAAAAAAAGHK!
BY THE UNDOING OF DEEDS.
HNGH.
THE BURNED ARE IN THE BUSINESS OF BREAKING SPIRITS, BLOODSHOT. AND SPIRITS ARE BROKEN BY FAILURE.
ENTRY REQUESTED.

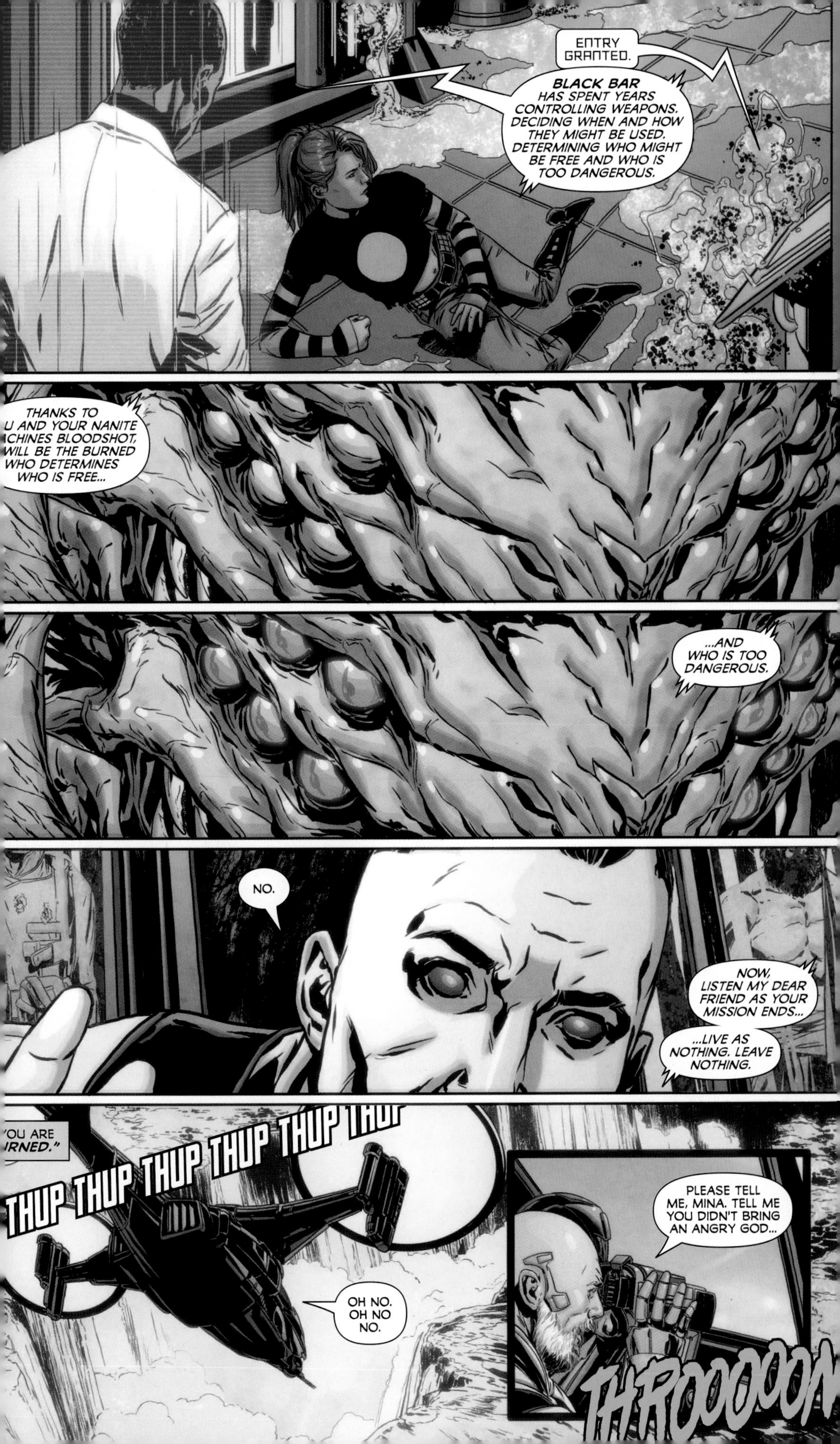
ENTRY GRANTED.
BLACK BAR HAS SPENT YEARS CONTROLLING WEAPONS. DECIDING WHEN AND HOW THEY MIGHT BE USED. DETERMINING WHO MIGHT BE FREE AND WHO IS TOO DANGEROUS.
THANKS TO U AND YOUR NANITE ACHINES BLOODSHOT, WILL BE THE BURNED WHO DETERMINES WHO IS FREE...
...AND WHO IS TOO DANGEROUS.
NO.
NOW, LISTEN MY DEAR FRIEND AS YOUR MISSION ENDS...
...LIVE AS NOTHING. LEAVE NOTHING.
YOU ARE IRNED."
THUP THUP THUP THUP THUP
PLEASE TELL ME, MINA. TELL ME YOU DIDN'T BRING AN ANGRY GOD...
OH NO. OH NO NO.
THROOOOON

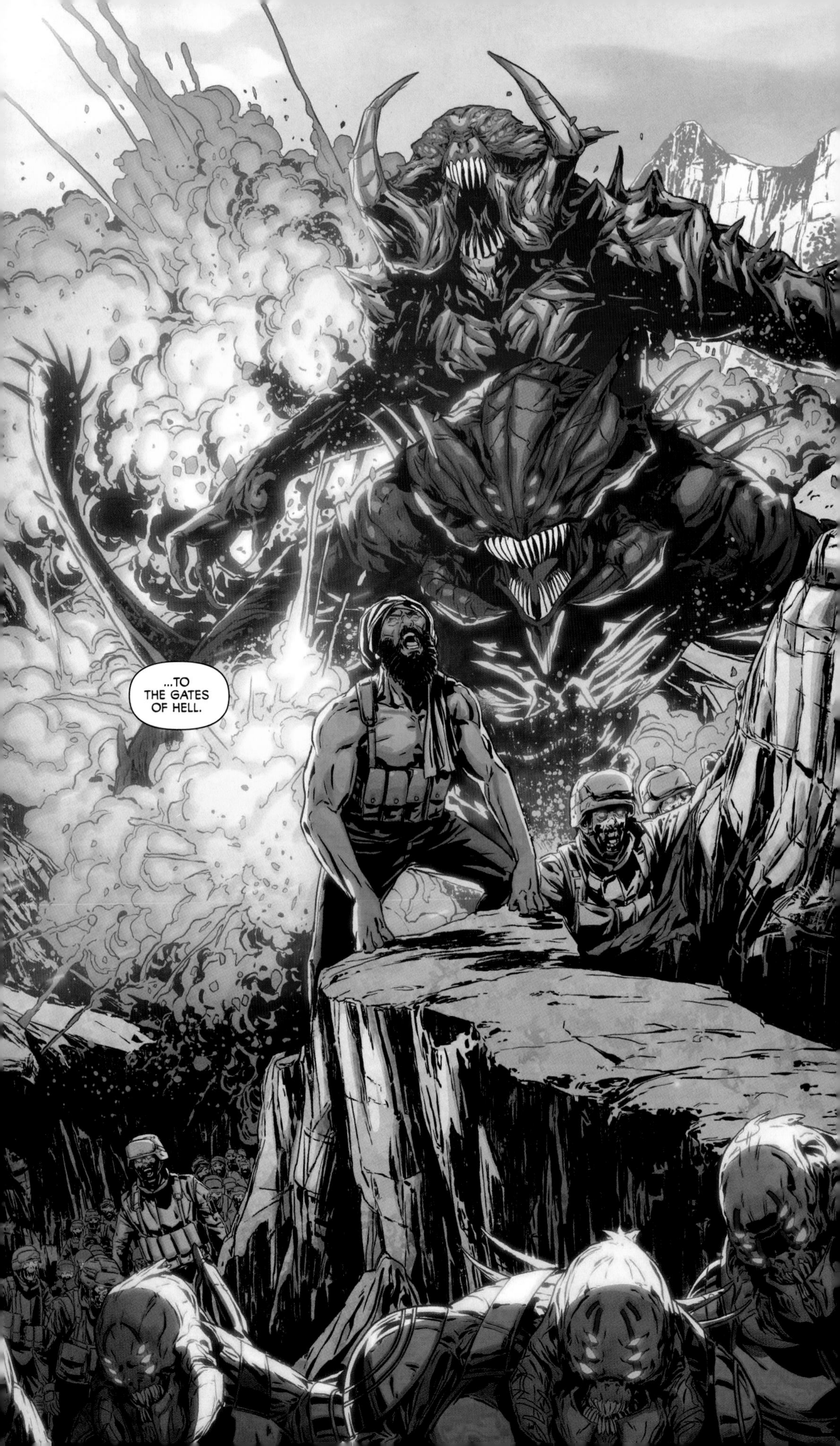
...TO THE GATES OF HELL.

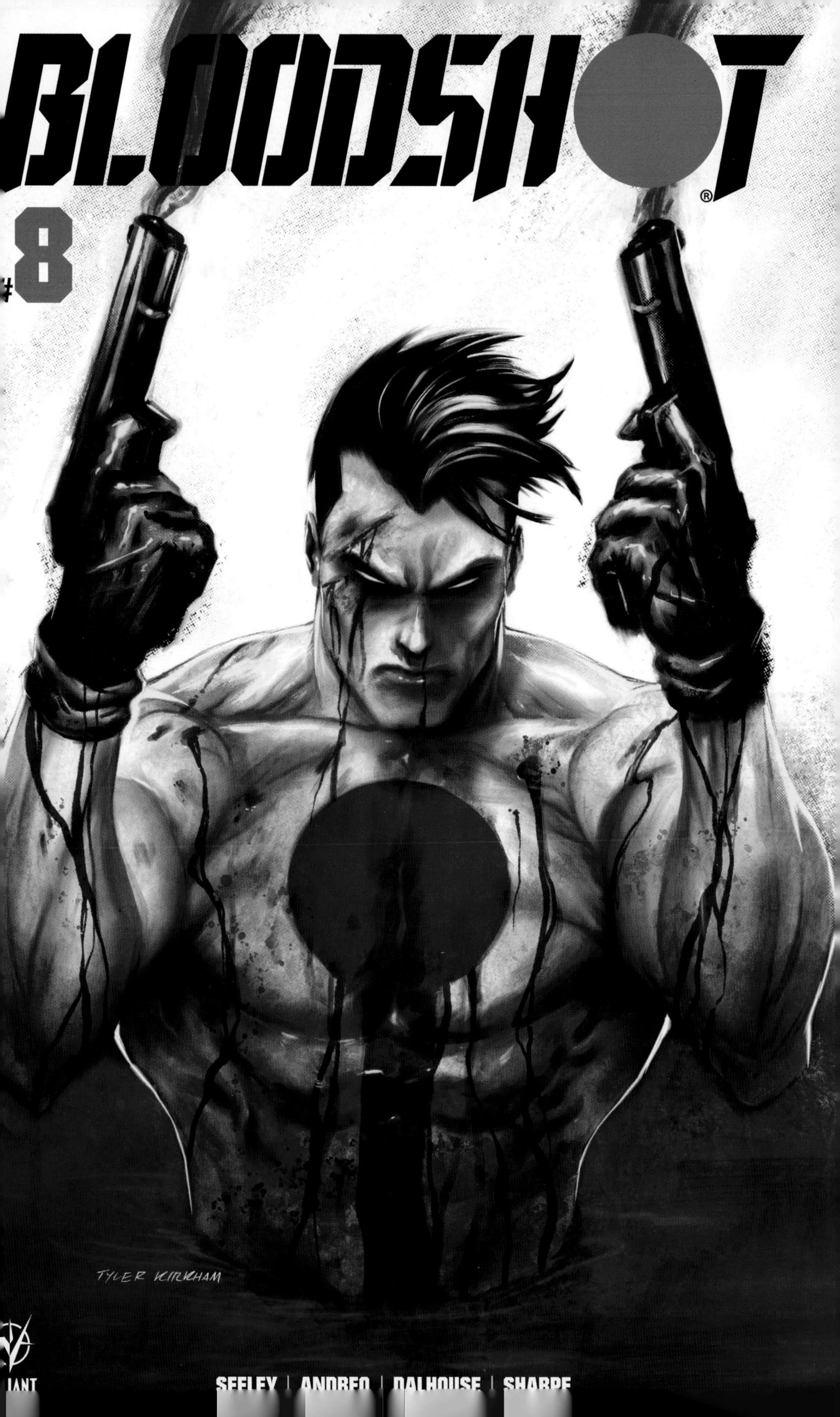
BLOODSHOT®
#8
TYLER KIRKHAM
VALIANT
SEELEY | ANDREO | DALHOUSE | SHARPE

"Burned, Part 2"

BLOODSHOT #8

WRITER: Tim Seeley
ARTIST: Pedro Andreo
COLORIST: Andrew Dalhouse
LETTERER: Dave Sharpe
COVER ARTIST: Tyler Kirkham
ASSISTANT EDITOR: Drew Baumgartner
SENIOR EDITOR: Lysa Hawkins

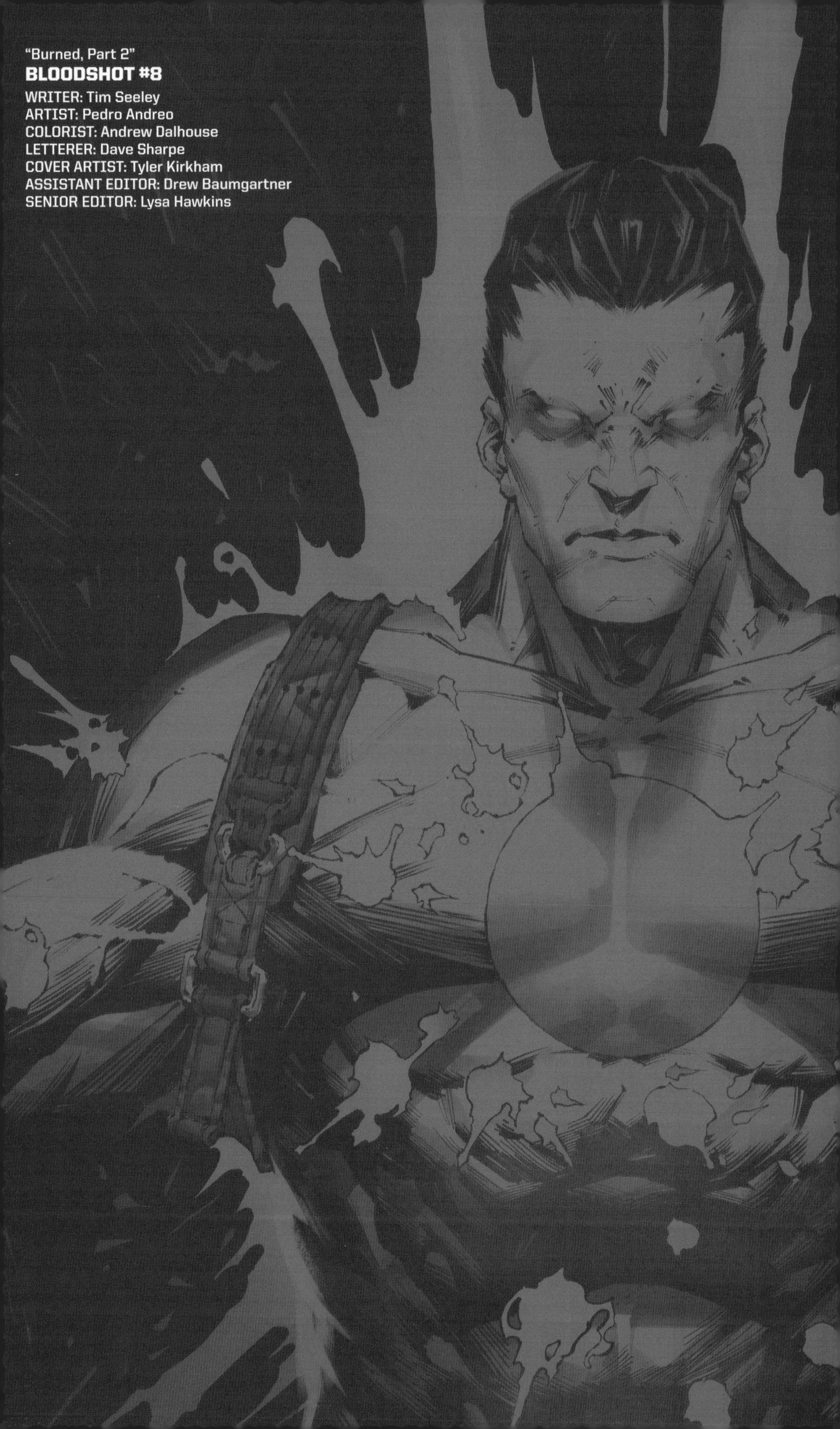

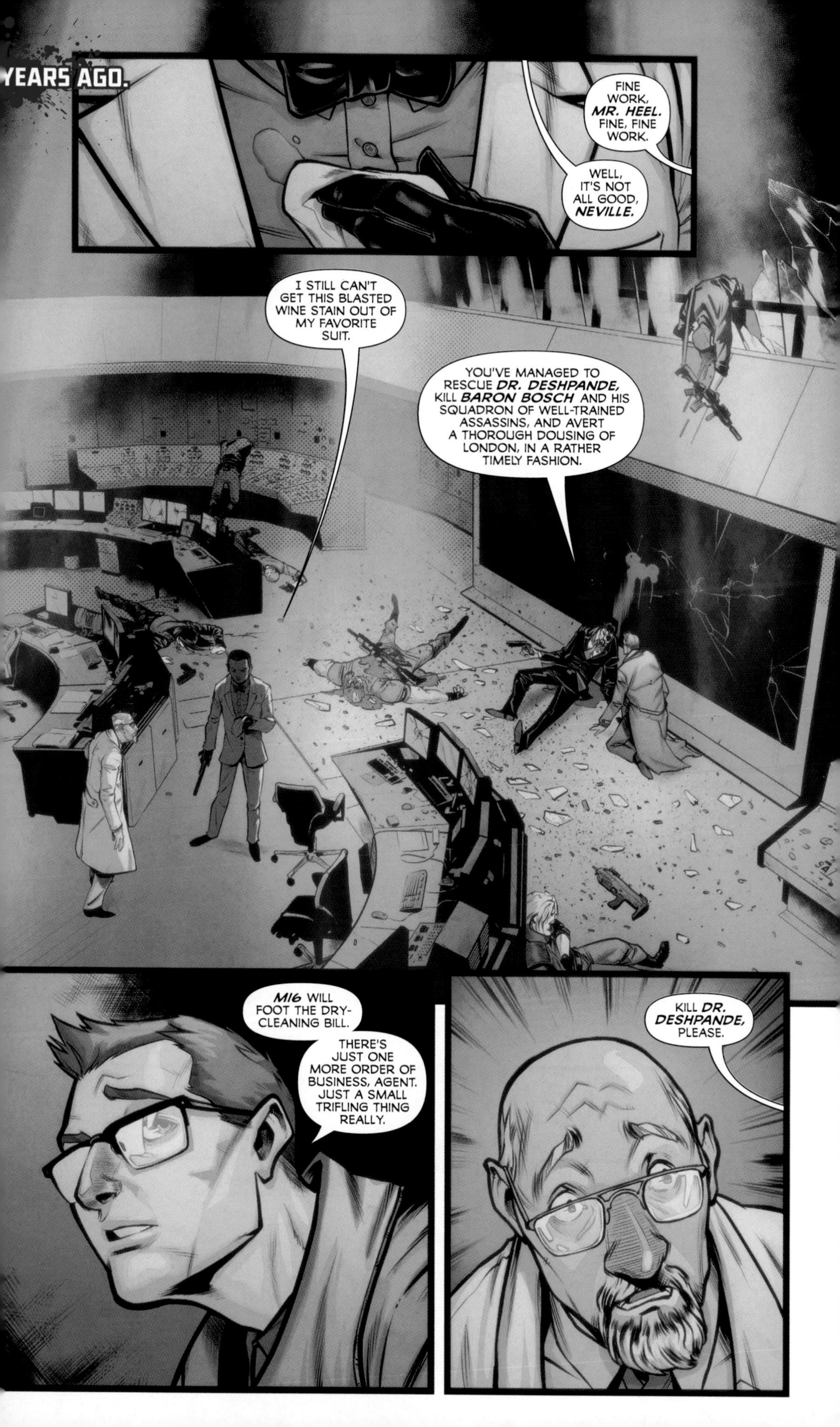
YEARS AGO.
FINE WORK, MR. HEEL. FINE, FINE WORK.
WELL, IT'S NOT ALL GOOD, NEVILLE.
I STILL CAN'T GET THIS BLASTED WINE STAIN OUT OF MY FAVORITE SUIT.
YOU'VE MANAGED TO RESCUE DR. DESHPANDE, KILL BARON BOSCH AND HIS SQUADRON OF WELL-TRAINED ASSASSINS, AND AVERT A THOROUGH DOUSING OF LONDON, IN A RATHER TIMELY FASHION.
MI6 WILL FOOT THE DRY-CLEANING BILL.
THERE'S JUST ONE MORE ORDER OF BUSINESS, AGENT. JUST A SMALL TRIFLING THING REALLY.
KILL DR. DESHPANDE, PLEASE.

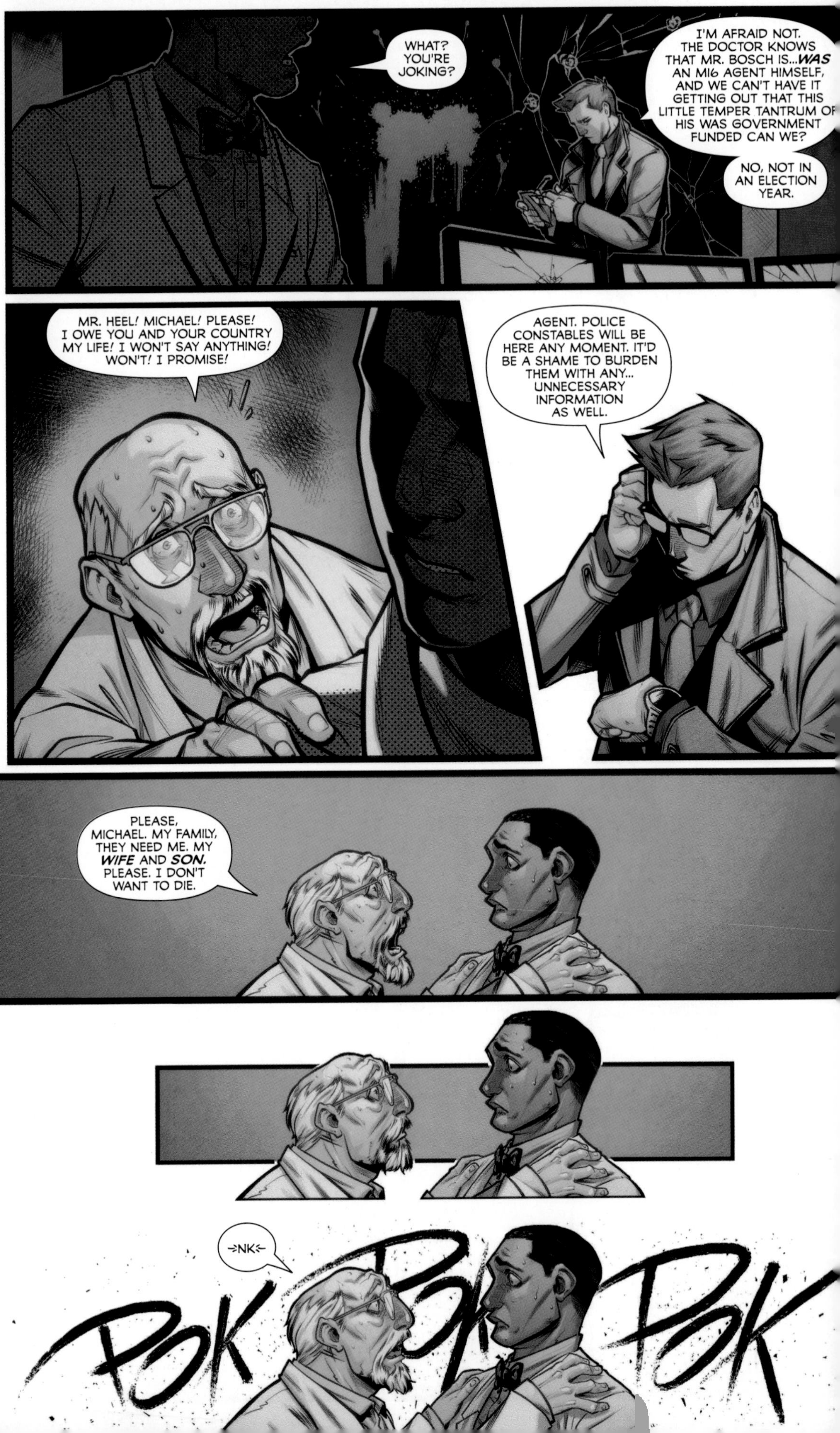
WHAT? YOU'RE JOKING?
I'M AFRAID NOT. THE DOCTOR KNOWS THAT MR. BOSCH IS...WAS AN MI6 AGENT HIMSELF, AND WE CAN'T HAVE IT GETTING OUT THAT THIS LITTLE TEMPER TANTRUM OF HIS WAS GOVERNMENT FUNDED CAN WE?
NO, NOT IN AN ELECTION YEAR.
MR. HEEL! MICHAEL! PLEASE! I OWE YOU AND YOUR COUNTRY MY LIFE! I WON'T SAY ANYTHING! WON'T! I PROMISE!
AGENT. POLICE CONSTABLES WILL BE HERE ANY MOMENT. IT'D BE A SHAME TO BURDEN THEM WITH ANY... UNNECESSARY INFORMATION AS WELL.
PLEASE, MICHAEL. MY FAMILY, THEY NEED ME. MY WIFE AND SON. PLEASE. I DON'T WANT TO DIE.
NK
POK POK POK

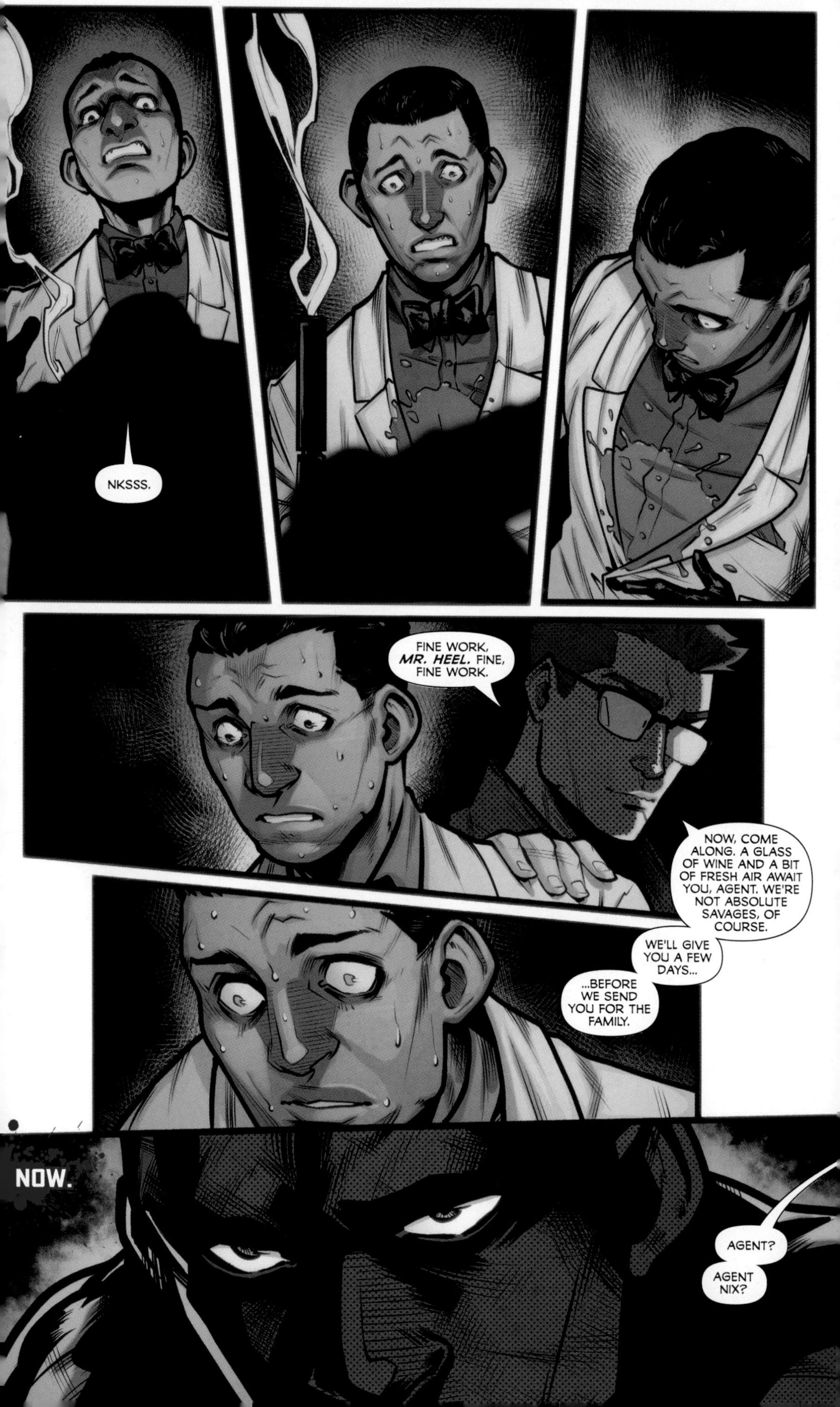
NKSSS.
FINE WORK, ***MR. HEEL.*** FINE, FINE WORK.
NOW, COME ALONG. A GLASS OF WINE AND A BIT OF FRESH AIR AWAIT YOU, AGENT. WE'RE NOT ABSOLUTE SAVAGES, OF COURSE.
WE'LL GIVE YOU A FEW DAYS...
...BEFORE WE SEND YOU FOR THE FAMILY.
NOW.
AGENT?
AGENT NIX?

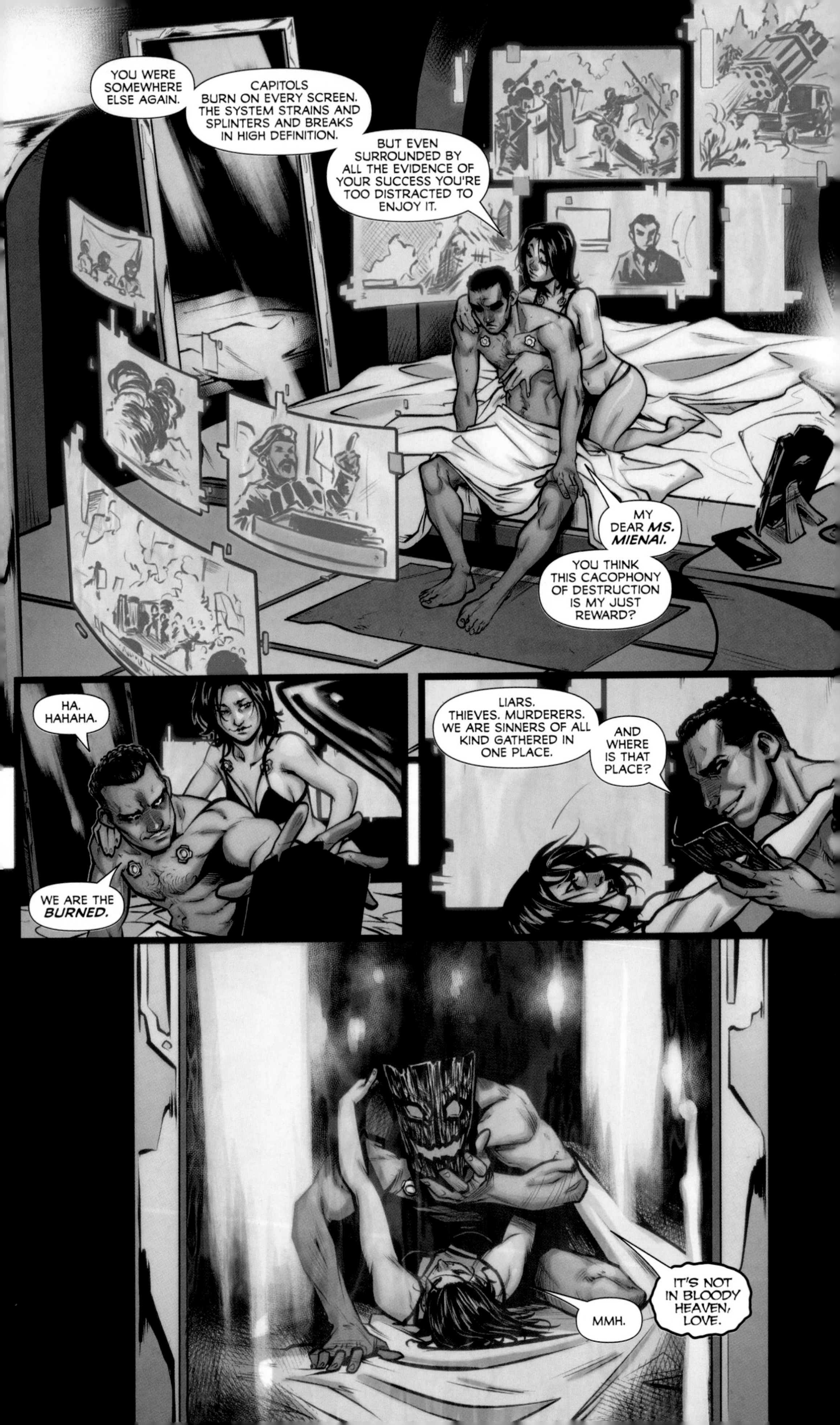
YOU WERE SOMEWHERE ELSE AGAIN.
CAPITOLS BURN ON EVERY SCREEN. THE SYSTEM STRAINS AND SPLINTERS AND BREAKS IN HIGH DEFINITION.
BUT EVEN SURROUNDED BY ALL THE EVIDENCE OF YOUR SUCCESS YOU'RE TOO DISTRACTED TO ENJOY IT.
MY DEAR ***MS. MIENAI.***
YOU THINK THIS CACOPHONY OF DESTRUCTION IS MY JUST REWARD?
HA. HAHAHA.
WE ARE THE ***BURNED.***
LIARS. THIEVES. MURDERERS. WE ARE SINNERS OF ALL KIND GATHERED IN ONE PLACE.
AND WHERE IS THAT PLACE?
MMH.
IT'S NOT IN BLOODY HEAVEN, LOVE.

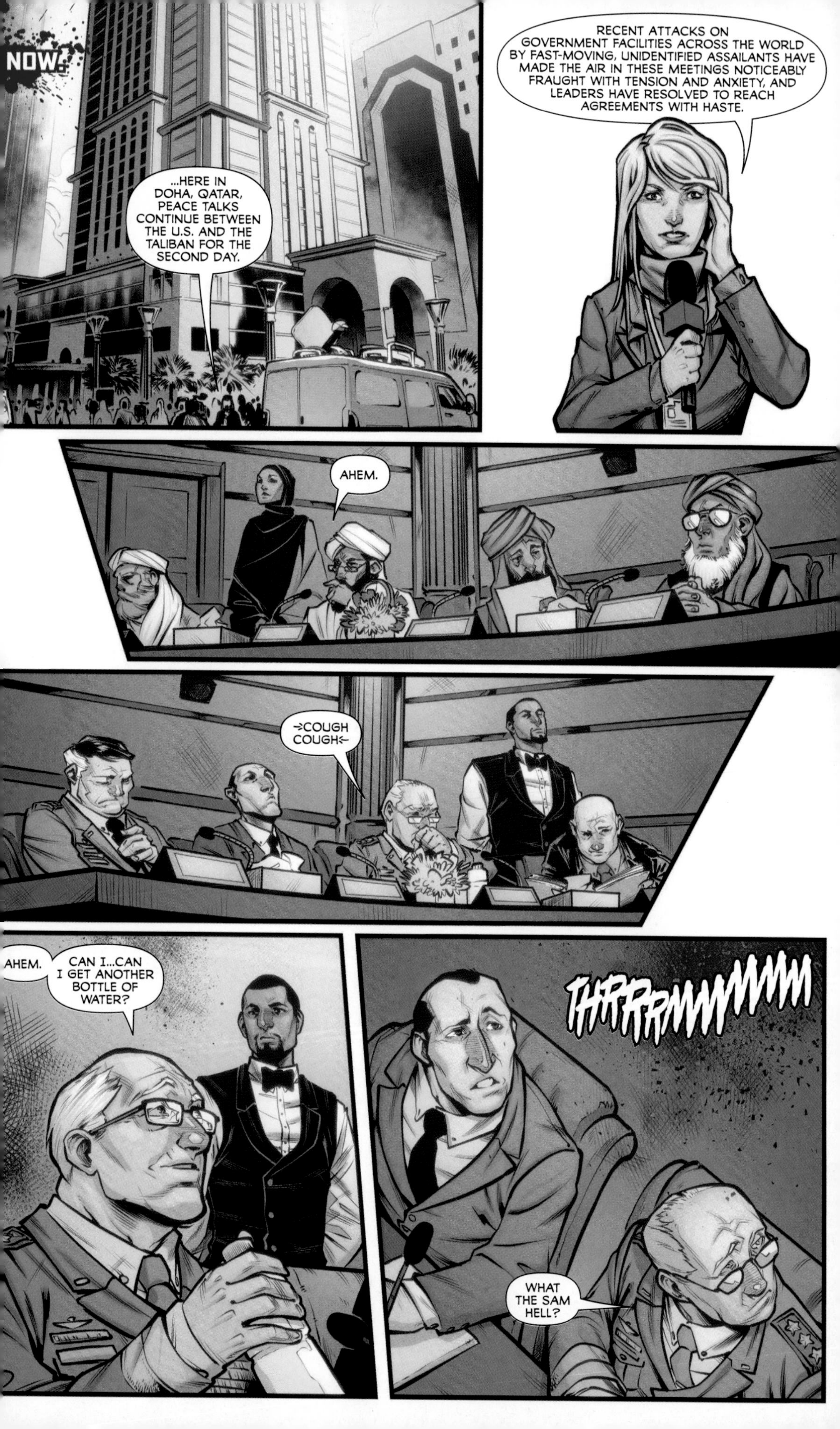
NOW:
...HERE IN DOHA, QATAR, PEACE TALKS CONTINUE BETWEEN THE U.S. AND THE TALIBAN FOR THE SECOND DAY.
RECENT ATTACKS ON GOVERNMENT FACILITIES ACROSS THE WORLD BY FAST-MOVING, UNIDENTIFIED ASSAILANTS HAVE MADE THE AIR IN THESE MEETINGS NOTICEABLY FRAUGHT WITH TENSION AND ANXIETY, AND LEADERS HAVE RESOLVED TO REACH AGREEMENTS WITH HASTE.
AHEM.
→COUGH COUGH←
AHEM.
CAN I...CAN I GET ANOTHER BOTTLE OF WATER?
THRRRMMWWMM
WHAT THE SAM HELL?

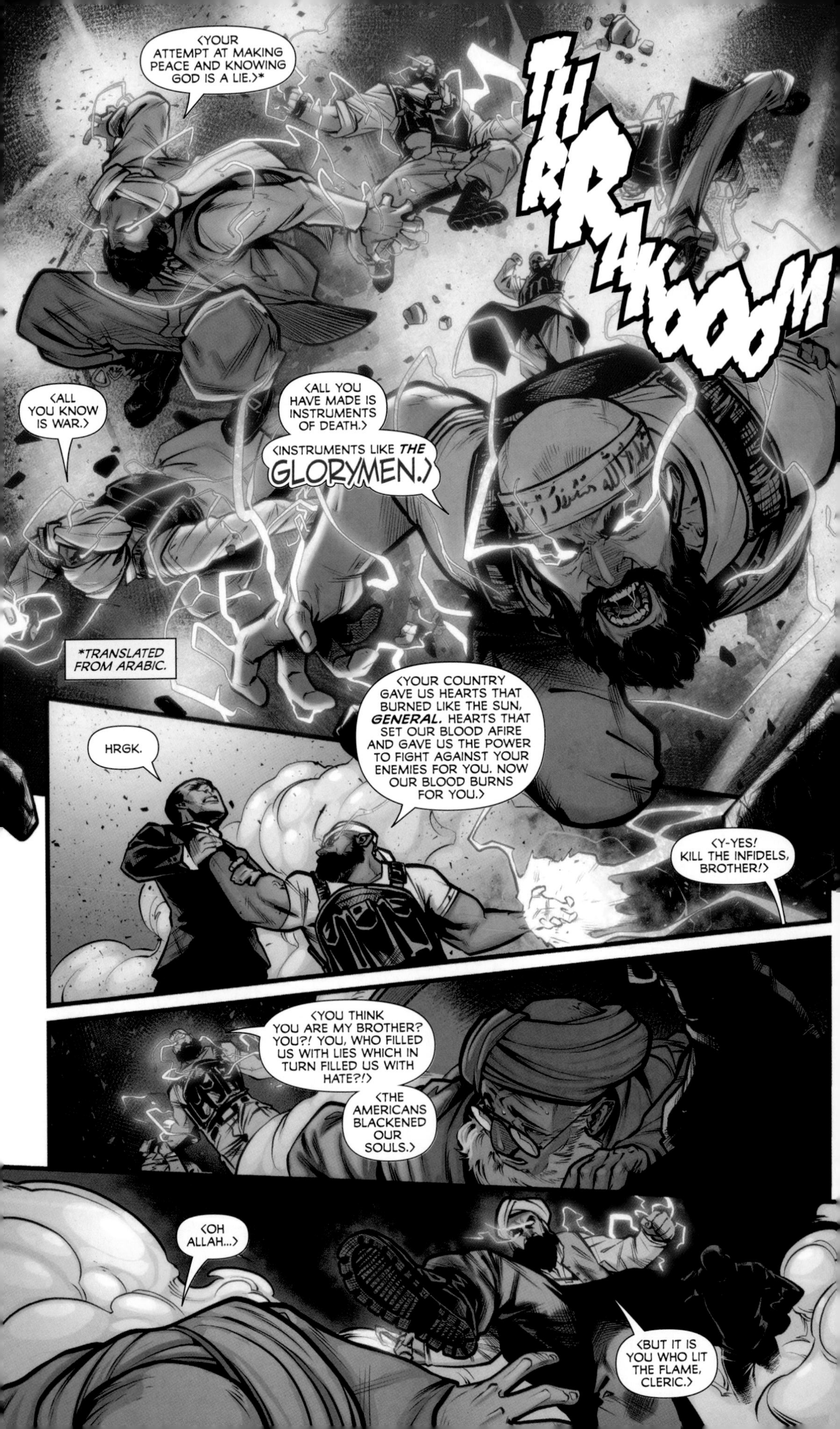
<YOUR ATTEMPT AT MAKING PEACE AND KNOWING GOD IS A LIE.>*
THRRAKOOOM
<ALL YOU KNOW IS WAR.>
<ALL YOU HAVE MADE IS INSTRUMENTS OF DEATH.>
<INSTRUMENTS LIKE *THE* GLORYMEN.>
*TRANSLATED FROM ARABIC.
<YOUR COUNTRY GAVE US HEARTS THAT BURNED LIKE THE SUN, ***GENERAL.*** HEARTS THAT SET OUR BLOOD AFIRE AND GAVE US THE POWER TO FIGHT AGAINST YOUR ENEMIES FOR YOU. NOW OUR BLOOD BURNS FOR YOU.>
HRGK.
<Y-YES*!* KILL THE INFIDELS, BROTHER*!*>
<YOU THINK YOU ARE MY BROTHER? YOU?*!* YOU, WHO FILLED US WITH LIES WHICH IN TURN FILLED US WITH HATE?*!*>
<THE AMERICANS BLACKENED OUR SOULS.>
<OH ALLAH...>
<BUT IT IS YOU WHO LIT THE FLAME, CLERIC.>

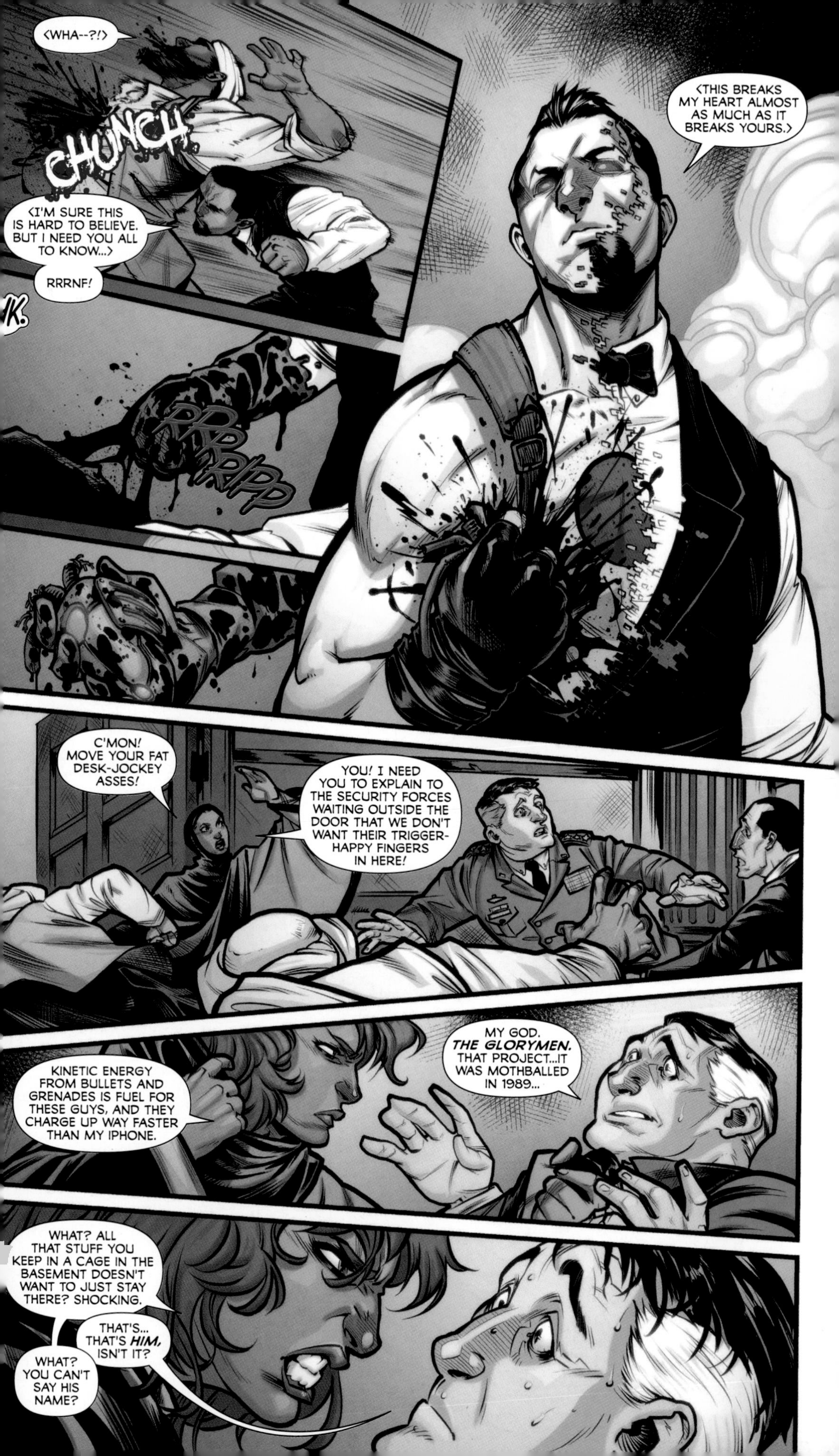

<WHA--?!>
CHUNCH
<I'M SURE THIS IS HARD TO BELIEVE. BUT I NEED YOU ALL TO KNOW...>
RRRNF!
<THIS BREAKS MY HEART ALMOST AS MUCH AS IT BREAKS YOURS.>
RRRRIPP
C'MON! MOVE YOUR FAT DESK-JOCKEY ASSES!
YOU! I NEED YOU TO EXPLAIN TO THE SECURITY FORCES WAITING OUTSIDE THE DOOR THAT WE DON'T WANT THEIR TRIGGER-HAPPY FINGERS IN HERE!
KINETIC ENERGY FROM BULLETS AND GRENADES IS FUEL FOR THESE GUYS, AND THEY CHARGE UP WAY FASTER THAN MY IPHONE.
MY GOD. THE GLORYMEN. THAT PROJECT...IT WAS MOTHBALLED IN 1989...
WHAT? ALL THAT STUFF YOU KEEP IN A CAGE IN THE BASEMENT DOESN'T WANT TO JUST STAY THERE? SHOCKING.
THAT'S... THAT'S HIM, ISN'T IT?
WHAT? YOU CAN'T SAY HIS NAME?

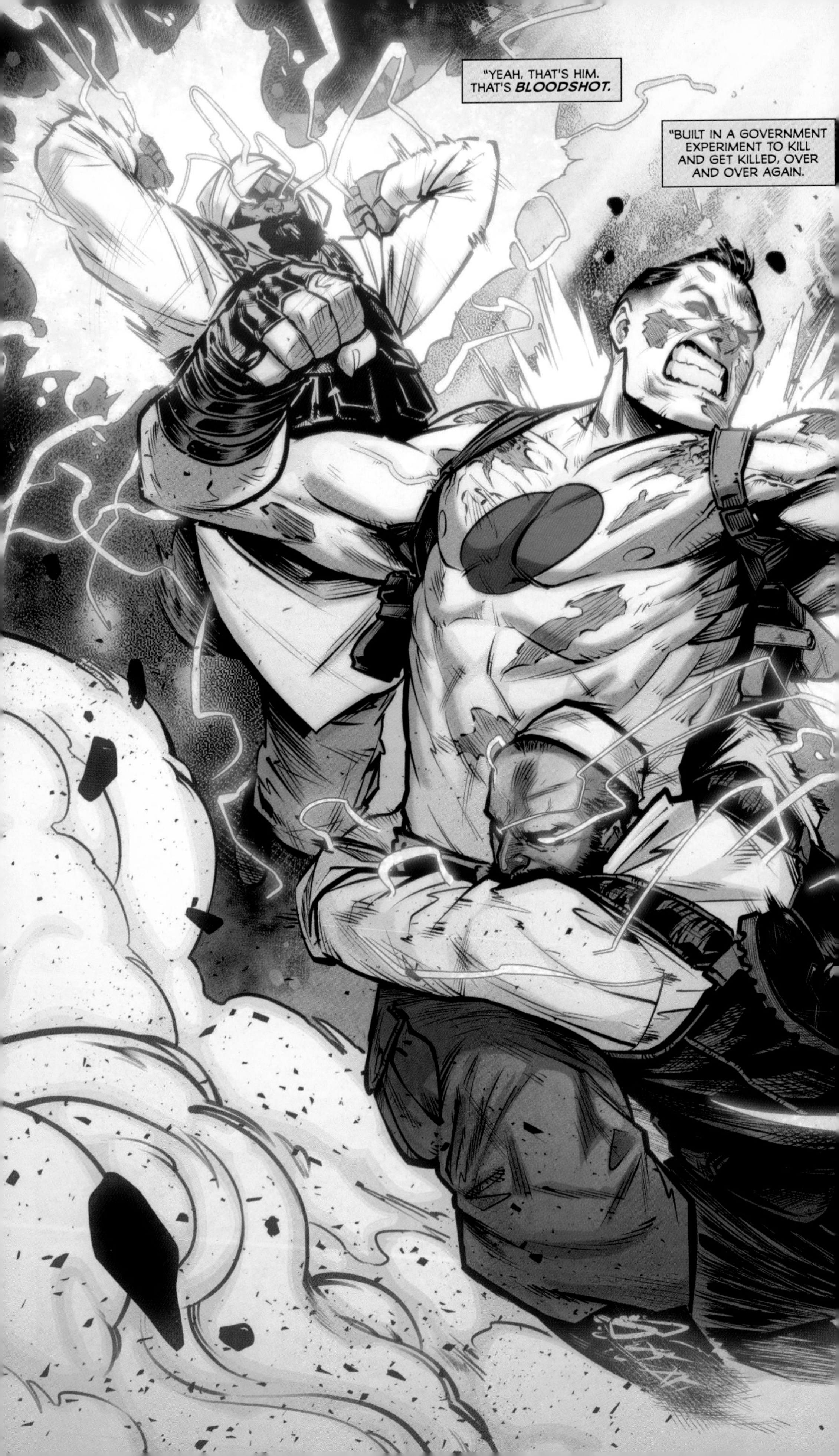
"YEAH, THAT'S HIM. THAT'S BLOODSHOT.
"BUILT IN A GOVERNMENT EXPERIMENT TO KILL AND GET KILLED, OVER AND OVER AGAIN.

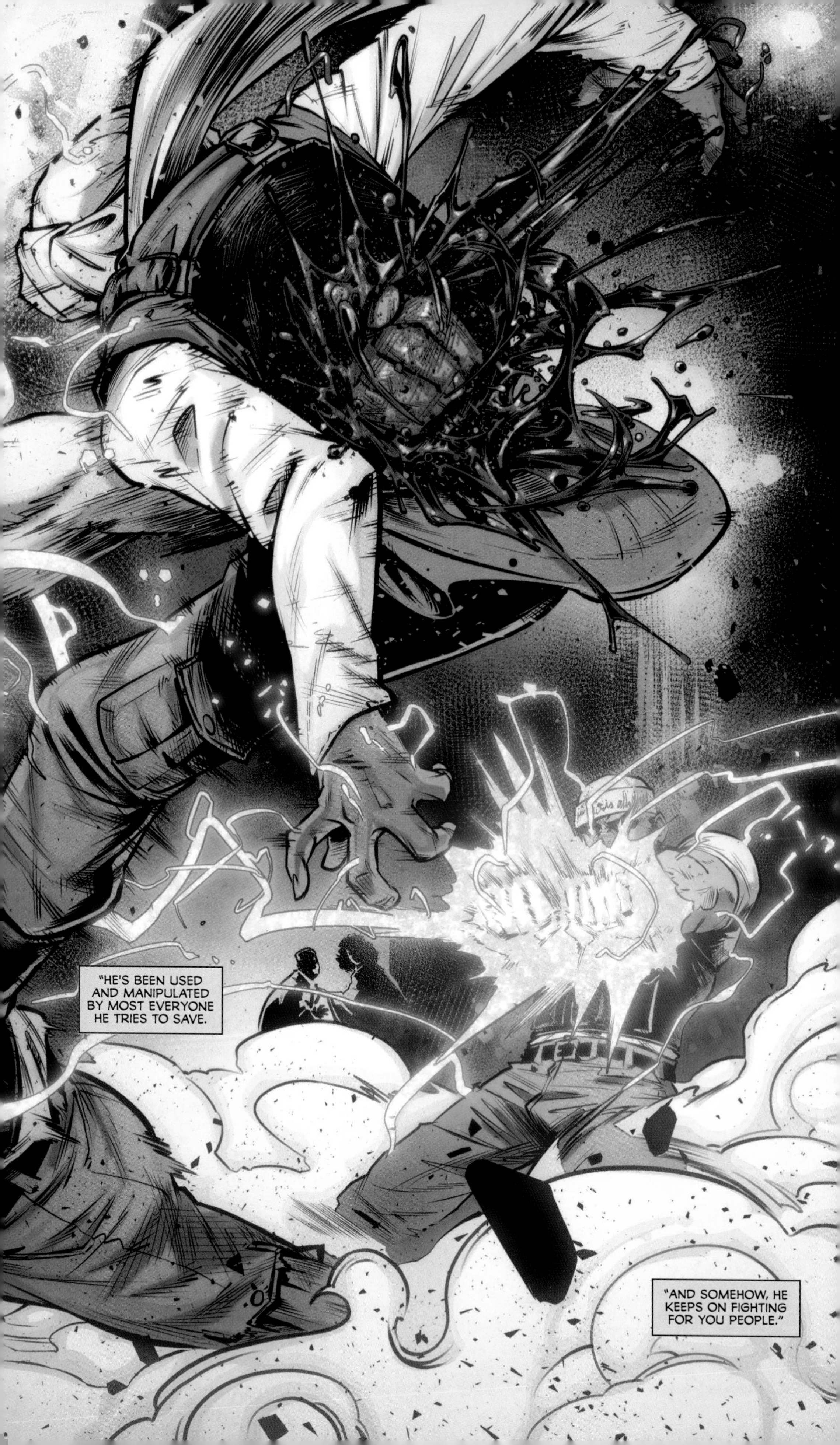
"HE'S BEEN USED AND MANIPULATED BY MOST EVERYONE HE TRIES TO SAVE.
"AND SOMEHOW, HE KEEPS ON FIGHTING FOR YOU PEOPLE."

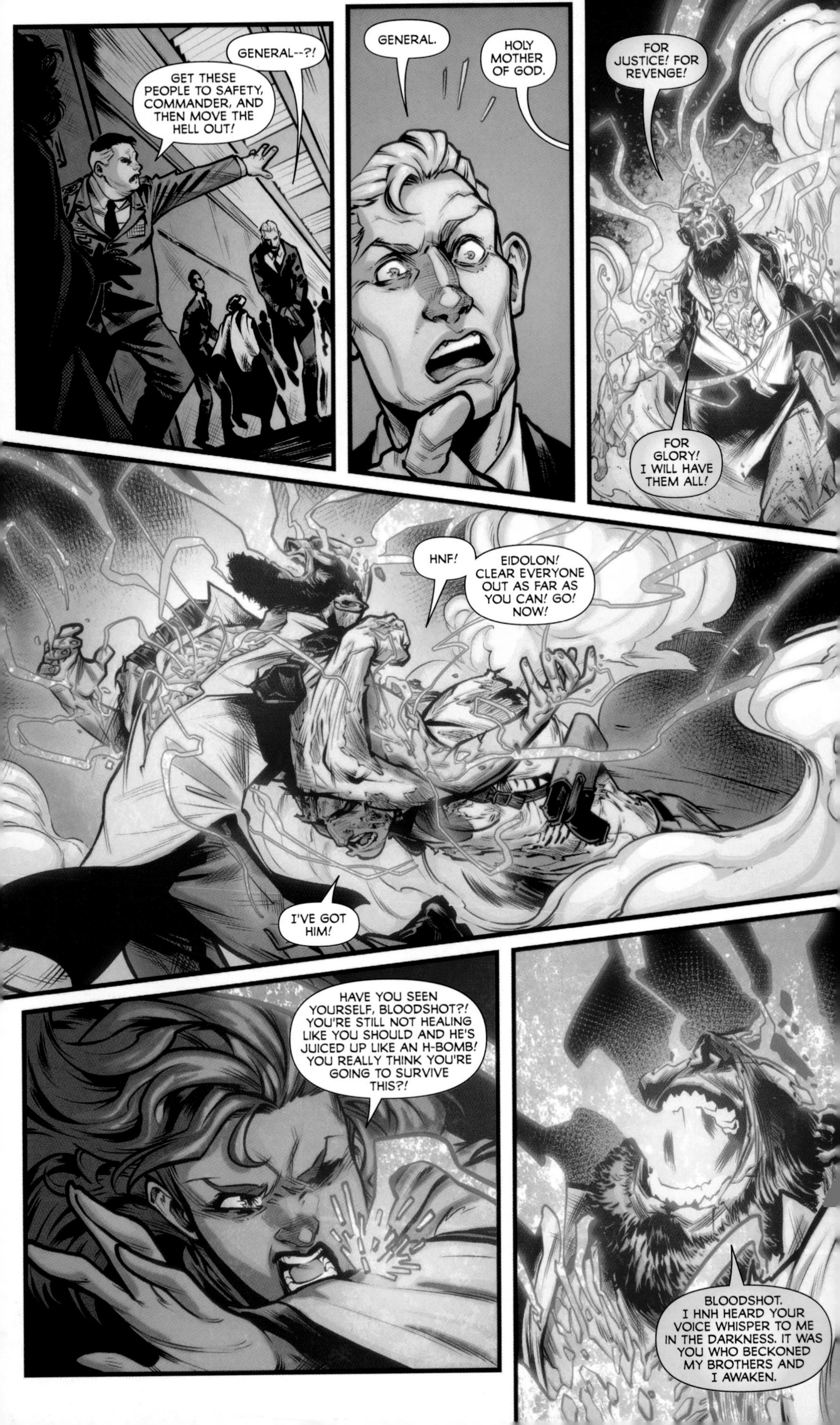
GENERAL--?!
GET THESE PEOPLE TO SAFETY, COMMANDER, AND THEN MOVE THE HELL OUT!
GENERAL.
HOLY MOTHER OF GOD.
FOR JUSTICE! FOR REVENGE!
FOR GLORY! I WILL HAVE THEM ALL!
HNF!
EIDOLON! CLEAR EVERYONE OUT AS FAR AS YOU CAN! GO! NOW!
I'VE GOT HIM!
HAVE YOU SEEN YOURSELF, BLOODSHOT?! YOU'RE STILL NOT HEALING LIKE YOU SHOULD AND HE'S JUICED UP LIKE AN H-BOMB! YOU REALLY THINK YOU'RE GOING TO SURVIVE THIS?!
BLOODSHOT. I HNH HEARD YOUR VOICE WHISPER TO ME IN THE DARKNESS. IT WAS YOU WHO BECKONED MY BROTHERS AND I AWAKEN.

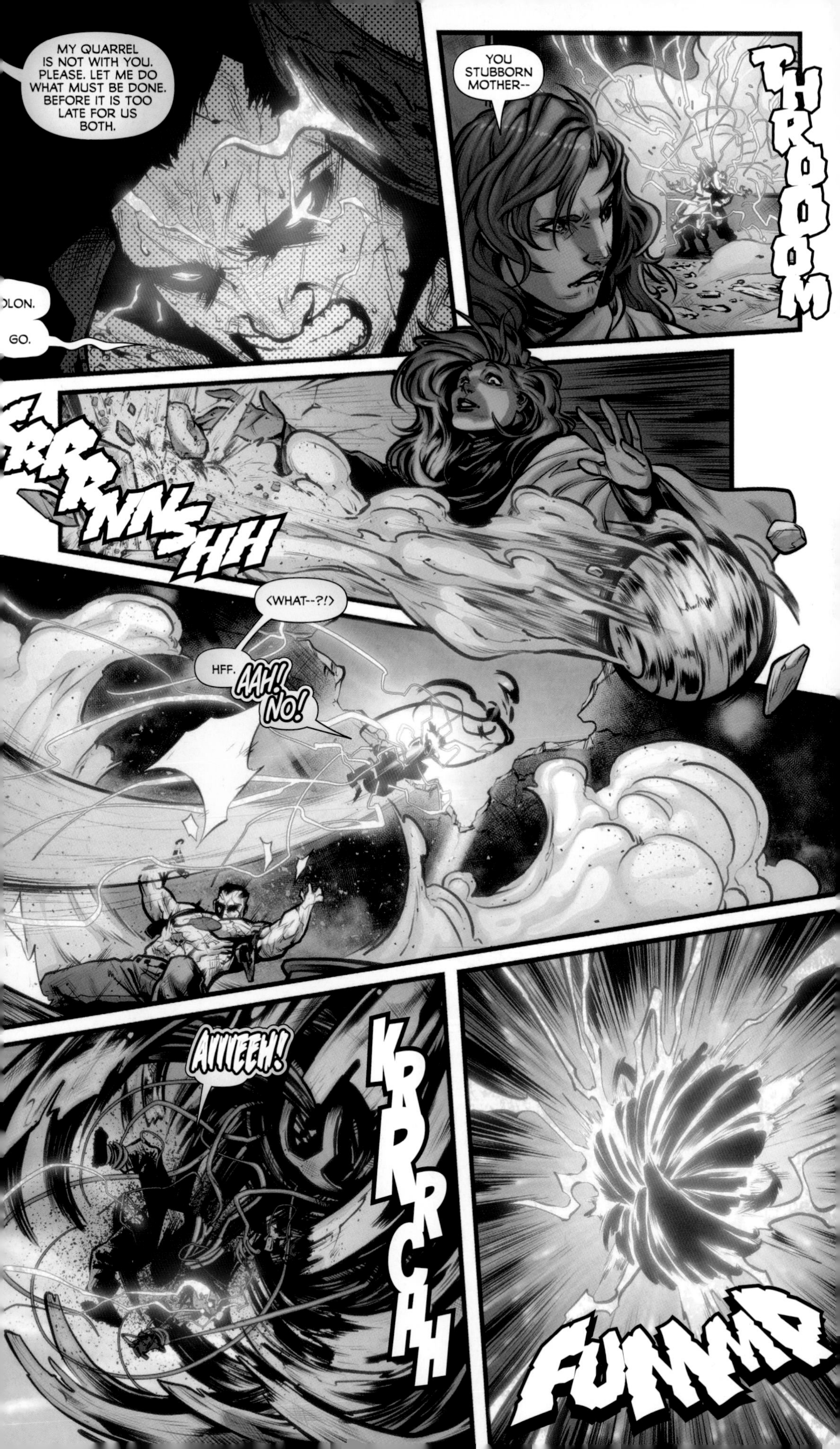
MY QUARREL IS NOT WITH YOU. PLEASE. LET ME DO WHAT MUST BE DONE. BEFORE IT IS TOO LATE FOR US BOTH.
OLON.
GO.
YOU STUBBORN MOTHER--
THROOOOM
RRRNNSHH
<WHAT--?!>
HFF.
AAH! NO!
AIIIEEH!
KRRRCHH
FUMMP

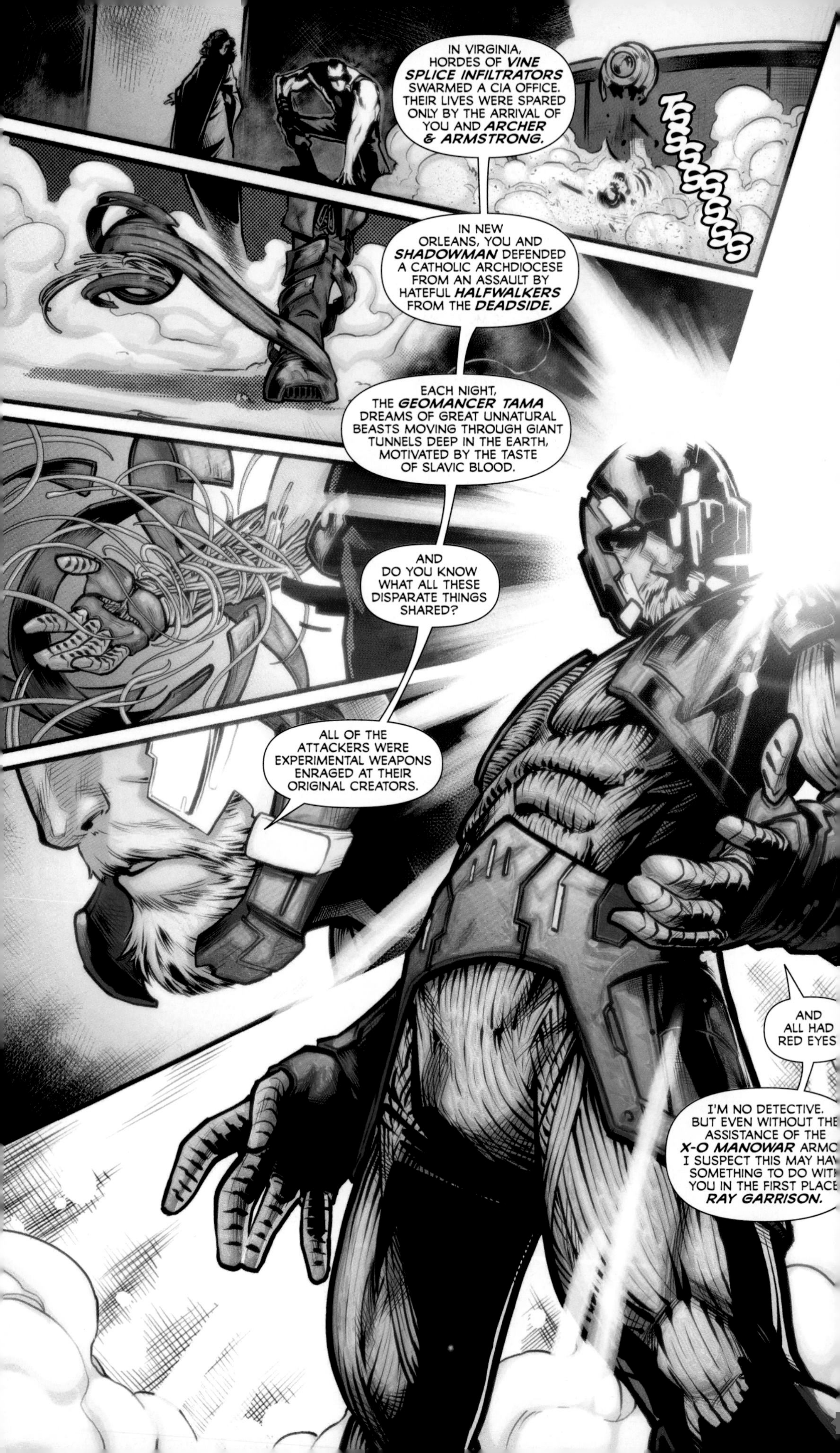
IN VIRGINIA, HORDES OF VINE SPLICE INFILTRATORS SWARMED A CIA OFFICE. THEIR LIVES WERE SPARED ONLY BY THE ARRIVAL OF YOU AND ARCHER & ARMSTRONG.
TSSSSSSS
IN NEW ORLEANS, YOU AND SHADOWMAN DEFENDED A CATHOLIC ARCHDIOCESE FROM AN ASSAULT BY HATEFUL HALFWALKERS FROM THE DEADSIDE.
EACH NIGHT, THE GEOMANCER TAMA DREAMS OF GREAT UNNATURAL BEASTS MOVING THROUGH GIANT TUNNELS DEEP IN THE EARTH, MOTIVATED BY THE TASTE OF SLAVIC BLOOD.
AND DO YOU KNOW WHAT ALL THESE DISPARATE THINGS SHARED?
ALL OF THE ATTACKERS WERE EXPERIMENTAL WEAPONS ENRAGED AT THEIR ORIGINAL CREATORS.
AND ALL HAD RED EYES
I'M NO DETECTIVE. BUT EVEN WITHOUT THE ASSISTANCE OF THE X-O MANOWAR ARMO I SUSPECT THIS MAY HAV SOMETHING TO DO WIT YOU IN THE FIRST PLACE RAY GARRISON.

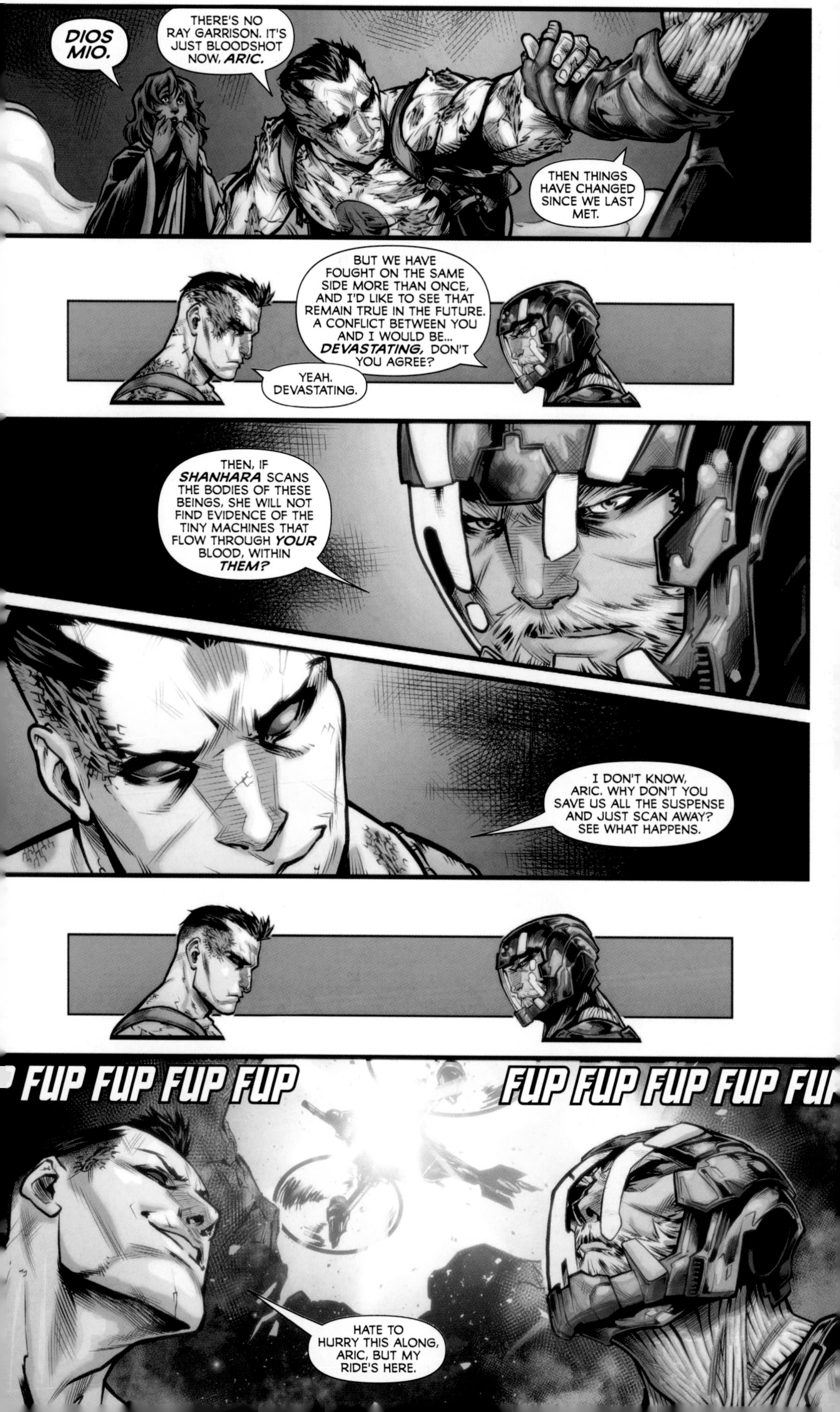
DIOS MIO.
THERE'S NO RAY GARRISON. IT'S JUST BLOODSHOT NOW, ARIC.
THEN THINGS HAVE CHANGED SINCE WE LAST MET.
BUT WE HAVE FOUGHT ON THE SAME SIDE MORE THAN ONCE, AND I'D LIKE TO SEE THAT REMAIN TRUE IN THE FUTURE. A CONFLICT BETWEEN YOU AND I WOULD BE... DEVASTATING, DON'T YOU AGREE?
YEAH. DEVASTATING.
THEN, IF SHANHARA SCANS THE BODIES OF THESE BEINGS, SHE WILL NOT FIND EVIDENCE OF THE TINY MACHINES THAT FLOW THROUGH YOUR BLOOD, WITHIN THEM?
I DON'T KNOW, ARIC. WHY DON'T YOU SAVE US ALL THE SUSPENSE AND JUST SCAN AWAY? SEE WHAT HAPPENS.
FUP FUP FUP FUP
FUP FUP FUP FUP
HATE TO HURRY THIS ALONG, ARIC, BUT MY RIDE'S HERE.

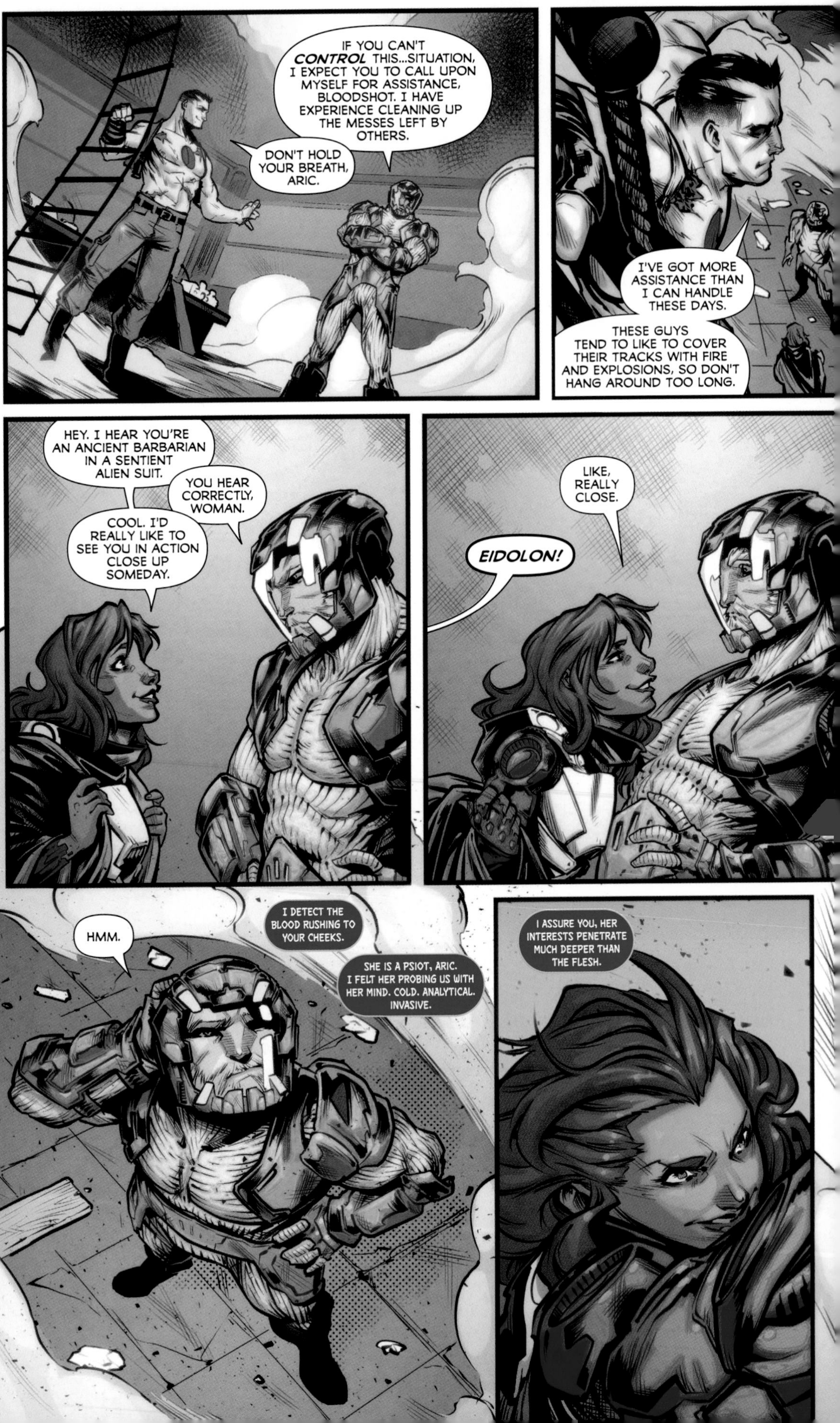
IF YOU CAN'T CONTROL THIS...SITUATION, I EXPECT YOU TO CALL UPON MYSELF FOR ASSISTANCE, BLOODSHOT. I HAVE EXPERIENCE CLEANING UP THE MESSES LEFT BY OTHERS.
DON'T HOLD YOUR BREATH, ARIC.
I'VE GOT MORE ASSISTANCE THAN I CAN HANDLE THESE DAYS.
THESE GUYS TEND TO LIKE TO COVER THEIR TRACKS WITH FIRE AND EXPLOSIONS, SO DON'T HANG AROUND TOO LONG.
HEY. I HEAR YOU'RE AN ANCIENT BARBARIAN IN A SENTIENT ALIEN SUIT.
YOU HEAR CORRECTLY, WOMAN.
COOL. I'D REALLY LIKE TO SEE YOU IN ACTION CLOSE UP SOMEDAY.
LIKE, REALLY CLOSE.
EIDOLON!
HMM.
I DETECT THE BLOOD RUSHING TO YOUR CHEEKS.
SHE IS A PSIOT, ARIC. I FELT HER PROBING US WITH HER MIND. COLD. ANALYTICAL. INVASIVE.
I ASSURE YOU, HER INTERESTS PENETRATE MUCH DEEPER THAN THE FLESH.

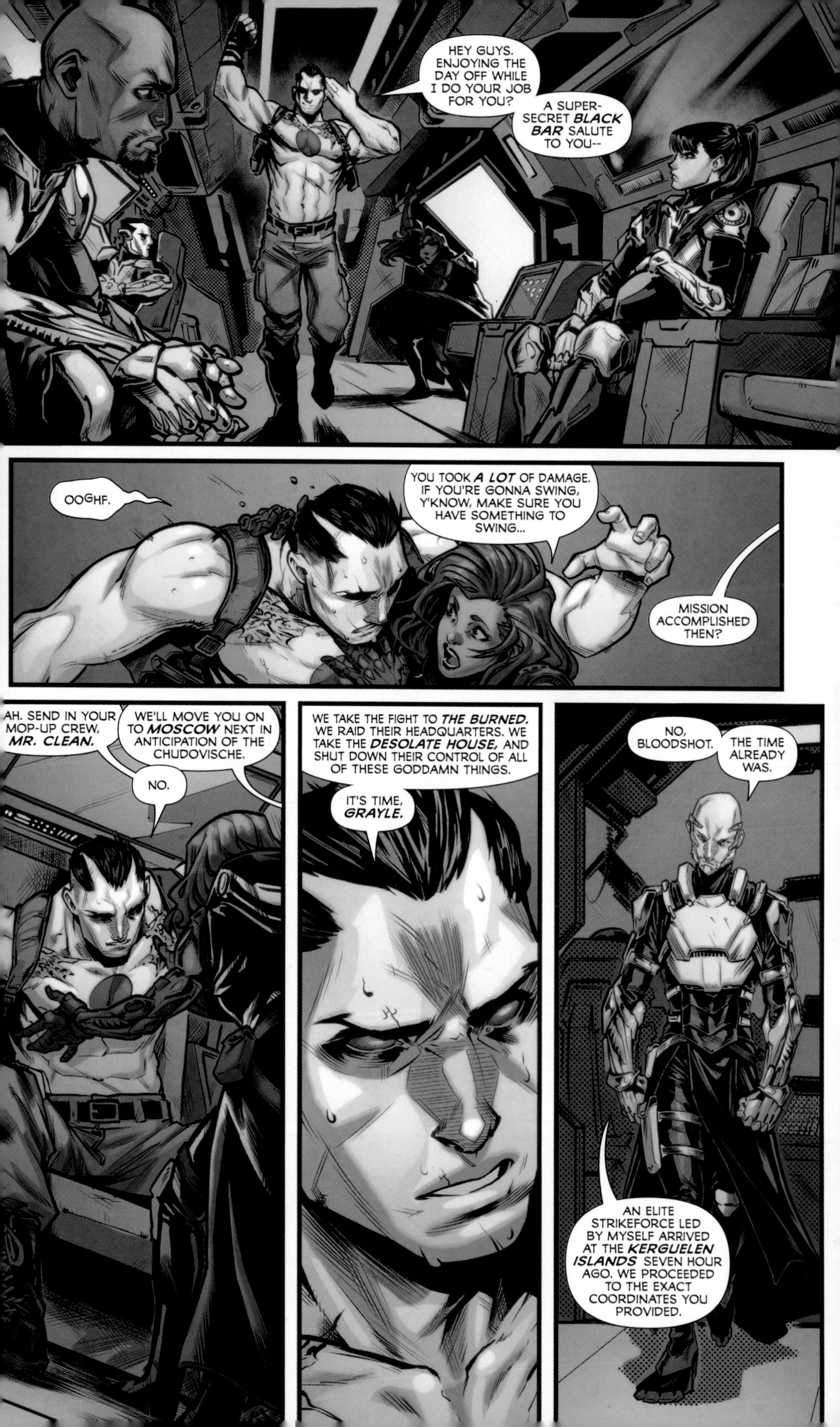
HEY GUYS. ENJOYING THE DAY OFF WHILE I DO YOUR JOB FOR YOU?
A SUPER-SECRET BLACK BAR SALUTE TO YOU--
OOGHF.
YOU TOOK A LOT OF DAMAGE. IF YOU'RE GONNA SWING, Y'KNOW, MAKE SURE YOU HAVE SOMETHING TO SWING...
MISSION ACCOMPLISHED THEN?
AH. SEND IN YOUR MOP-UP CREW, MR. CLEAN.
WE'LL MOVE YOU ON TO MOSCOW NEXT IN ANTICIPATION OF THE CHUDOVISCHE.
NO.
WE TAKE THE FIGHT TO THE BURNED. WE RAID THEIR HEADQUARTERS. WE TAKE THE DESOLATE HOUSE, AND SHUT DOWN THEIR CONTROL OF ALL OF THESE GODDAMN THINGS.
IT'S TIME, GRAYLE.
NO, BLOODSHOT.
THE TIME ALREADY WAS.
AN ELITE STRIKEFORCE LED BY MYSELF ARRIVED AT THE KERGUELEN ISLANDS SEVEN HOUR AGO. WE PROCEEDED TO THE EXACT COORDINATES YOU PROVIDED.

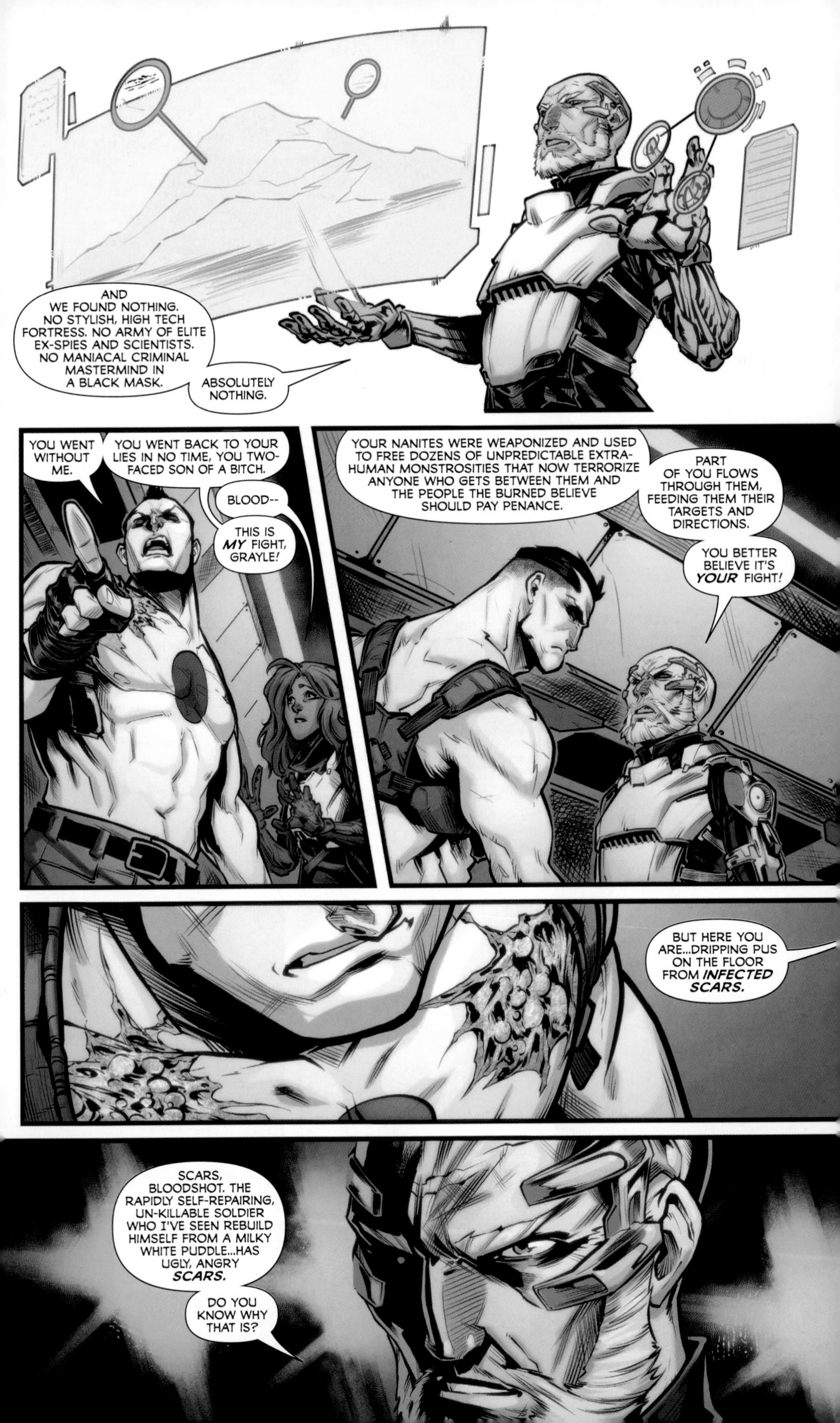
AND WE FOUND NOTHING. NO STYLISH, HIGH TECH FORTRESS. NO ARMY OF ELITE EX-SPIES AND SCIENTISTS. NO MANIACAL CRIMINAL MASTERMIND IN A BLACK MASK.
ABSOLUTELY NOTHING.
YOU WENT WITHOUT ME.
YOU WENT BACK TO YOUR LIES IN NO TIME, YOU TWO-FACED SON OF A BITCH.
BLOOD--
THIS IS *MY* FIGHT, GRAYLE!
YOUR NANITES WERE WEAPONIZED AND USED TO FREE DOZENS OF UNPREDICTABLE EXTRA-HUMAN MONSTROSITIES THAT NOW TERRORIZE ANYONE WHO GETS BETWEEN THEM AND THE PEOPLE THE BURNED BELIEVE SHOULD PAY PENANCE.
PART OF YOU FLOWS THROUGH THEM, FEEDING THEM THEIR TARGETS AND DIRECTIONS.
YOU BETTER BELIEVE IT'S ***YOUR*** FIGHT!
BUT HERE YOU ARE...DRIPPING PUS ON THE FLOOR FROM ***INFECTED SCARS.***
SCARS, BLOODSHOT. THE RAPIDLY SELF-REPAIRING, UN-KILLABLE SOLDIER WHO I'VE SEEN REBUILD HIMSELF FROM A MILKY WHITE PUDDLE...HAS UGLY, ANGRY ***SCARS.***
DO YOU KNOW WHY THAT IS?

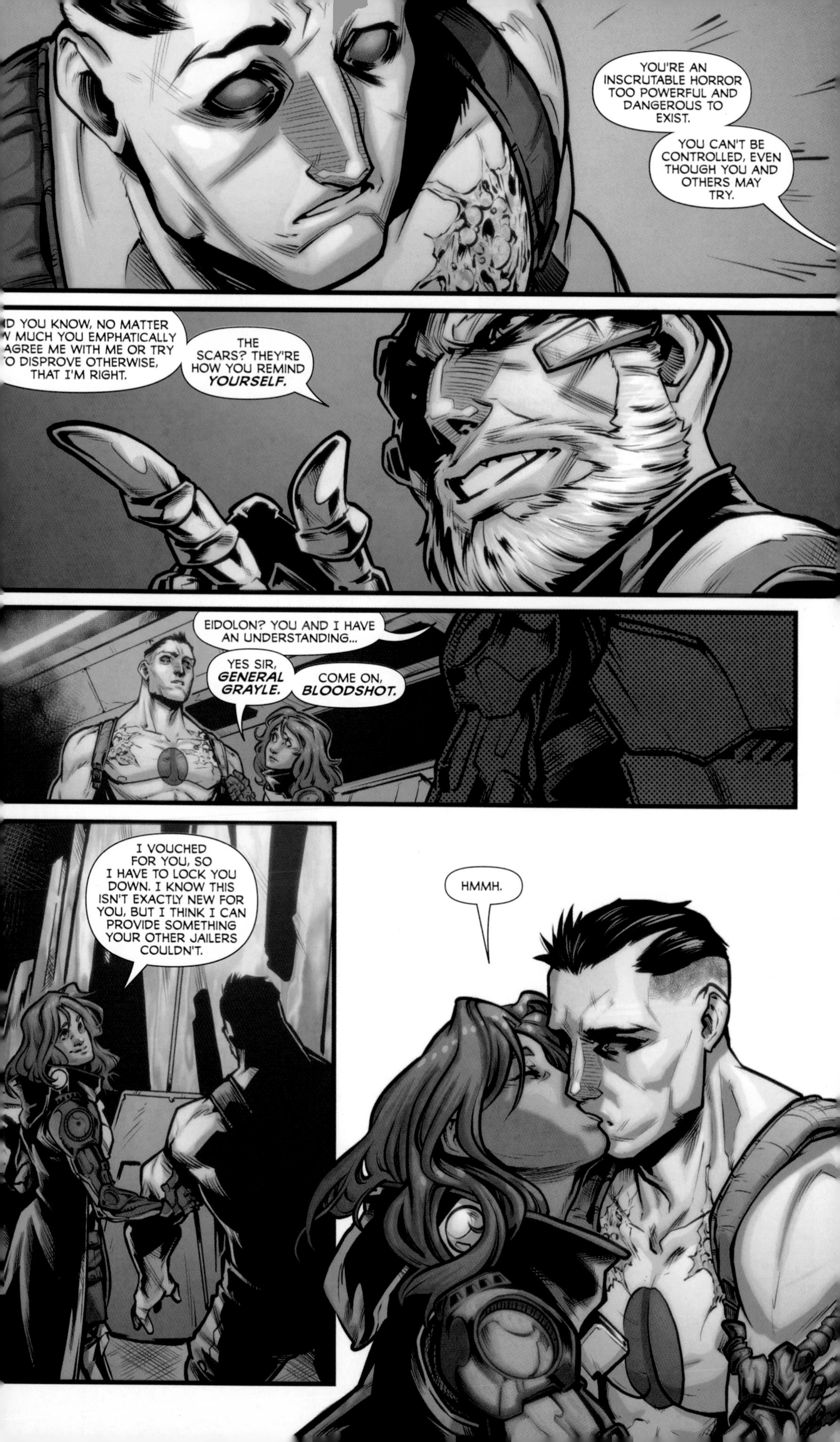
YOU'RE AN INSCRUTABLE HORROR TOO POWERFUL AND DANGEROUS TO EXIST.
YOU CAN'T BE CONTROLLED, EVEN THOUGH YOU AND OTHERS MAY TRY.
D YOU KNOW, NO MATTER V MUCH YOU EMPHATICALLY AGREE ME WITH ME OR TRY O DISPROVE OTHERWISE, THAT I'M RIGHT.
THE SCARS? THEY'RE HOW YOU REMIND ***YOURSELF.***
EIDOLON? YOU AND I HAVE AN UNDERSTANDING...
YES SIR, ***GENERAL GRAYLE.***
COME ON, ***BLOODSHOT.***
I VOUCHED FOR YOU, SO I HAVE TO LOCK YOU DOWN. I KNOW THIS ISN'T EXACTLY NEW FOR YOU, BUT I THINK I CAN PROVIDE SOMETHING YOUR OTHER JAILERS COULDN'T.
HMMH.

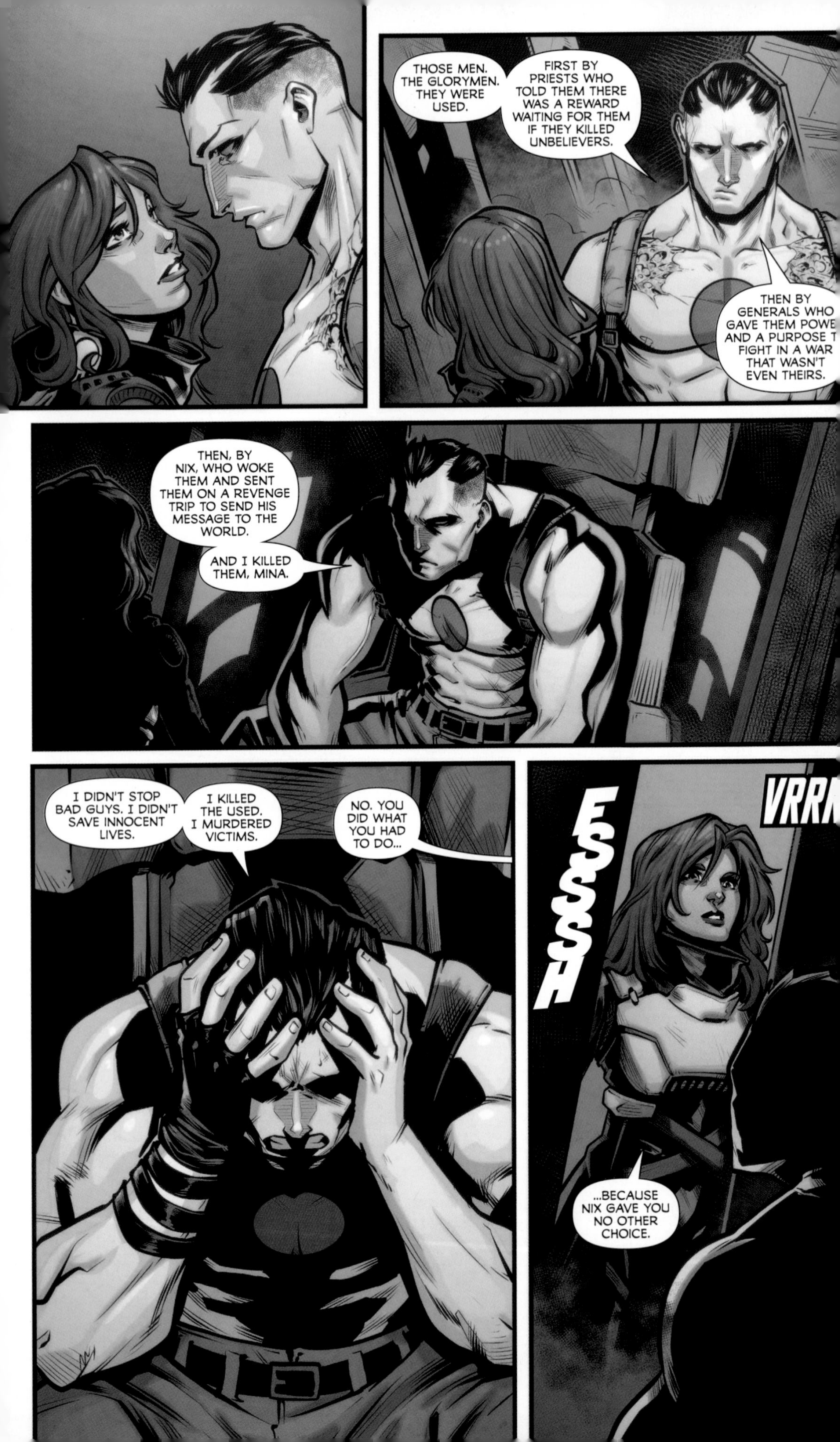
THOSE MEN. THE GLORYMEN. THEY WERE USED.
FIRST BY PRIESTS WHO TOLD THEM THERE WAS A REWARD WAITING FOR THEM IF THEY KILLED UNBELIEVERS.
THEN BY GENERALS WHO GAVE THEM POWE AND A PURPOSE T FIGHT IN A WAR THAT WASN'T EVEN THEIRS.
THEN, BY NIX, WHO WOKE THEM AND SENT THEM ON A REVENGE TRIP TO SEND HIS MESSAGE TO THE WORLD.
AND I KILLED THEM, MINA.
I DIDN'T STOP BAD GUYS. I DIDN'T SAVE INNOCENT LIVES.
I KILLED THE USED. I MURDERED VICTIMS.
NO. YOU DID WHAT YOU HAD TO DO...
ESSSH
VRRR
...BECAUSE NIX GAVE YOU NO OTHER CHOICE.

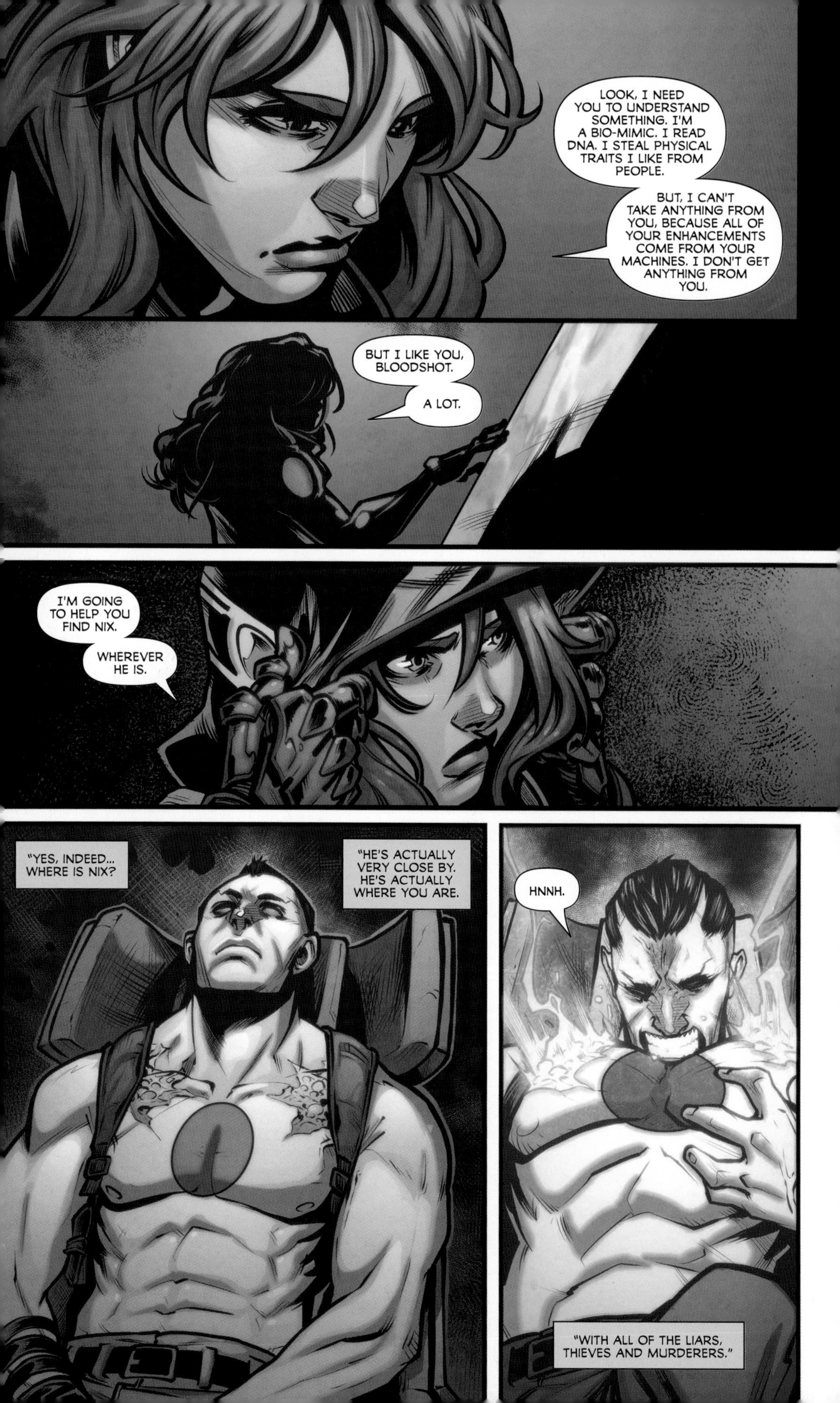
LOOK, I NEED YOU TO UNDERSTAND SOMETHING. I'M A BIO-MIMIC. I READ DNA. I STEAL PHYSICAL TRAITS I LIKE FROM PEOPLE.
BUT, I CAN'T TAKE ANYTHING FROM YOU, BECAUSE ALL OF YOUR ENHANCEMENTS COME FROM YOUR MACHINES. I DON'T GET ANYTHING FROM YOU.
BUT I LIKE YOU, BLOODSHOT.
A LOT.
I'M GOING TO HELP YOU FIND NIX.
WHEREVER HE IS.
"YES, INDEED... WHERE IS NIX?
"HE'S ACTUALLY VERY CLOSE BY. HE'S ACTUALLY WHERE YOU ARE.
HNNH.
"WITH ALL OF THE LIARS, THIEVES AND MURDERERS."

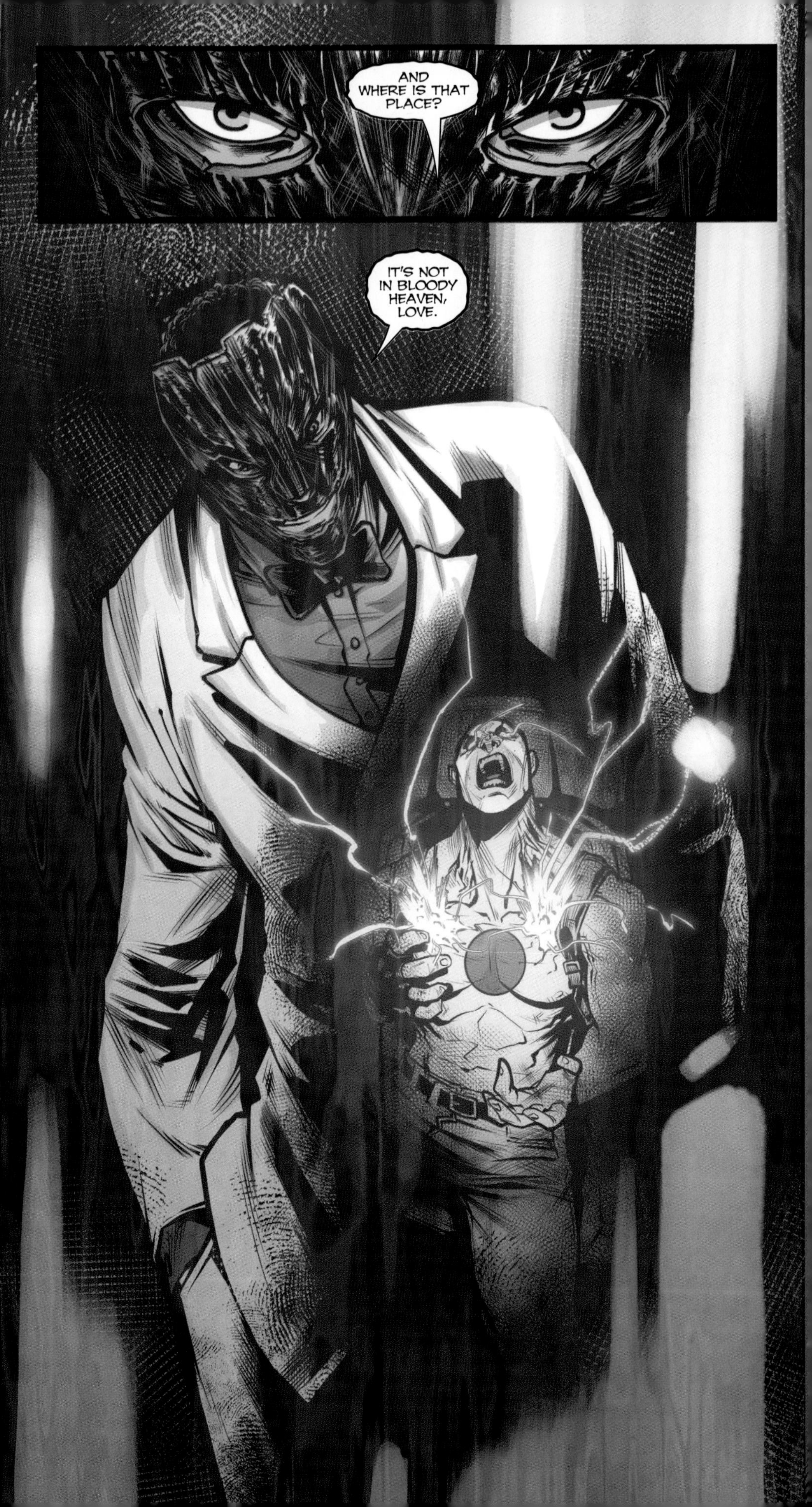
AND WHERE IS THAT PLACE?
IT'S NOT IN BLOODY HEAVEN, LOVE.

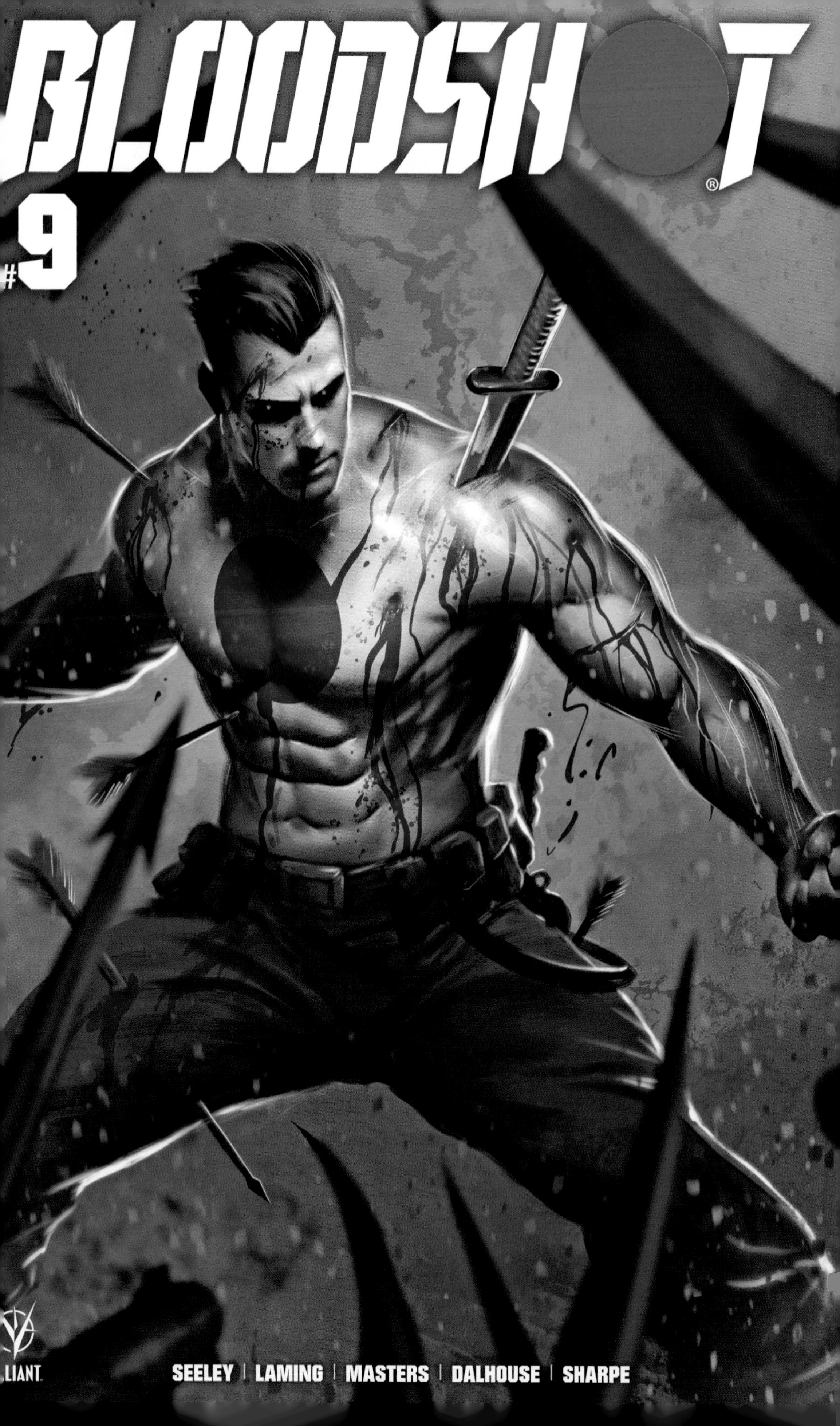
BLOODSHOT®
#9
VALIANT
SEELEY | LAMING | MASTERS | DALHOUSE | SHARPE

"Burned, Part 3"

BLOODSHOT #9

WRITER: Tim Seeley
ARTISTS: Mark Laming and Jason Masters
COLORIST: Andrew Dalhouse
LETTERER: Dave Sharpe
COVER ARTIST: Tyler Kirkham
ASSISTANT EDITOR: Drew Baumgartner
SENIOR EDITOR: Lysa Hawkins

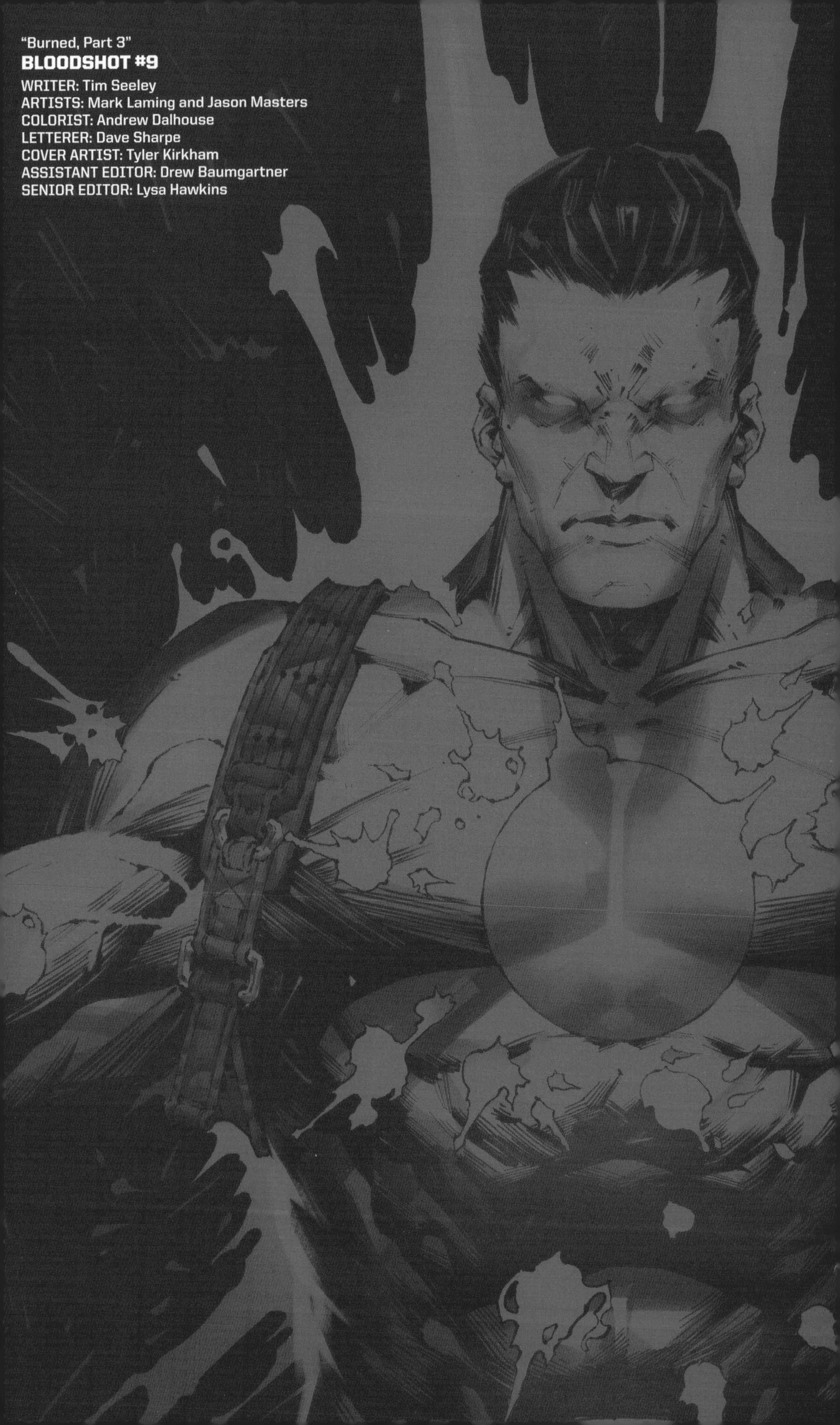

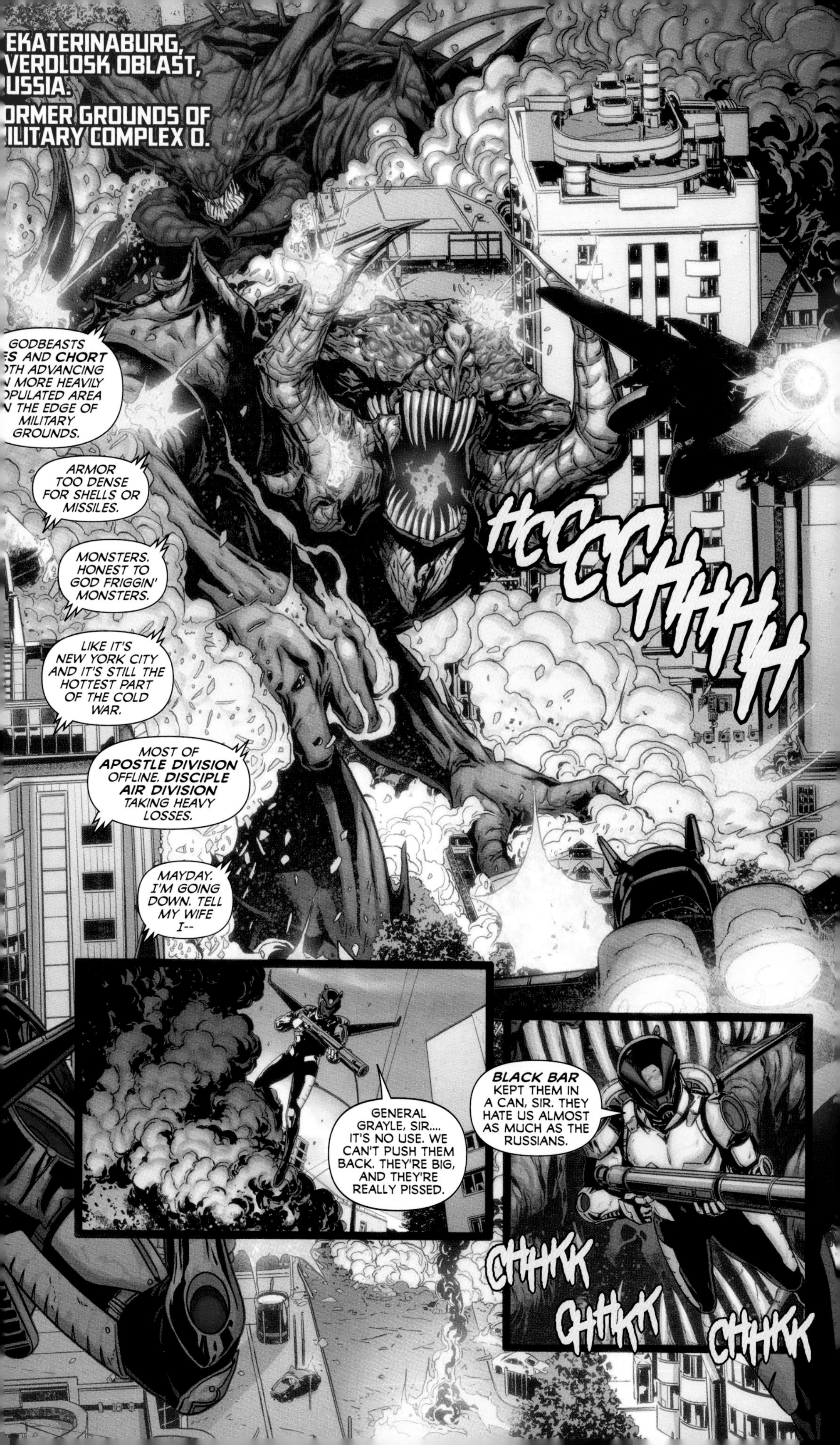

EKATERINABURG, VERDLOSK OBLAST, USSIA.
ORMER GROUNDS OF ILITARY COMPLEX 0.
GODBEASTS ES AND CHORT OTH ADVANCING N MORE HEAVILY OPULATED AREA N THE EDGE OF MILITARY GROUNDS.
ARMOR TOO DENSE FOR SHELLS OR MISSILES.
MONSTERS. HONEST TO GOD FRIGGIN' MONSTERS.
LIKE IT'S NEW YORK CITY AND IT'S STILL THE HOTTEST PART OF THE COLD WAR.
MOST OF APOSTLE DIVISION OFFLINE. DISCIPLE AIR DIVISION TAKING HEAVY LOSSES.
MAYDAY. I'M GOING DOWN. TELL MY WIFE I--
GENERAL GRAYLE, SIR.... IT'S NO USE. WE CAN'T PUSH THEM BACK. THEY'RE BIG, AND THEY'RE REALLY PISSED.
BLACK BAR KEPT THEM IN A CAN, SIR. THEY HATE US ALMOST AS MUCH AS THE RUSSIANS.
CHHKK
CHHKK
CHHKK

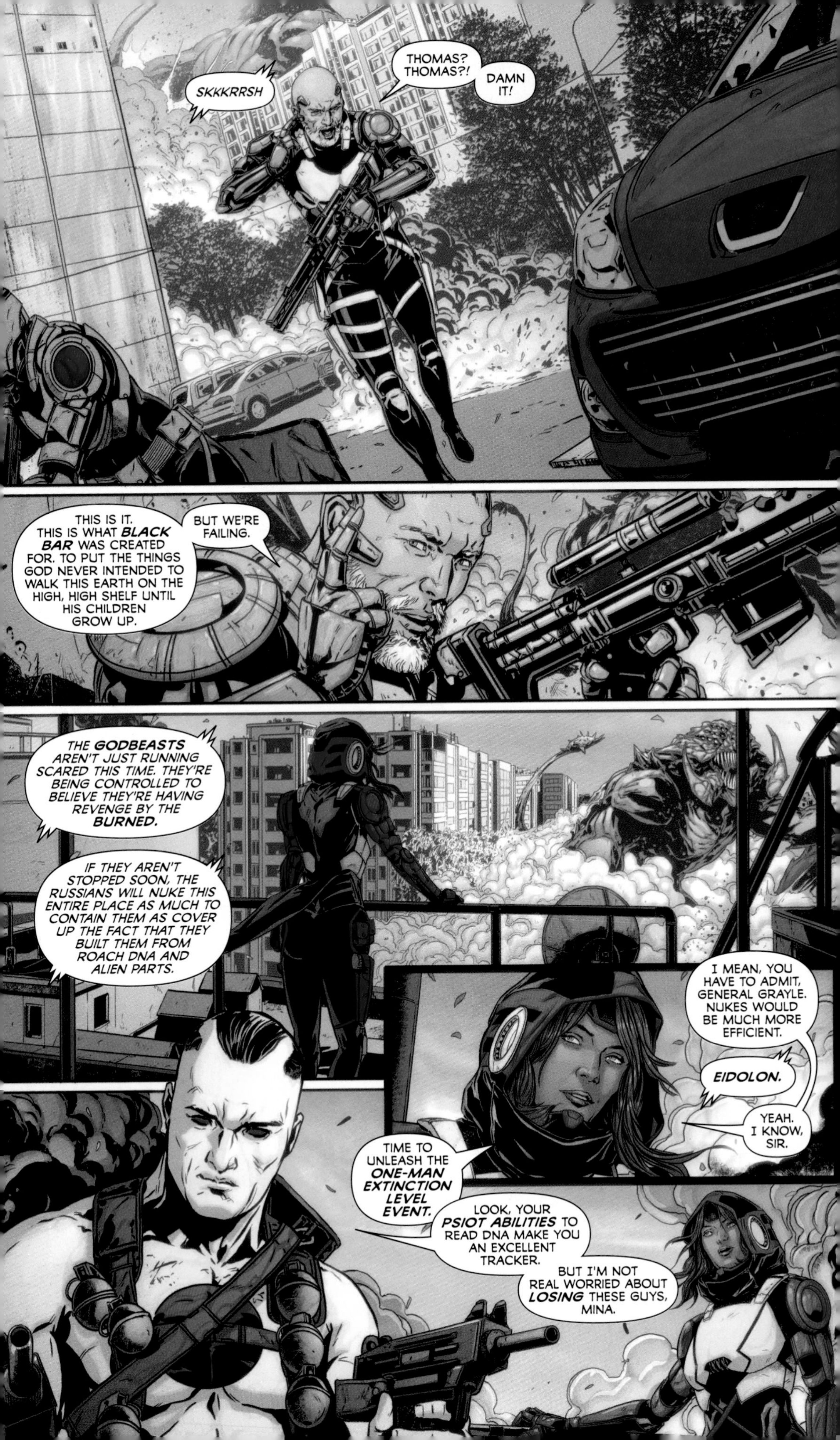
SKKKRRSH
THOMAS? THOMAS?!
DAMN IT!
THIS IS IT. THIS IS WHAT BLACK BAR WAS CREATED FOR. TO PUT THE THINGS GOD NEVER INTENDED TO WALK THIS EARTH ON THE HIGH, HIGH SHELF UNTIL HIS CHILDREN GROW UP.
BUT WE'RE FAILING.
THE GODBEASTS AREN'T JUST RUNNING SCARED THIS TIME. THEY'RE BEING CONTROLLED TO BELIEVE THEY'RE HAVING REVENGE BY THE BURNED.
IF THEY AREN'T STOPPED SOON, THE RUSSIANS WILL NUKE THIS ENTIRE PLACE AS MUCH TO CONTAIN THEM AS COVER UP THE FACT THAT THEY BUILT THEM FROM ROACH DNA AND ALIEN PARTS.
I MEAN, YOU HAVE TO ADMIT, GENERAL GRAYLE. NUKES WOULD BE MUCH MORE EFFICIENT.
EIDOLON.
YEAH. I KNOW, SIR.
TIME TO UNLEASH THE ONE-MAN EXTINCTION LEVEL EVENT.
LOOK, YOUR PSIOT ABILITIES TO READ DNA MAKE YOU AN EXCELLENT TRACKER.
BUT I'M NOT REAL WORRIED ABOUT LOSING THESE GUYS, MINA.

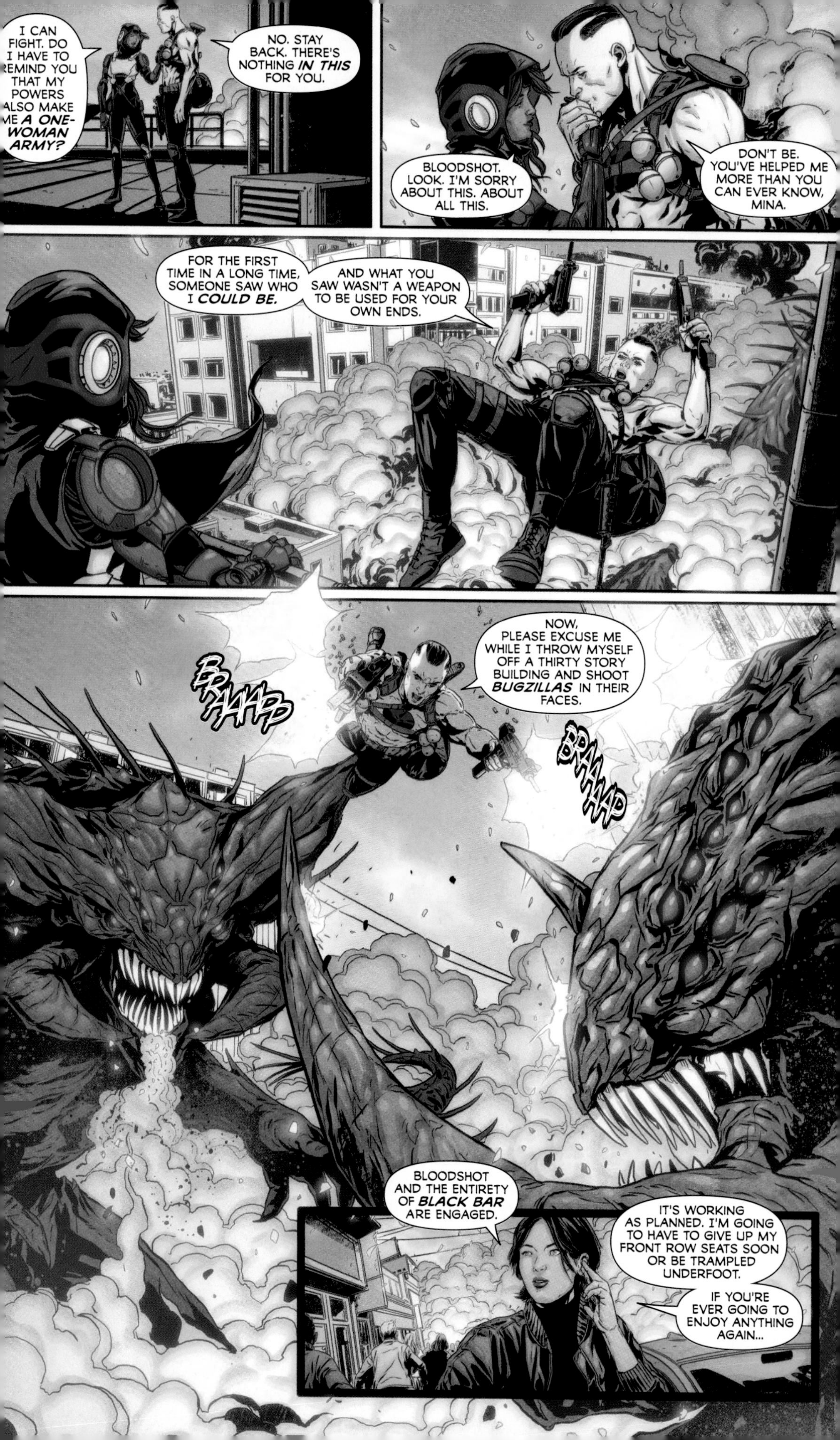

I CAN FIGHT. DO I HAVE TO REMIND YOU THAT MY POWERS ALSO MAKE ME *A ONE-WOMAN ARMY?*
NO. STAY BACK. THERE'S NOTHING *IN THIS* FOR YOU.
BLOODSHOT. LOOK. I'M SORRY ABOUT THIS. ABOUT ALL THIS.
DON'T BE. YOU'VE HELPED ME MORE THAN YOU CAN EVER KNOW, MINA.
FOR THE FIRST TIME IN A LONG TIME, SOMEONE SAW WHO I *COULD BE.*
AND WHAT YOU SAW WASN'T A WEAPON TO BE USED FOR YOUR OWN ENDS.
BRAAAPP
NOW, PLEASE EXCUSE ME WHILE I THROW MYSELF OFF A THIRTY STORY BUILDING AND SHOOT *BUGZILLAS* IN THEIR FACES.
BRAAAAP
BLOODSHOT AND THE ENTIRETY OF *BLACK BAR* ARE ENGAGED.
IT'S WORKING AS PLANNED. I'M GOING TO HAVE TO GIVE UP MY FRONT ROW SEATS SOON OR BE TRAMPLED UNDERFOOT.
IF YOU'RE EVER GOING TO ENJOY ANYTHING AGAIN...

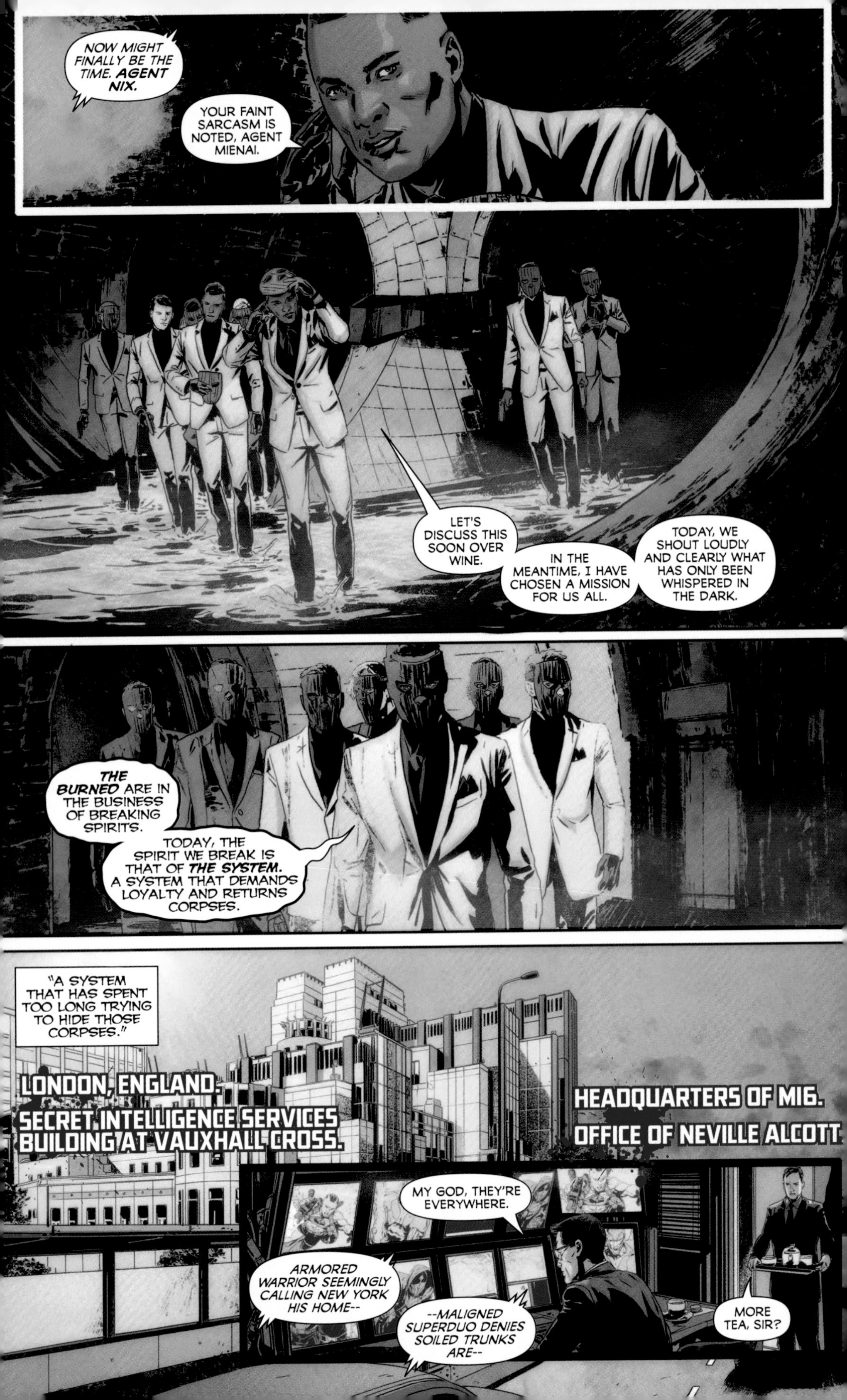
NOW MIGHT FINALLY BE THE TIME. AGENT NIX.
YOUR FAINT SARCASM IS NOTED, AGENT MIENAI.
LET'S DISCUSS THIS SOON OVER WINE.
IN THE MEANTIME, I HAVE CHOSEN A MISSION FOR US ALL.
TODAY, WE SHOUT LOUDLY AND CLEARLY WHAT HAS ONLY BEEN WHISPERED IN THE DARK.
THE BURNED ARE IN THE BUSINESS OF BREAKING SPIRITS.
TODAY, THE SPIRIT WE BREAK IS THAT OF THE SYSTEM. A SYSTEM THAT DEMANDS LOYALTY AND RETURNS CORPSES.
"A SYSTEM THAT HAS SPENT TOO LONG TRYING TO HIDE THOSE CORPSES."
LONDON, ENGLAND.
SECRET INTELLIGENCE SERVICES BUILDING AT VAUXHALL CROSS.
HEADQUARTERS OF MI6.
OFFICE OF NEVILLE ALCOTT.
MY GOD, THEY'RE EVERYWHERE.
ARMORED WARRIOR SEEMINGLY CALLING NEW YORK HIS HOME--
--MALIGNED SUPERDUO DENIES SOILED TRUNKS ARE--
MORE TEA, SIR?

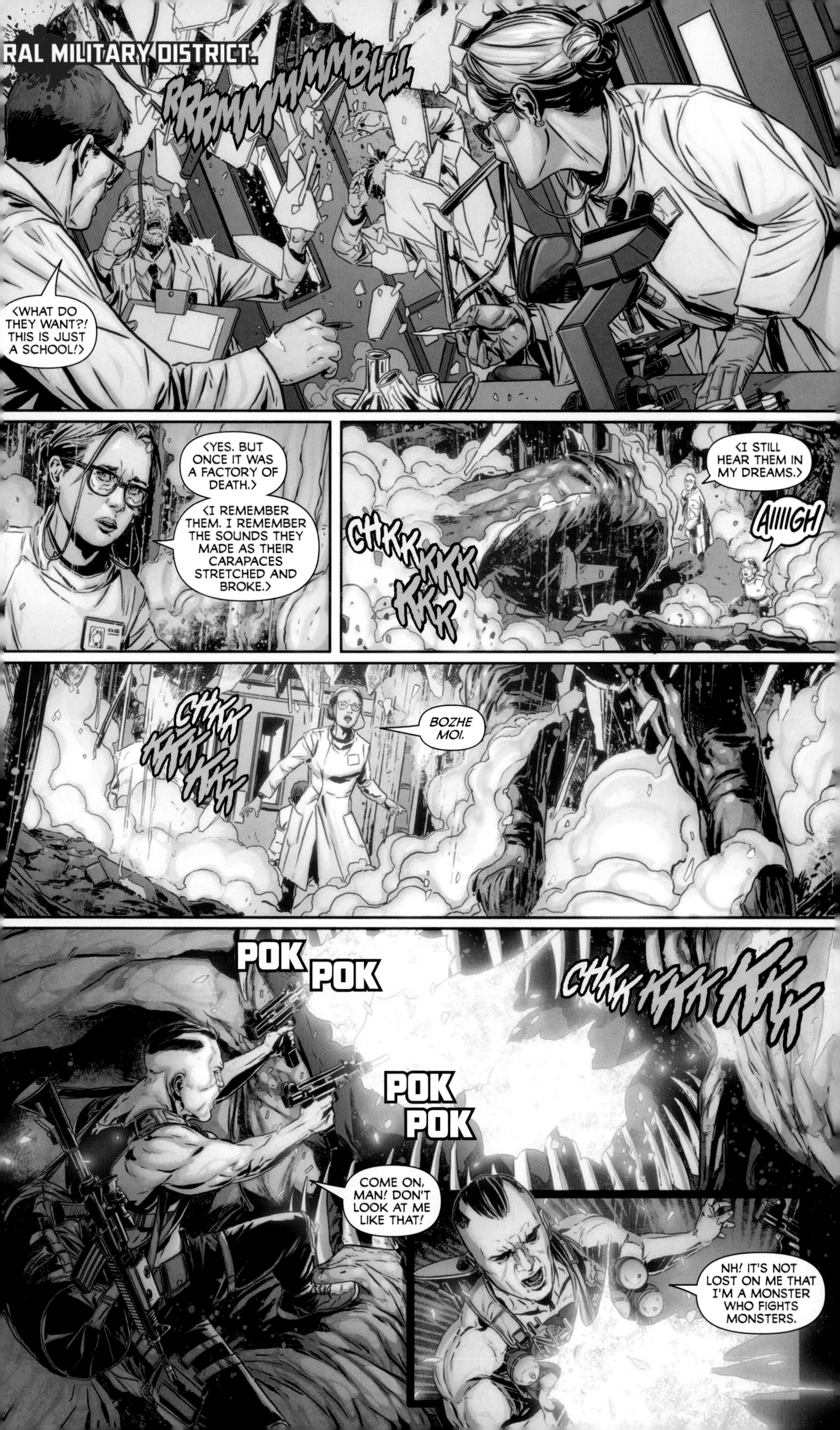
RAL MILITARY DISTRICT.
RRRMMMMMMBLLL
<WHAT DO THEY WANT?! THIS IS JUST A SCHOOL!>
<YES. BUT ONCE IT WAS A FACTORY OF DEATH.>
<I REMEMBER THEM. I REMEMBER THE SOUNDS THEY MADE AS THEIR CARAPACES STRETCHED AND BROKE.>
CHKKKKKKKKK
<I STILL HEAR THEM IN MY DREAMS.>
AIIIIGH
CHKKKKKKKKK
BOZHE MOI.
POK POK
CHKKKKKKKKK
POK POK
COME ON, MAN! DON'T LOOK AT ME LIKE THAT!
NH! IT'S NOT LOST ON ME THAT I'M A MONSTER WHO FIGHTS MONSTERS.

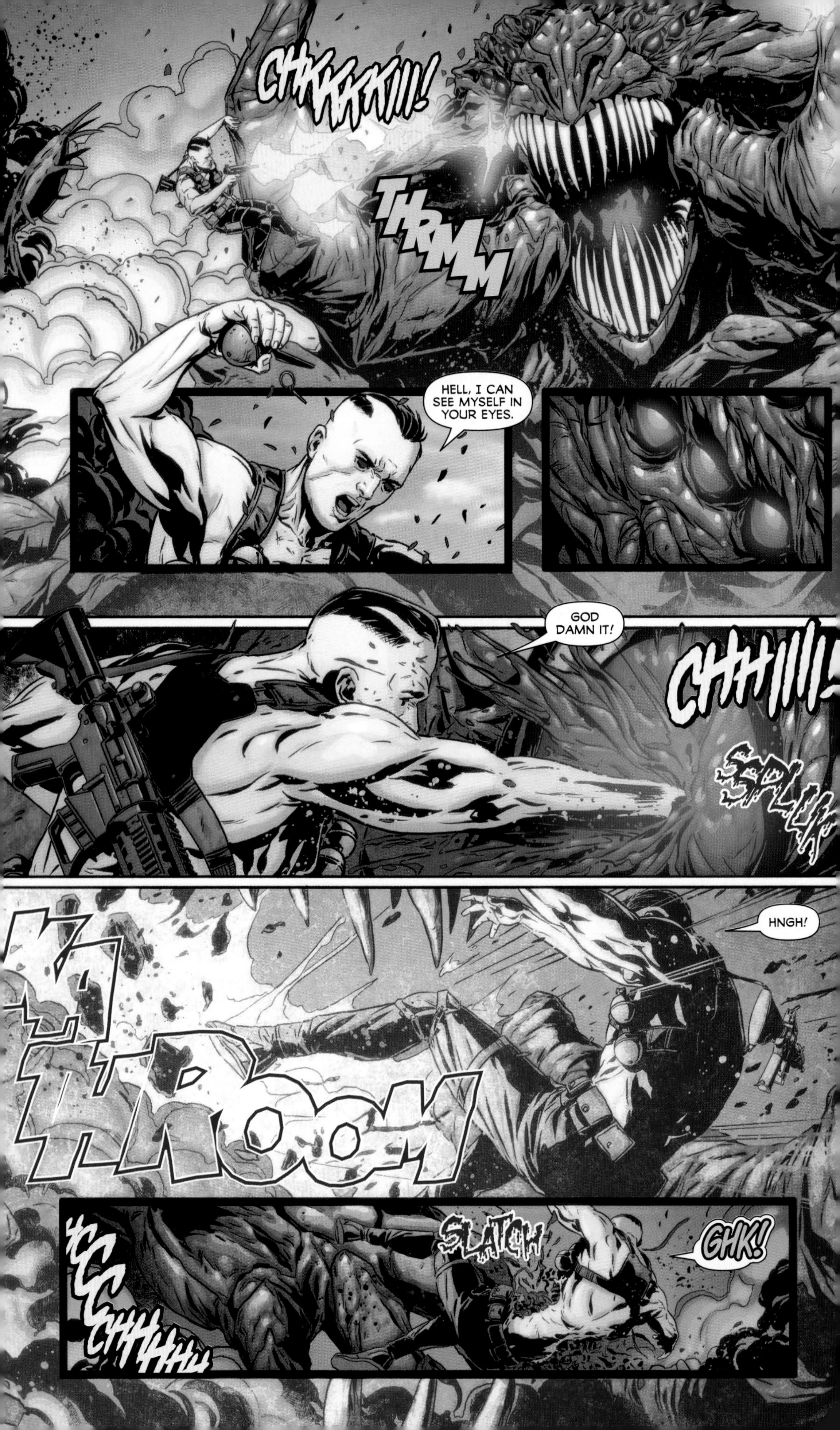
CHKKKKKIII!
THRMMM
HELL, I CAN SEE MYSELF IN YOUR EYES.
GOD DAMN IT!
CHHIIIII
SPLUK
HNGH!
KATHROOM
SLATCH
GHK!
KCCCHHHHHU

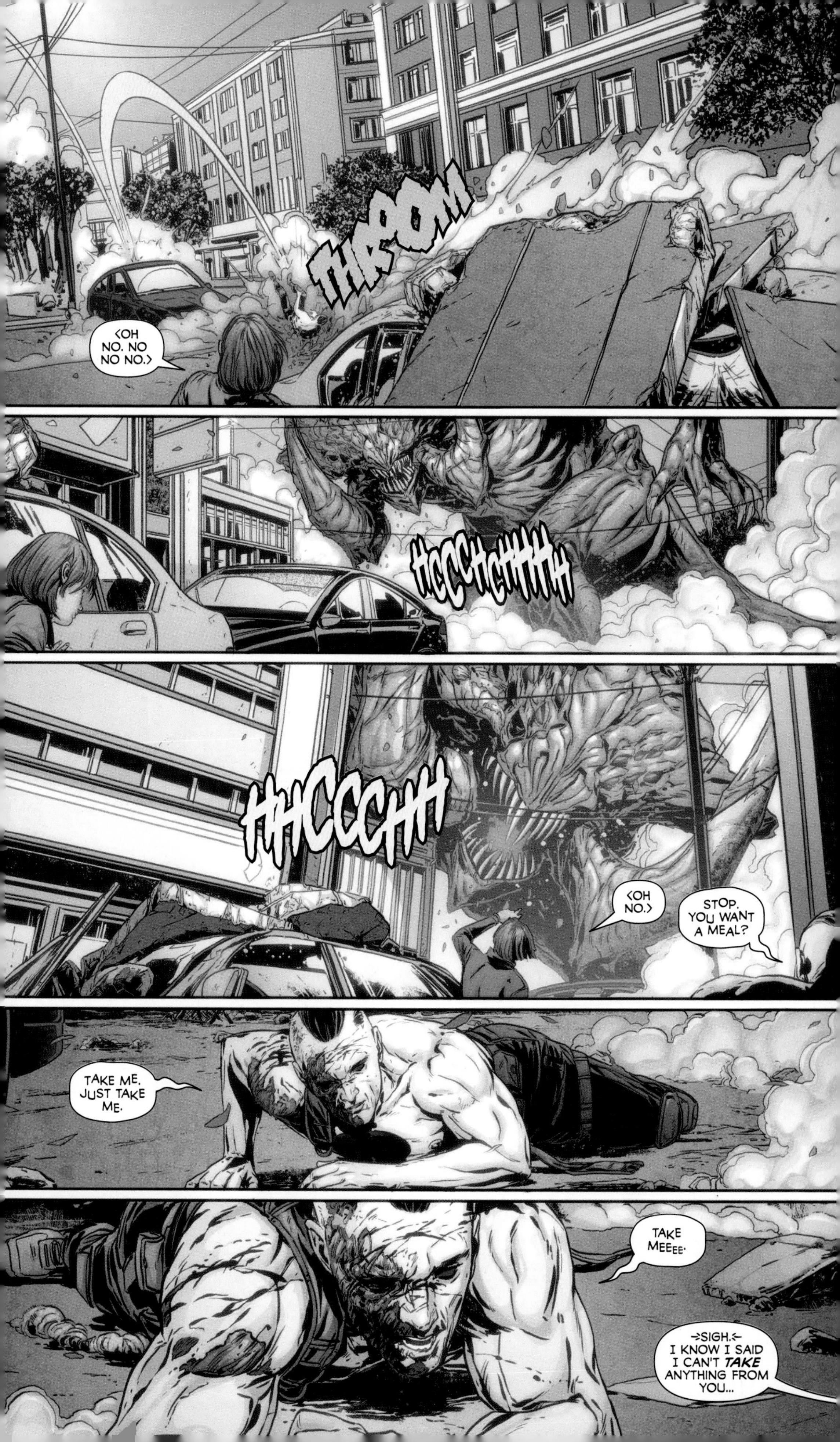
THROOM
<OH NO. NO NO NO.>
HCCCHCHHHH
HHCCCHH
<OH NO.>
STOP. YOU WANT A MEAL?
TAKE ME. JUST TAKE ME.
TAKE MEEEE.
SIGH. I KNOW I SAID I CAN'T ***TAKE*** ANYTHING FROM YOU...

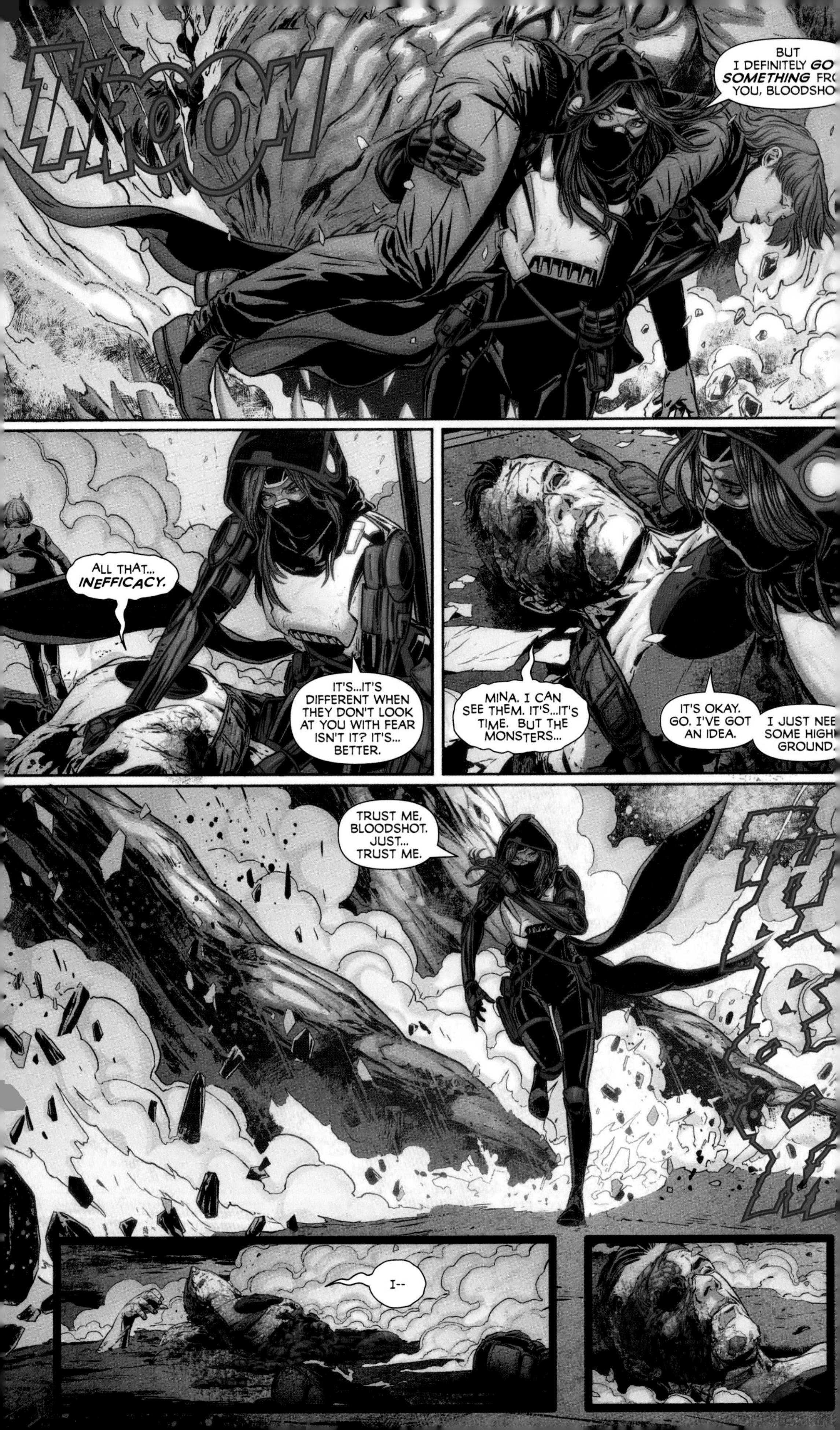
WHOOM
BUT I DEFINITELY GO SOMETHING FR YOU, BLOODSHO
ALL THAT... INEFFICACY.
IT'S...IT'S DIFFERENT WHEN THEY DON'T LOOK AT YOU WITH FEAR ISN'T IT? IT'S... BETTER.
MINA. I CAN SEE THEM. IT'S...IT'S TIME. BUT THE MONSTERS...
IT'S OKAY. GO. I'VE GOT AN IDEA.
I JUST NEE SOME HIGH GROUND.
TRUST ME, BLOODSHOT. JUST... TRUST ME.
I--

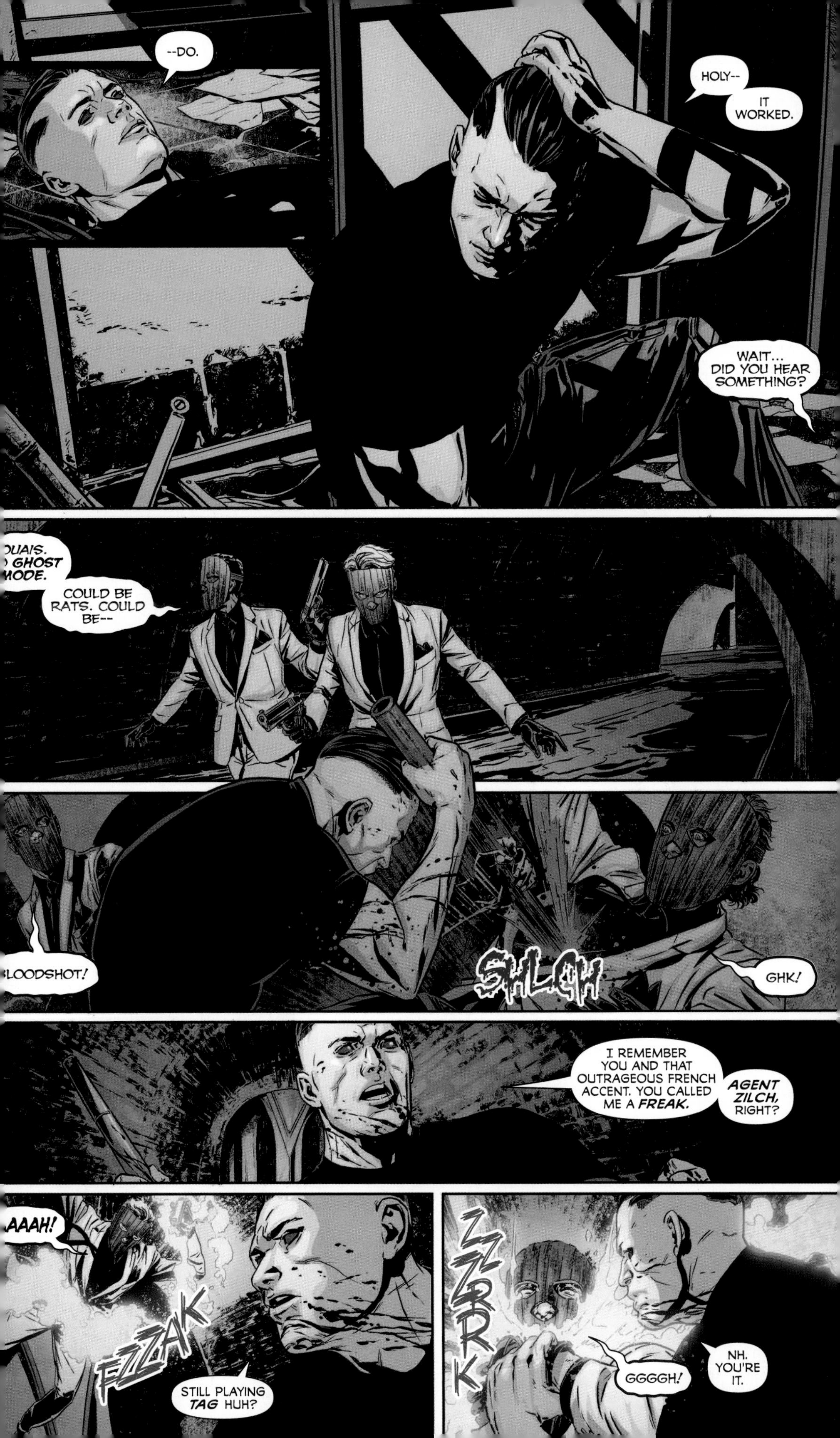
--DO.
HOLY--
IT WORKED.
WAIT... DID YOU HEAR SOMETHING?
OUAIS. GHOST MODE.
COULD BE RATS. COULD BE--
LOODSHOT!
SHLCH
GHK!
I REMEMBER YOU AND THAT OUTRAGEOUS FRENCH ACCENT. YOU CALLED ME A FREAK.
AGENT ZILCH, RIGHT?
AAAH!
FZZZAK
STILL PLAYING TAG HUH?
ZZZRRK
GGGGH!
NH. YOU'RE IT.

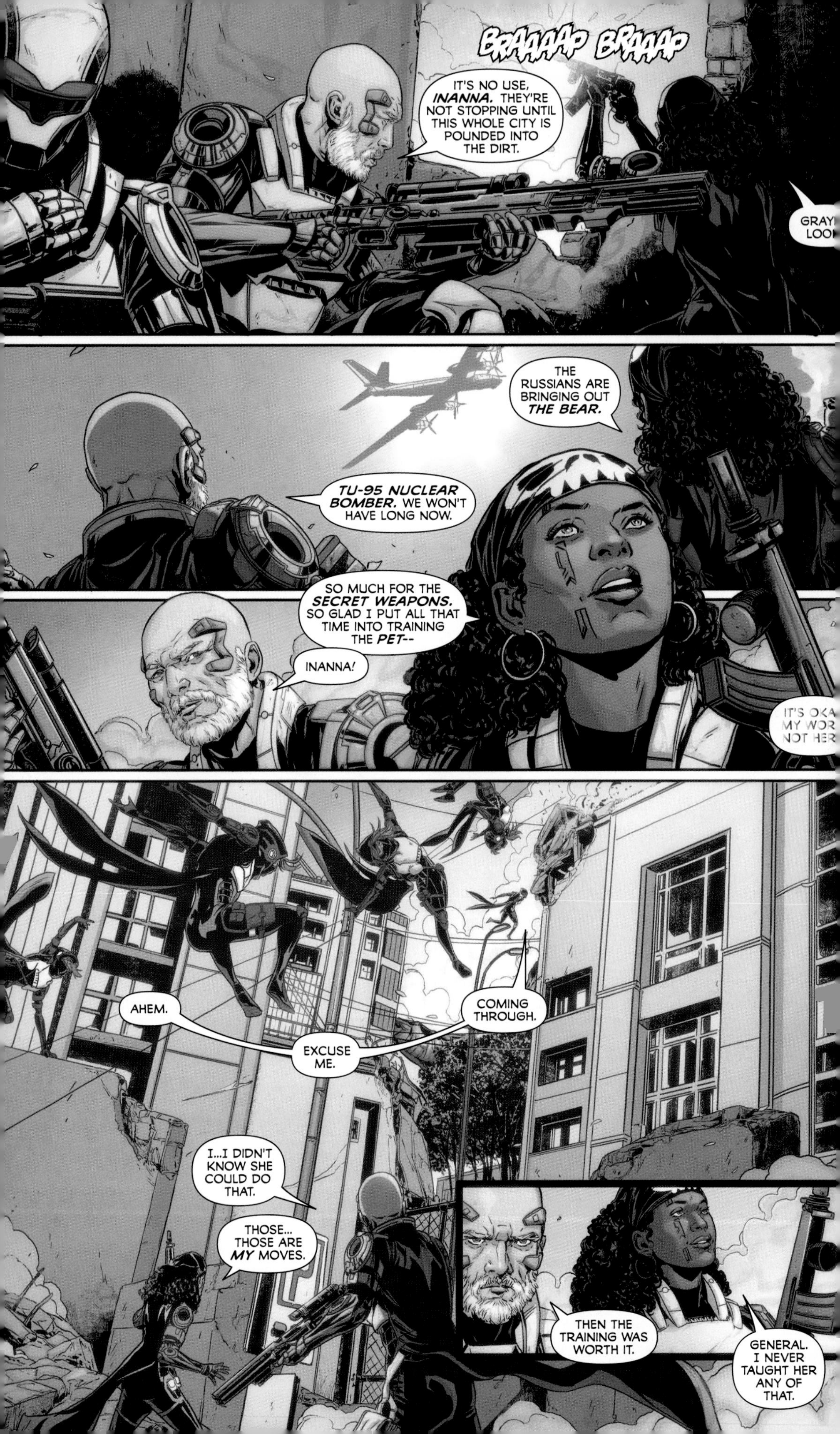
BRAAAAP BRAAAP
IT'S NO USE, INANNA. THEY'RE NOT STOPPING UNTIL THIS WHOLE CITY IS POUNDED INTO THE DIRT.
THE RUSSIANS ARE BRINGING OUT THE BEAR.
TU-95 NUCLEAR BOMBER. WE WON'T HAVE LONG NOW.
SO MUCH FOR THE SECRET WEAPONS. SO GLAD I PUT ALL THAT TIME INTO TRAINING THE PET--
INANNA!
AHEM.
EXCUSE ME.
COMING THROUGH.
I...I DIDN'T KNOW SHE COULD DO THAT.
THOSE... THOSE ARE MY MOVES.
THEN THE TRAINING WAS WORTH IT.
GENERAL. I NEVER TAUGHT HER ANY OF THAT.

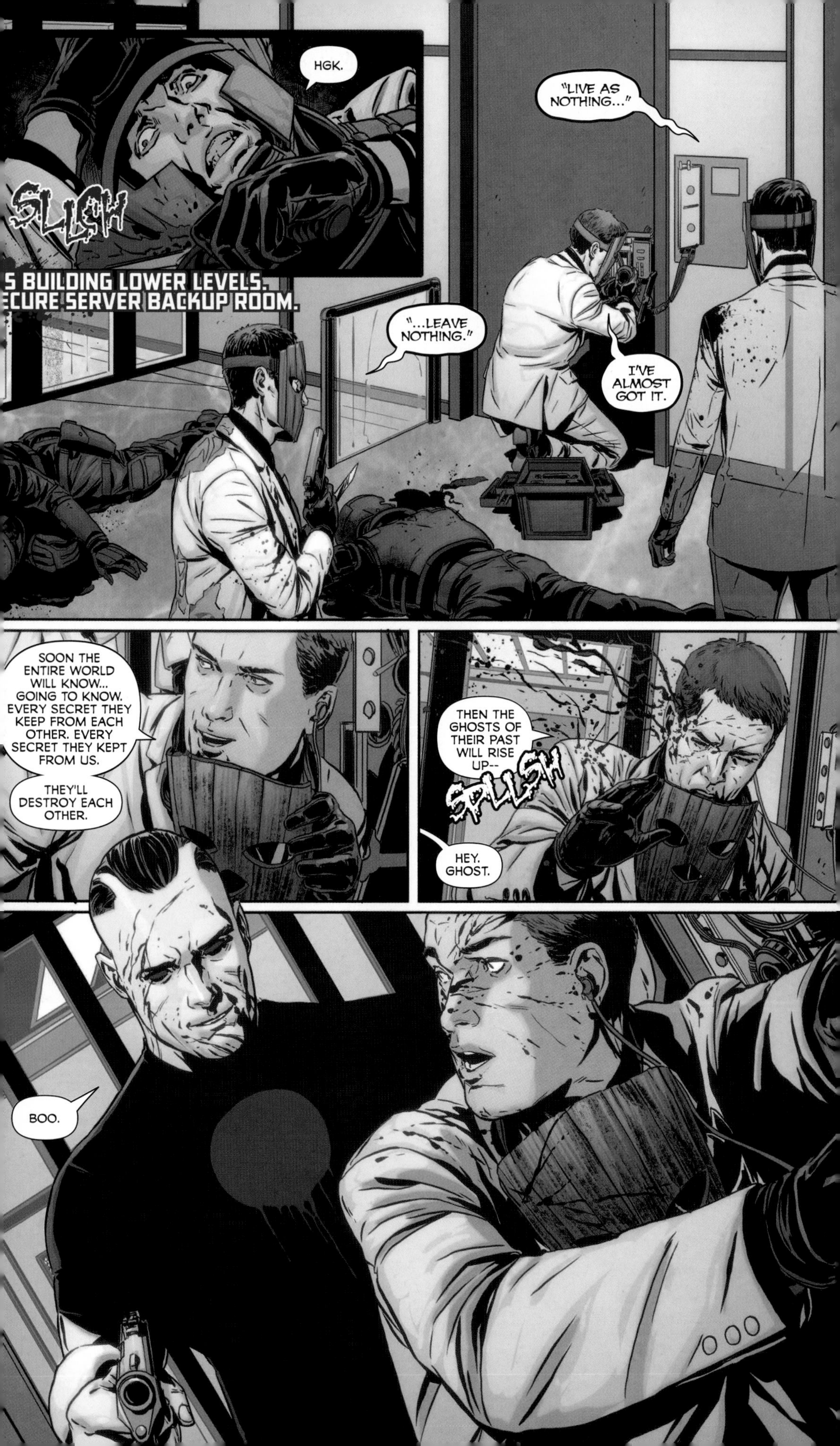

HGK.
SLLSH
S BUILDING LOWER LEVELS.
ECURE SERVER BACKUP ROOM.
"LIVE AS NOTHING..."
"...LEAVE NOTHING."
I'VE ALMOST GOT IT.
SOON THE ENTIRE WORLD WILL KNOW... GOING TO KNOW. EVERY SECRET THEY KEEP FROM EACH OTHER. EVERY SECRET THEY KEPT FROM US.
THEY'LL DESTROY EACH OTHER.
THEN THE GHOSTS OF THEIR PAST WILL RISE UP--
SPLLSH
HEY. GHOST.
BOO.

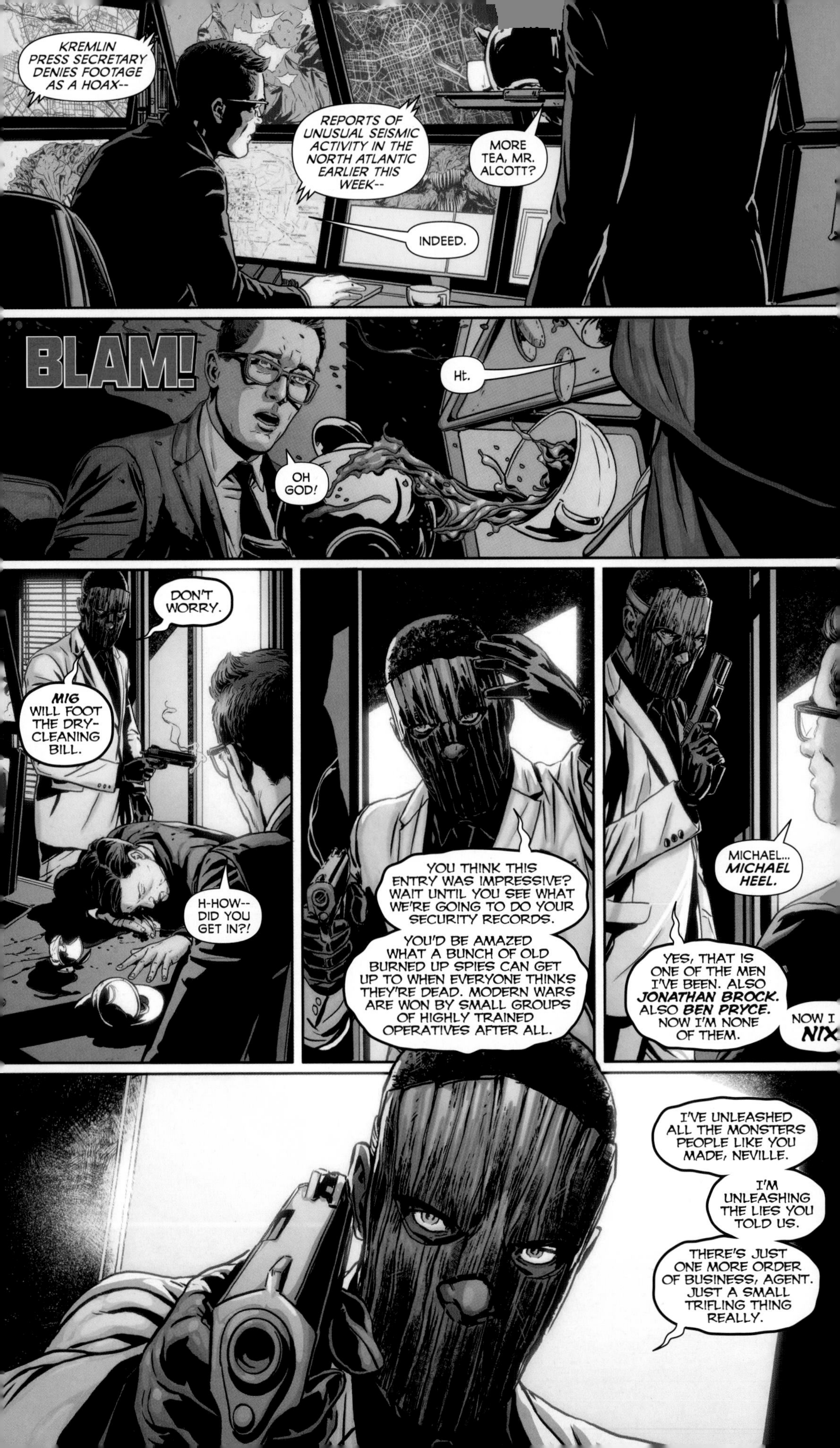
KREMLIN PRESS SECRETARY DENIES FOOTAGE AS A HOAX--
REPORTS OF UNUSUAL SEISMIC ACTIVITY IN THE NORTH ATLANTIC EARLIER THIS WEEK--
MORE TEA, MR. ALCOTT?
INDEED.
BLAM!
Ht.
OH GOD!
DON'T WORRY.
MI6 WILL FOOT THE DRY-CLEANING BILL.
H-HOW-- DID YOU GET IN?!
YOU THINK THIS ENTRY WAS IMPRESSIVE? WAIT UNTIL YOU SEE WHAT WE'RE GOING TO DO YOUR SECURITY RECORDS.
YOU'D BE AMAZED WHAT A BUNCH OF OLD BURNED UP SPIES CAN GET UP TO WHEN EVERYONE THINKS THEY'RE DEAD. MODERN WARS ARE WON BY SMALL GROUPS OF HIGHLY TRAINED OPERATIVES AFTER ALL.
MICHAEL... MICHAEL HEEL.
YES, THAT IS ONE OF THE MEN I'VE BEEN. ALSO JONATHAN BROCK. ALSO BEN PRYCE. NOW I'M NONE OF THEM.
NOW I NIX
I'VE UNLEASHED ALL THE MONSTERS PEOPLE LIKE YOU MADE, NEVILLE.
I'M UNLEASHING THE LIES YOU TOLD US.
THERE'S JUST ONE MORE ORDER OF BUSINESS, AGENT. JUST A SMALL TRIFLING THING REALLY.

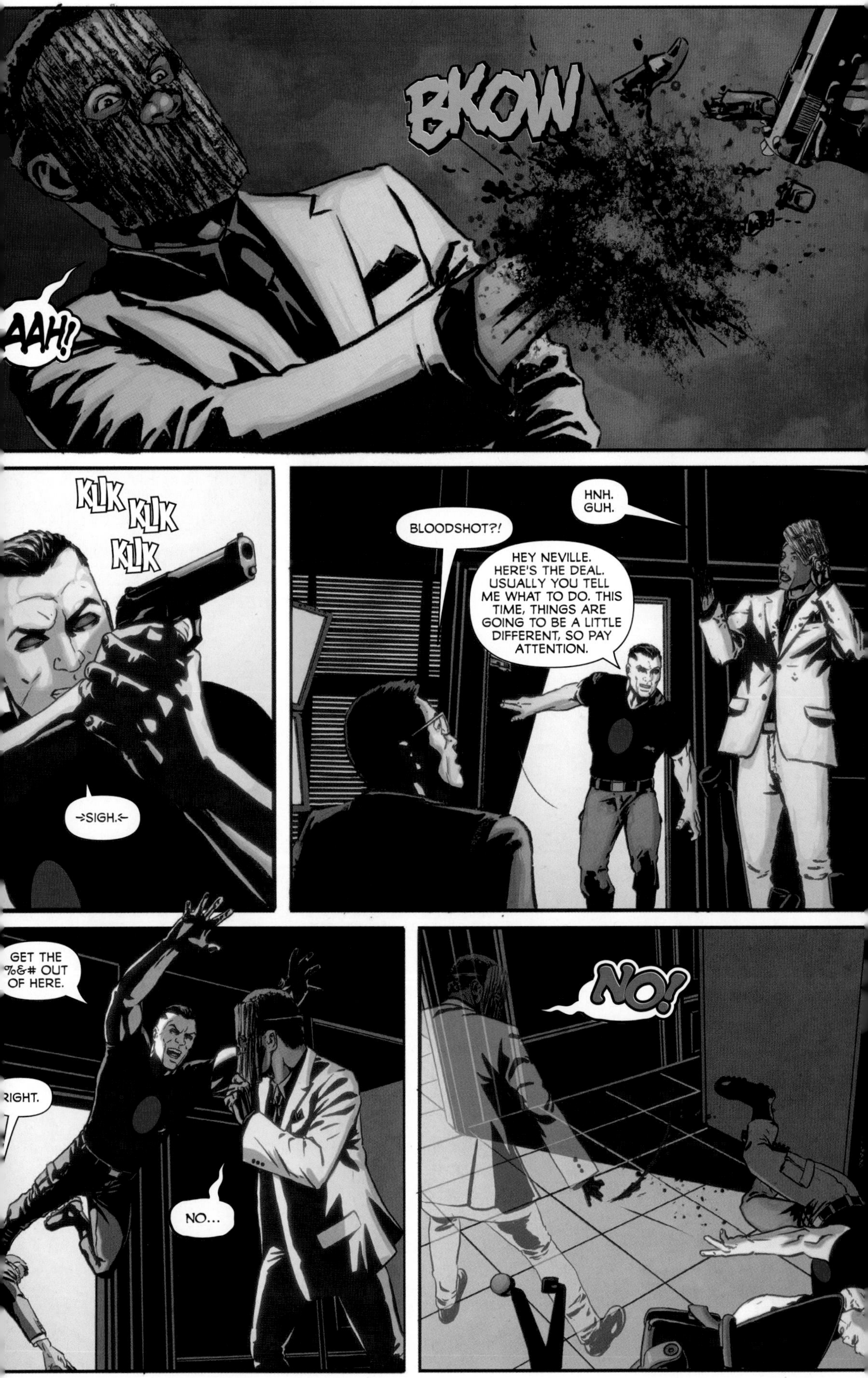
BKOW
AAH!!
KLIK KLIK KLIK
›SIGH.‹
BLOODSHOT?!
HNH. GUH.
HEY NEVILLE. HERE'S THE DEAL. USUALLY YOU TELL ME WHAT TO DO. THIS TIME, THINGS ARE GOING TO BE A LITTLE DIFFERENT, SO PAY ATTENTION.
GET THE %&# OUT OF HERE.
RIGHT.
NO...
NO!

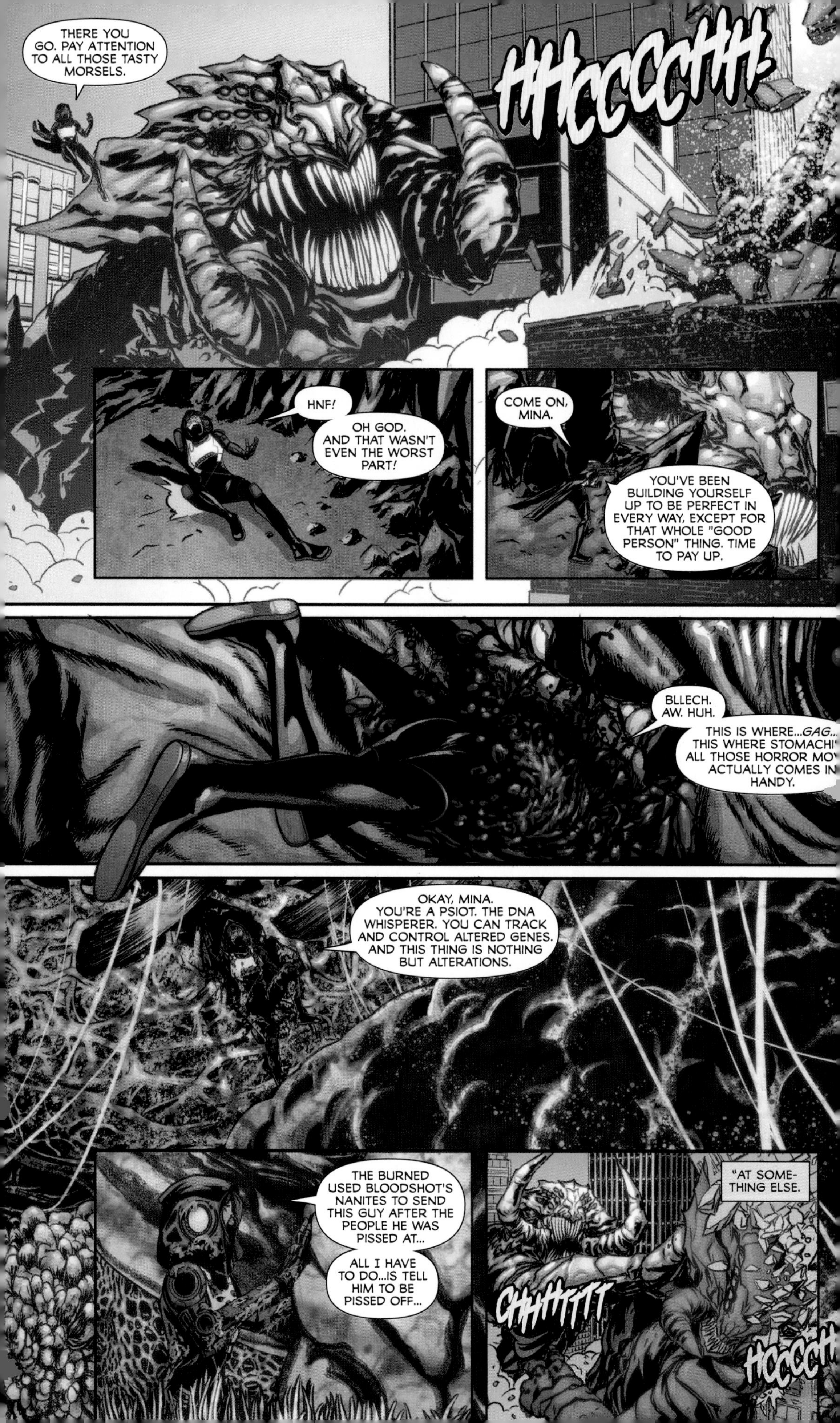
THERE YOU GO. PAY ATTENTION TO ALL THOSE TASTY MORSELS.
HHCCCCHH-
HNF!
OH GOD. AND THAT WASN'T EVEN THE WORST PART!
COME ON, MINA.
YOU'VE BEEN BUILDING YOURSELF UP TO BE PERFECT IN EVERY WAY, EXCEPT FOR THAT WHOLE "GOOD PERSON" THING. TIME TO PAY UP.
BLLECH. AW. HUH.
THIS IS WHERE...GAG...
THIS WHERE STOMACHI
ALL THOSE HORROR MO
ACTUALLY COMES IN
HANDY.
OKAY, MINA. YOU'RE A PSIOT. THE DNA WHISPERER. YOU CAN TRACK AND CONTROL ALTERED GENES. AND THIS THING IS NOTHING BUT ALTERATIONS.
THE BURNED USED BLOODSHOT'S NANITES TO SEND THIS GUY AFTER THE PEOPLE HE WAS PISSED AT...
ALL I HAVE TO DO...IS TELL HIM TO BE PISSED OFF...
"AT SOMETHING ELSE.
CHHHTTTT
HCCCH

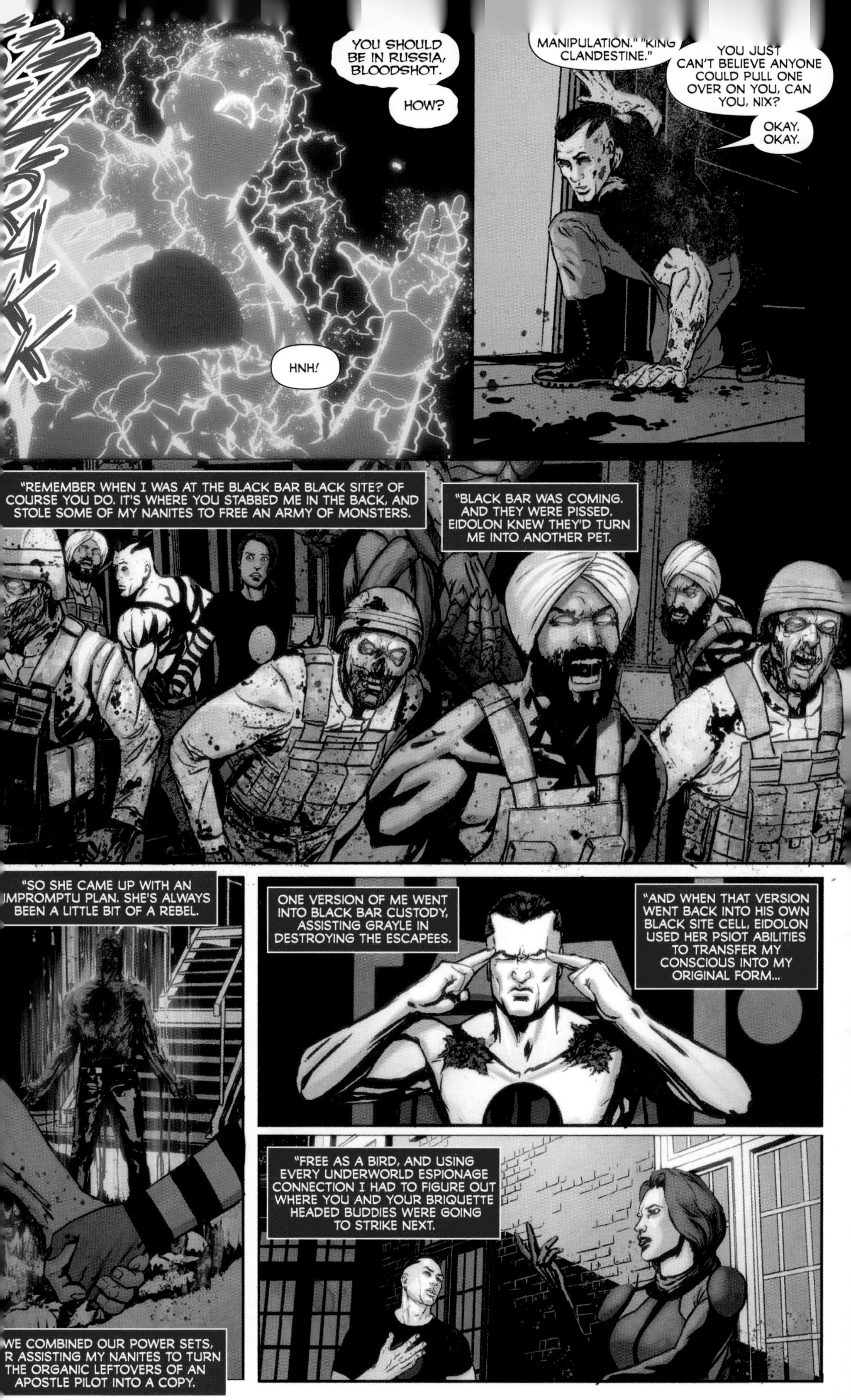

YOU SHOULD BE IN RUSSIA, BLOODSHOT.
HOW?
HNH!
MANIPULATION." "KING CLANDESTINE."
YOU JUST CAN'T BELIEVE ANYONE COULD PULL ONE OVER ON YOU, CAN YOU, NIX?
OKAY. OKAY.
"REMEMBER WHEN I WAS AT THE BLACK BAR BLACK SITE? OF COURSE YOU DO. IT'S WHERE YOU STABBED ME IN THE BACK, AND STOLE SOME OF MY NANITES TO FREE AN ARMY OF MONSTERS.
"BLACK BAR WAS COMING. AND THEY WERE PISSED. EIDOLON KNEW THEY'D TURN ME INTO ANOTHER PET.
"SO SHE CAME UP WITH AN IMPROMPTU PLAN. SHE'S ALWAYS BEEN A LITTLE BIT OF A REBEL.
WE COMBINED OUR POWER SETS, R ASSISTING MY NANITES TO TURN THE ORGANIC LEFTOVERS OF AN APOSTLE PILOT INTO A COPY.
ONE VERSION OF ME WENT INTO BLACK BAR CUSTODY, ASSISTING GRAYLE IN DESTROYING THE ESCAPEES.
"AND WHEN THAT VERSION WENT BACK INTO HIS OWN BLACK SITE CELL, EIDOLON USED HER PSIOT ABILITIES TO TRANSFER MY CONSCIOUS INTO MY ORIGINAL FORM...
"FREE AS A BIRD, AND USING EVERY UNDERWORLD ESPIONAGE CONNECTION I HAD TO FIGURE OUT WHERE YOU AND YOUR BRIQUETTE HEADED BUDDIES WERE GOING TO STRIKE NEXT.

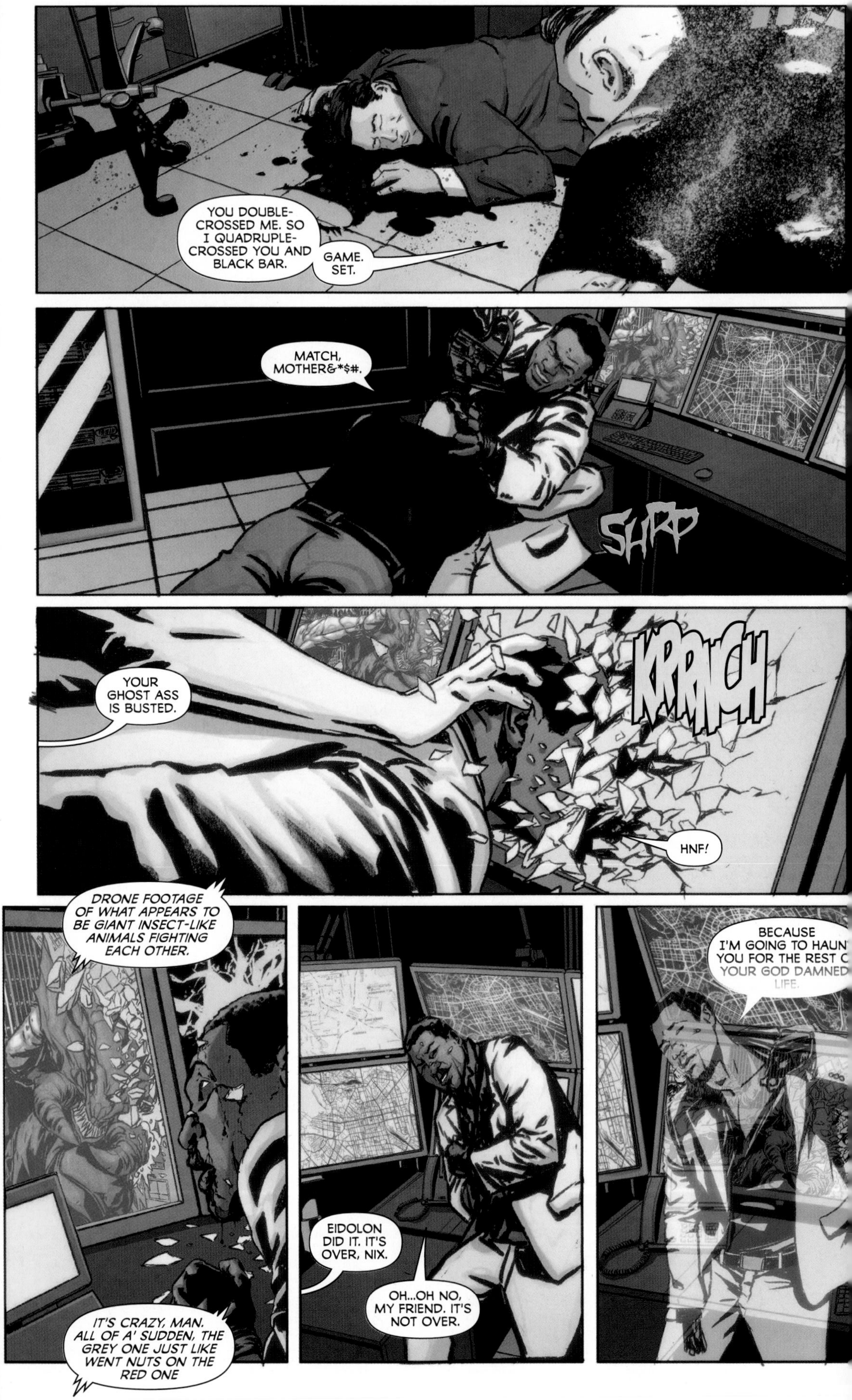
YOU DOUBLE-CROSSED ME. SO I QUADRUPLE-CROSSED YOU AND BLACK BAR.
GAME. SET.
MATCH, MOTHER&*$#.
SHRP
YOUR GHOST ASS IS BUSTED.
KRRNCH
HNF!
DRONE FOOTAGE OF WHAT APPEARS TO BE GIANT INSECT-LIKE ANIMALS FIGHTING EACH OTHER.
IT'S CRAZY, MAN. ALL OF A' SUDDEN, THE GREY ONE JUST LIKE WENT NUTS ON THE RED ONE
EIDOLON DID IT. IT'S OVER, NIX.
OH...OH NO, MY FRIEND. IT'S NOT OVER.
BECAUSE I'M GOING TO HAUN YOU FOR THE REST O YOUR GOD DAMNED LIFE.

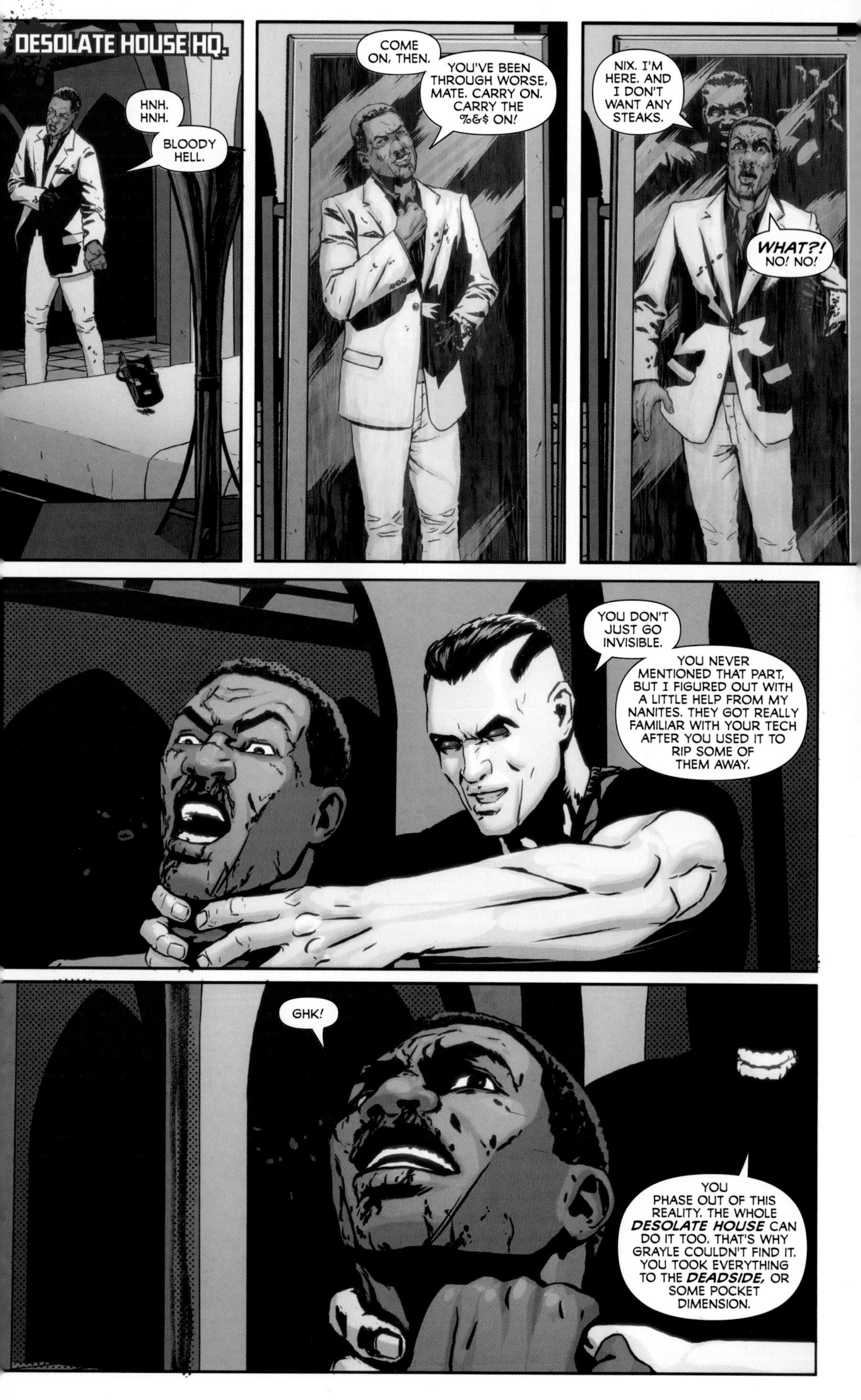
DESOLATE HOUSE HQ.
HNH. HNH.
BLOODY HELL.
COME ON, THEN.
YOU'VE BEEN THROUGH WORSE, MATE. CARRY ON. CARRY THE %&$ ON!
NIX. I'M HERE. AND I DON'T WANT ANY STEAKS.
WHAT?! NO! NO!
YOU DON'T JUST GO INVISIBLE.
YOU NEVER MENTIONED THAT PART, BUT I FIGURED OUT WITH A LITTLE HELP FROM MY NANITES. THEY GOT REALLY FAMILIAR WITH YOUR TECH AFTER YOU USED IT TO RIP SOME OF THEM AWAY.
GHK!
YOU PHASE OUT OF THIS REALITY. THE WHOLE DESOLATE HOUSE CAN DO IT TOO. THAT'S WHY GRAYLE COULDN'T FIND IT. YOU TOOK EVERYTHING TO THE DEADSIDE, OR SOME POCKET DIMENSION.

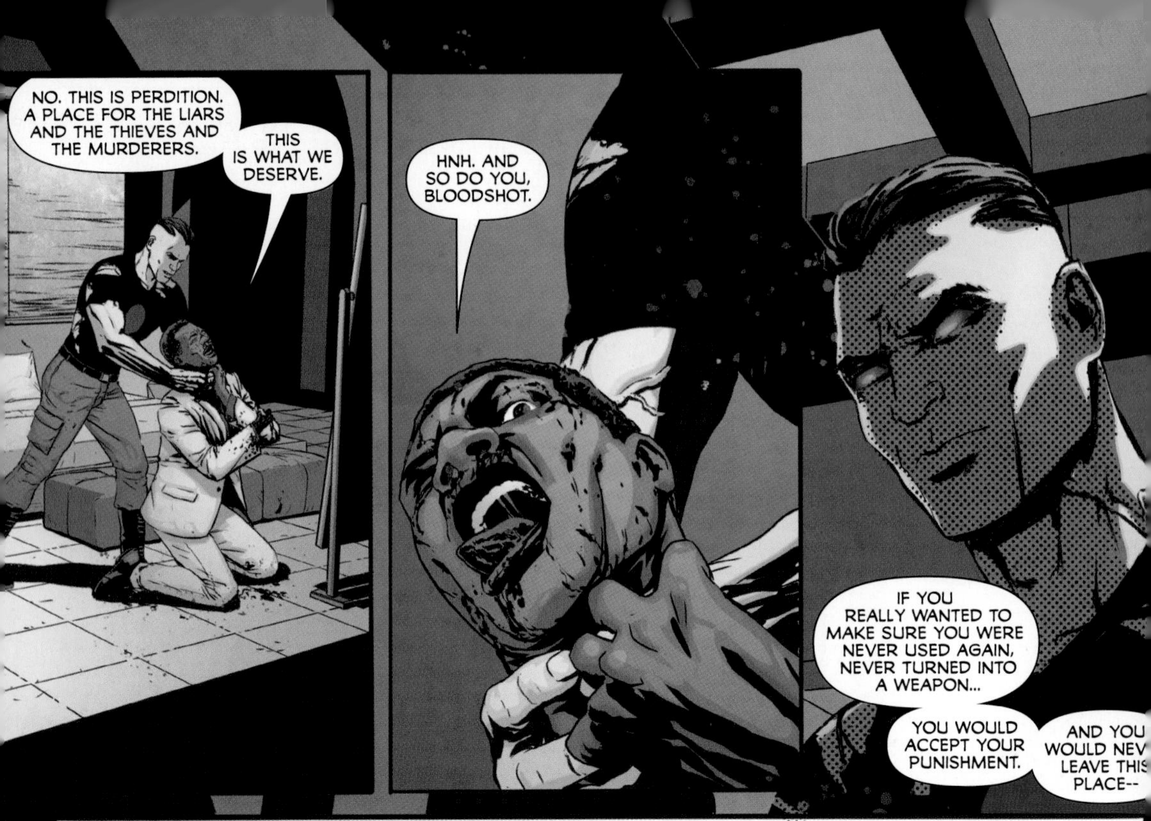
NO. THIS IS PERDITION. A PLACE FOR THE LIARS AND THE THIEVES AND THE MURDERERS.
THIS IS WHAT WE DESERVE.
HNH. AND SO DO YOU, BLOODSHOT.
IF YOU REALLY WANTED TO MAKE SURE YOU WERE NEVER USED AGAIN, NEVER TURNED INTO A WEAPON...
YOU WOULD ACCEPT YOUR PUNISHMENT.
AND YOU WOULD NEV LEAVE THIS PLACE--

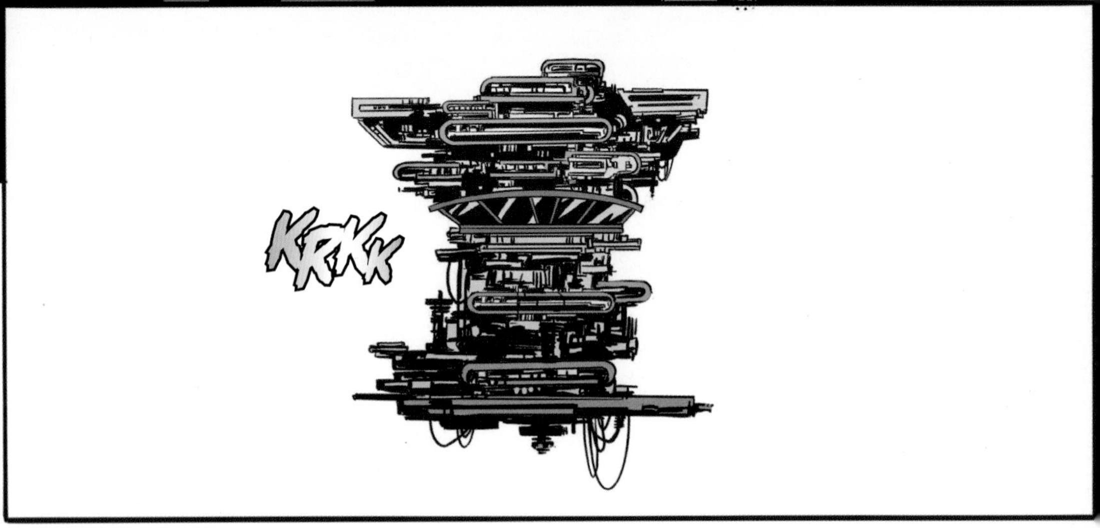
KRKK

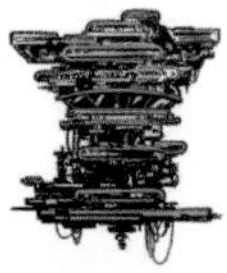

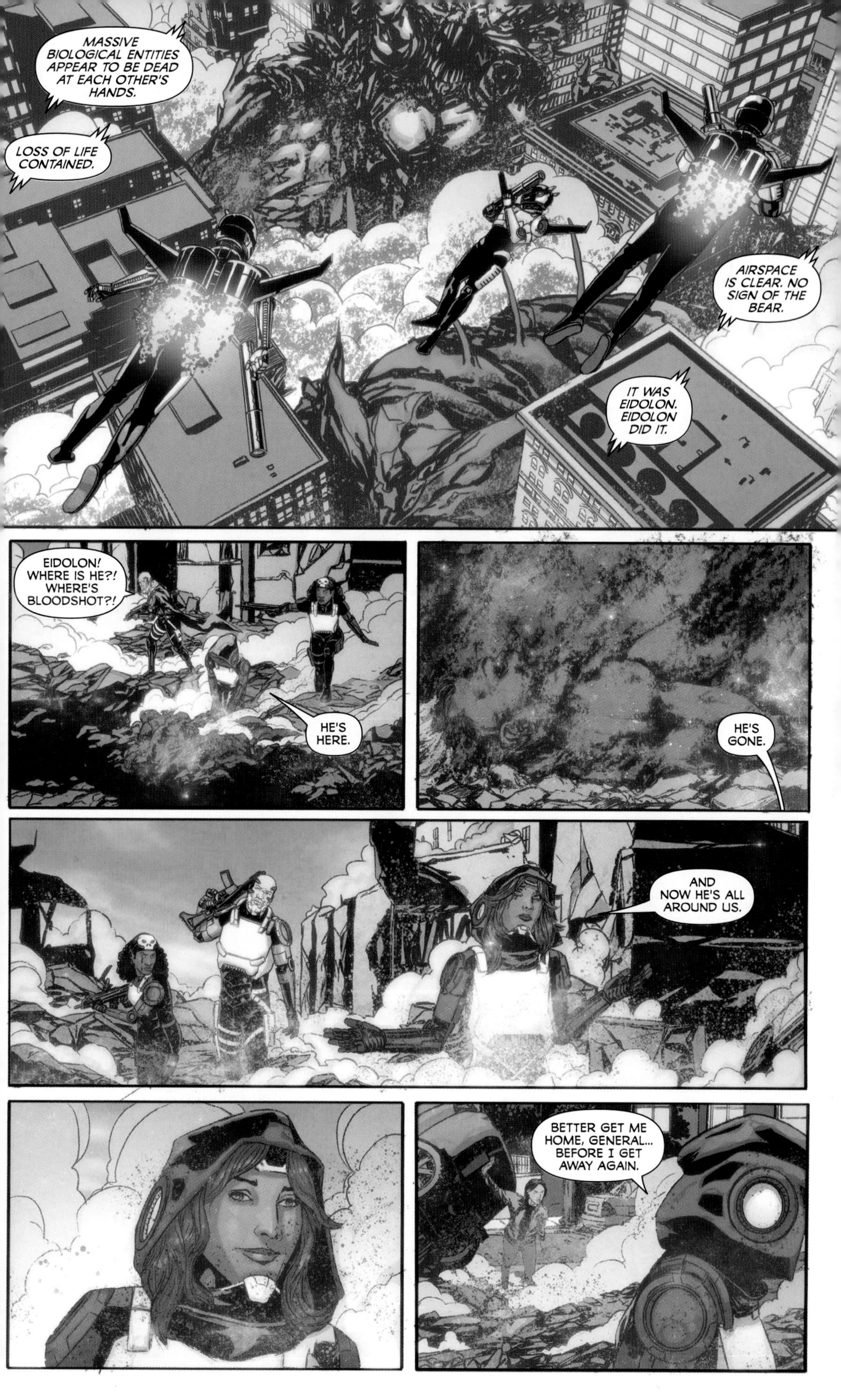
MASSIVE BIOLOGICAL ENTITIES APPEAR TO BE DEAD AT EACH OTHER'S HANDS.
LOSS OF LIFE CONTAINED.
AIRSPACE IS CLEAR. NO SIGN OF THE BEAR.
IT WAS EIDOLON. EIDOLON DID IT.
EIDOLON! WHERE IS HE?! WHERE'S BLOODSHOT?!
HE'S HERE.
HE'S GONE.
AND NOW HE'S ALL AROUND US.
BETTER GET ME HOME, GENERAL... BEFORE I GET AWAY AGAIN.

"YOU ARE BURNED..."
FWASSH
GOD DAMN IT.
I LIKED YOU, MAN.
HNH.
SHK
AAAGGH!
HNN. HNN. HNN.
TSSSK KKRT SSHOT
HNGH! WHAT THE--?!
HELLO? IS THIS THING ON? WHY'S THE RECEPTION SO POOR? WHERE ARE YOU?
GET THE-- WHO?!
THAT'S NOT IMPORTANT RIGHT NOW. ALL YOU NEED TO KNOW IS THAT I'M SMART ENOUGH TO HACK INTO YOUR HEAD. I KNOW THINGS.
MOST IMPORTANTLY I KNO YOU NEED TO RETUR FROM WHEREVER YOU ARE.

BECAUSE **PROJECT RISING SPIRIT** IS BACK.

NEXT: BOOK FOUR

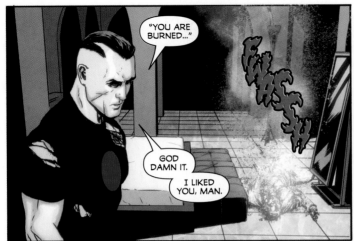

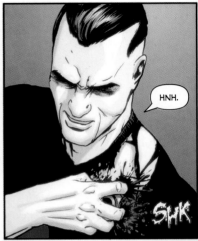

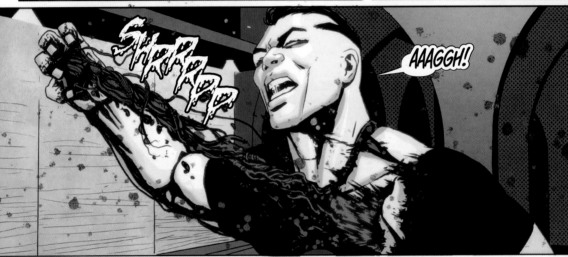

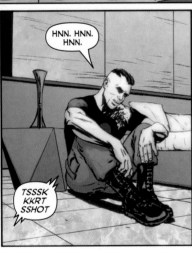

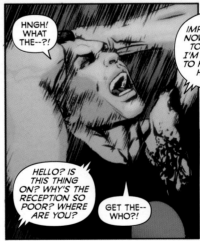

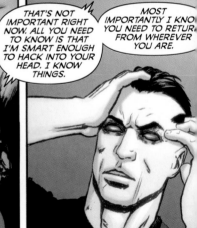

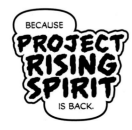

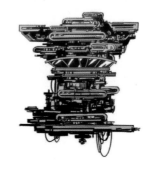

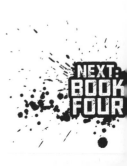

BLOODSHOT #0 COVER C
Art by FRANCIS PORTELA

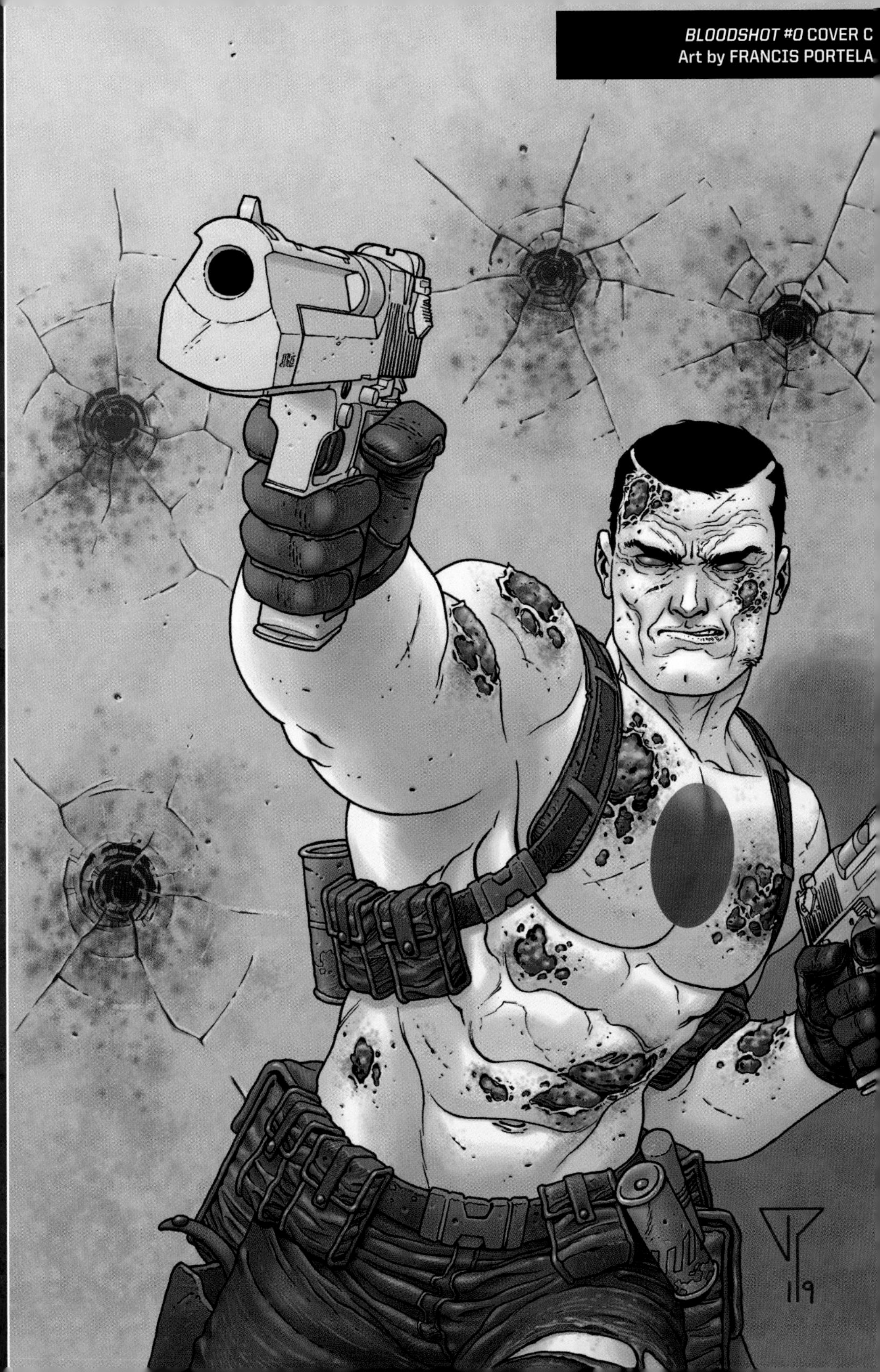

Art by NIK VIRELLA

BLOODSHOT #8 COVER C
Art by CRYSSY CHEUNG

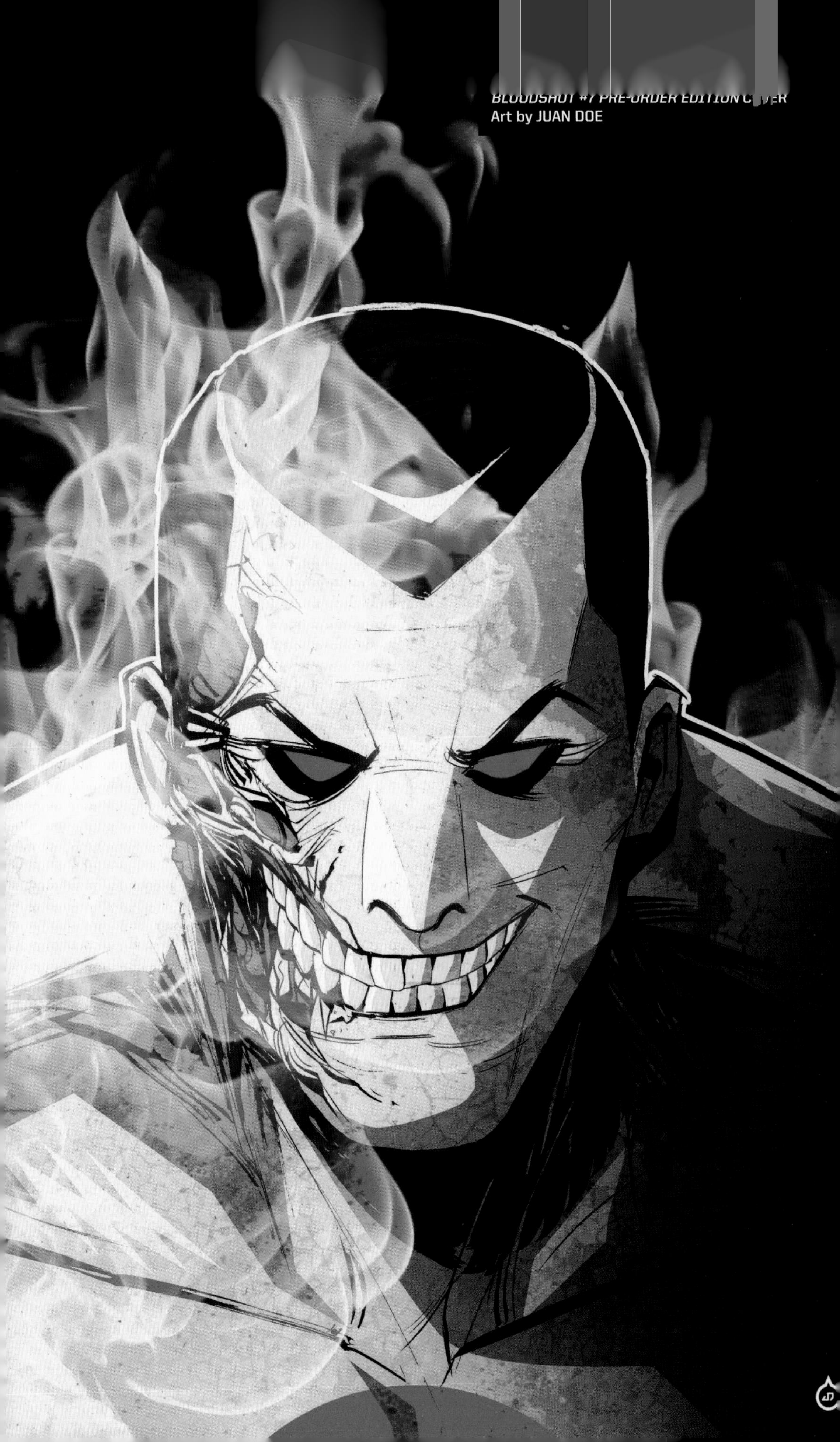

BLOODSHOT #7 PRE-ORDER EDITION COVER
Art by JUAN DOE

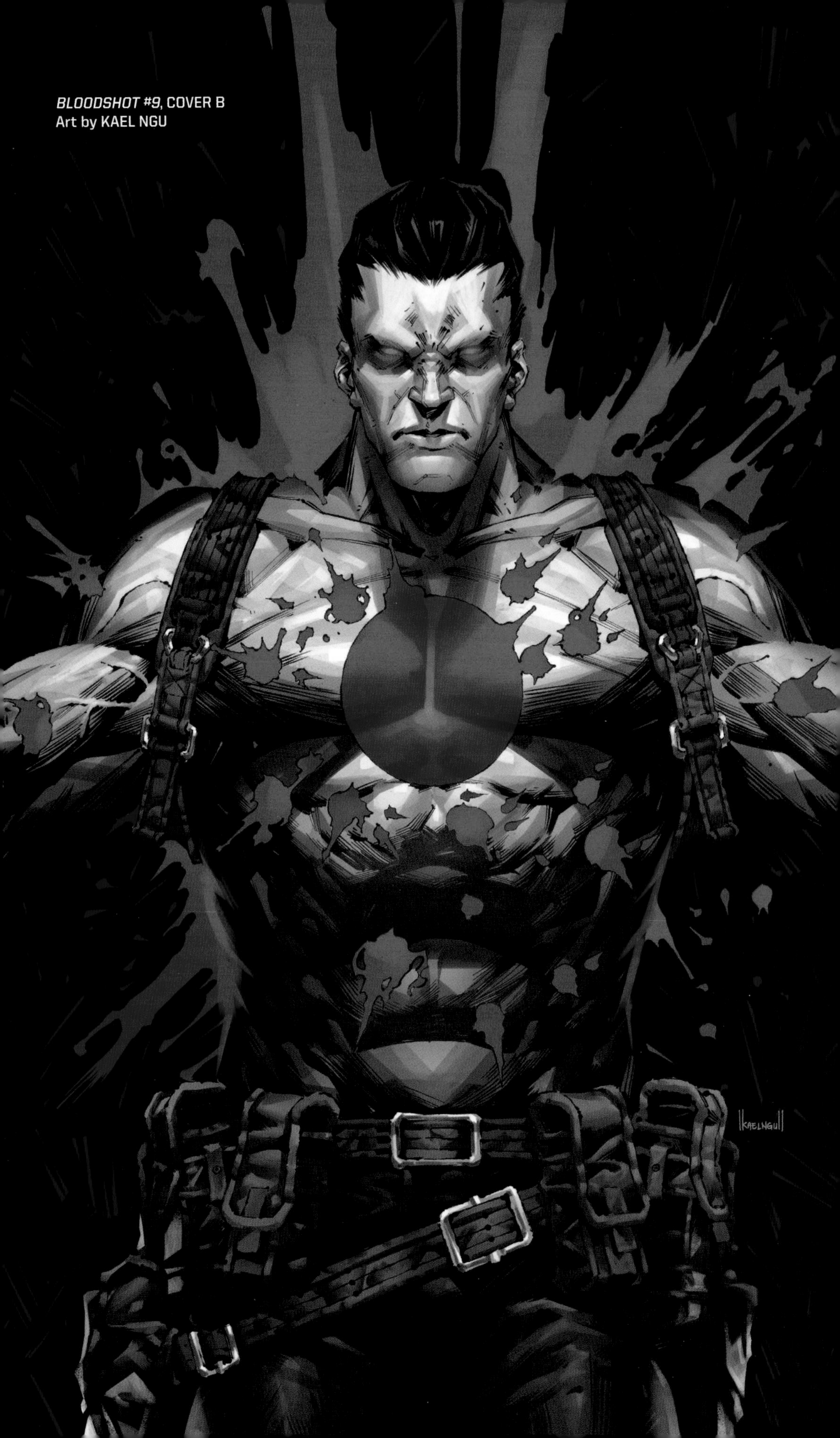
KAELNGU

BLOODSHOT #9, COVER B
Art by KAEL NGU

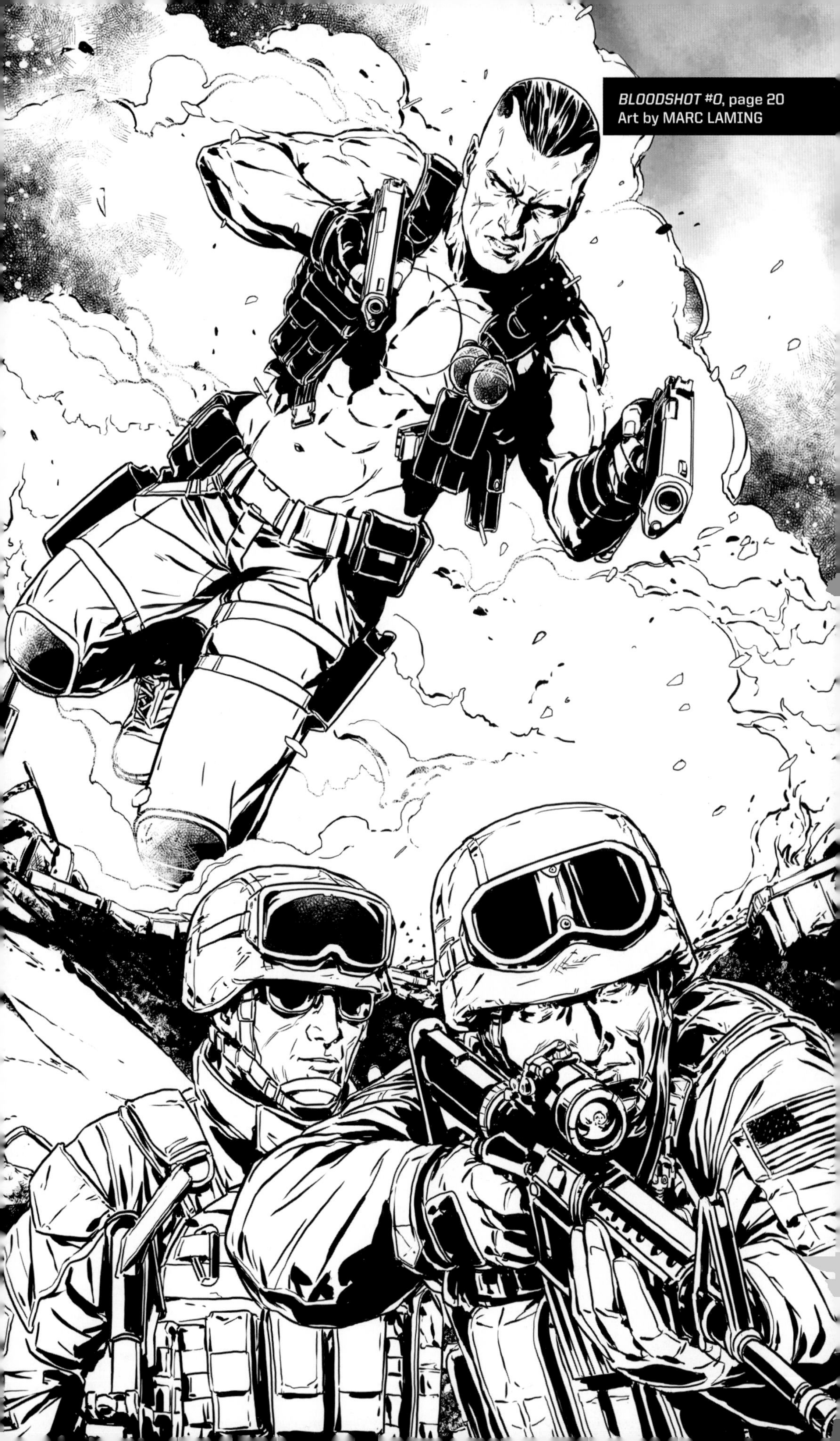

BLOODSHOT #0, page 20
Art by MARC LAMING

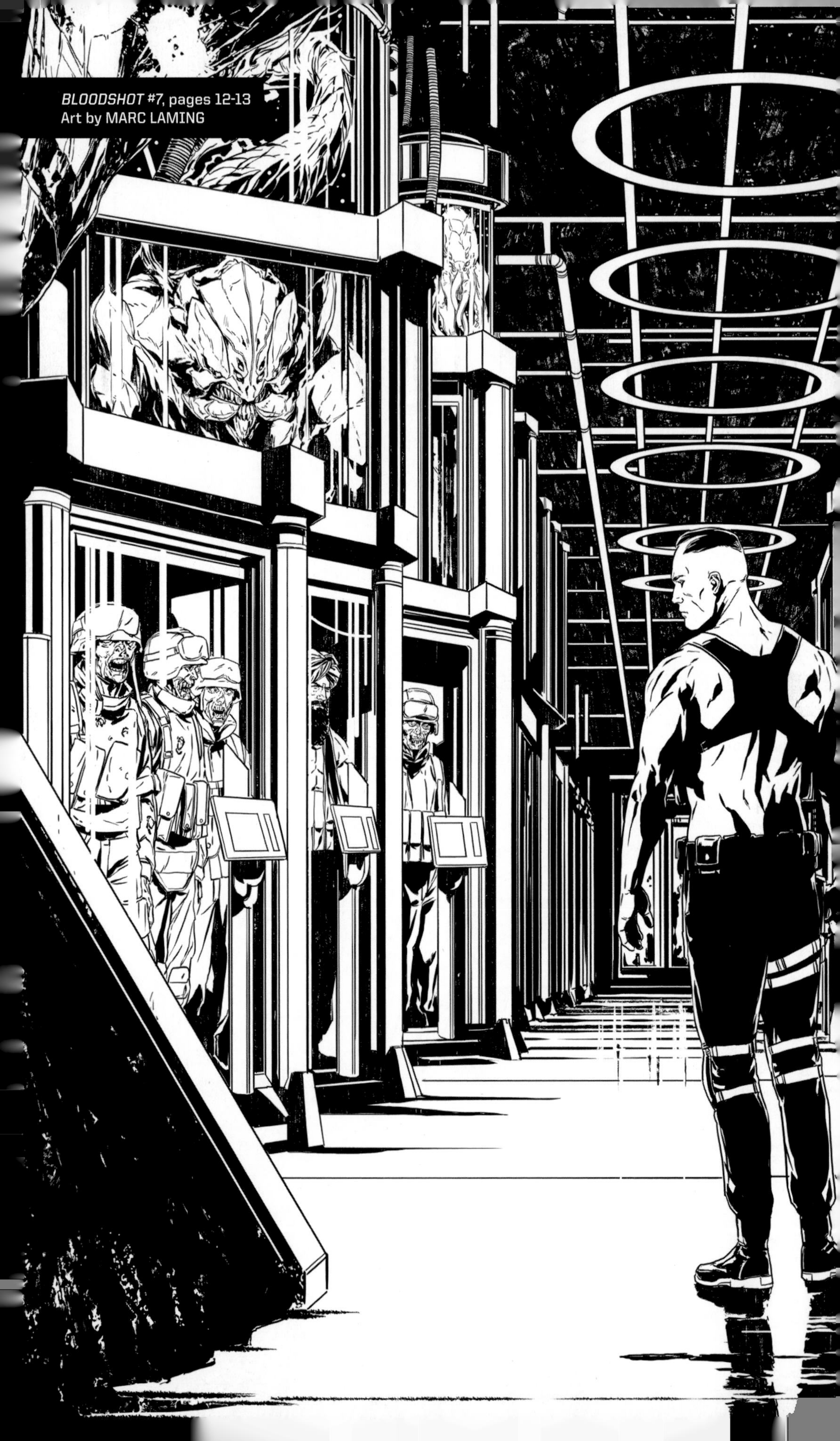

BLOODSHOT #7, pages 12-13
Art by MARC LAMING

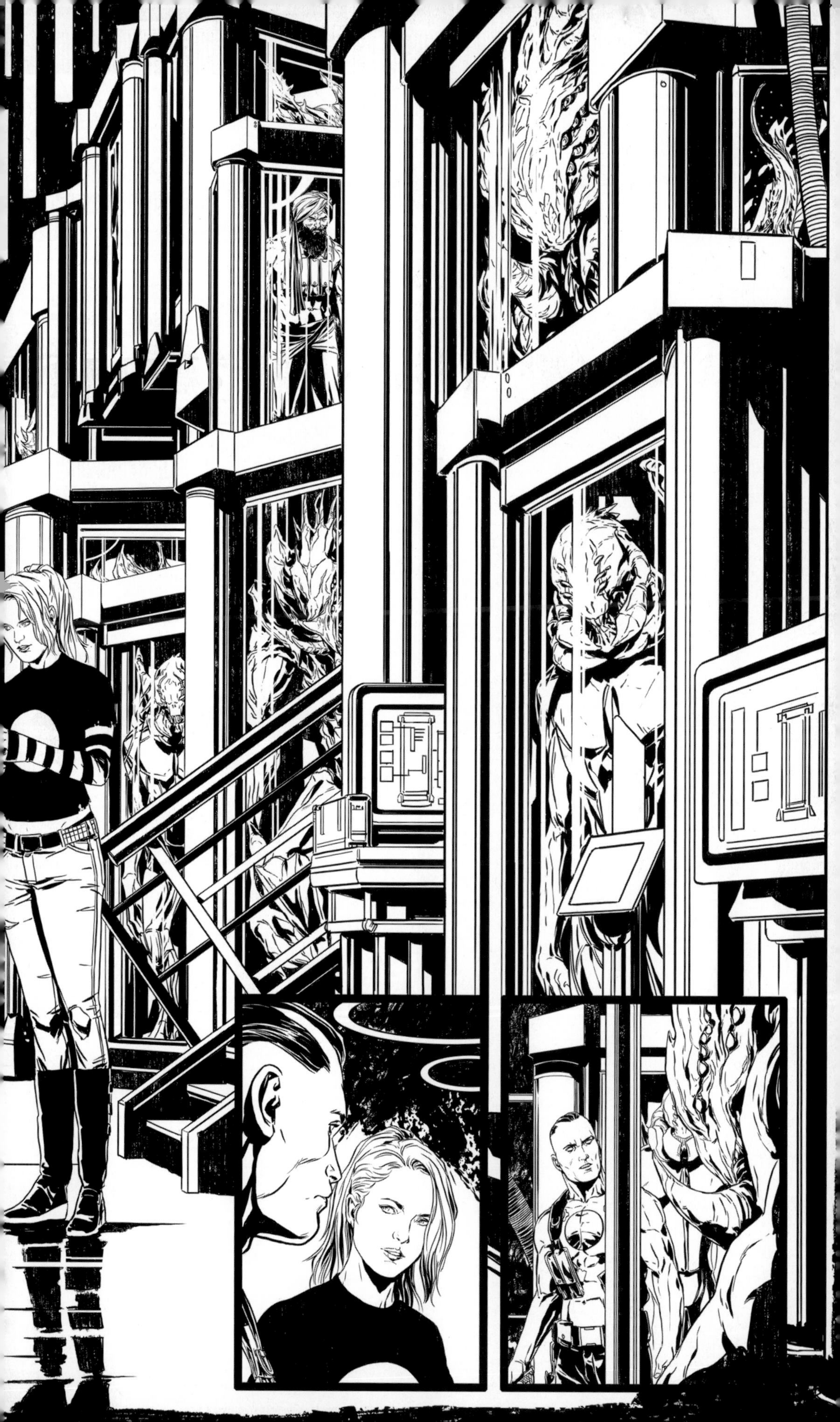

BLOODSHOT #7, pages 18, 19, and (facing) 20
Art by MARC LAMING

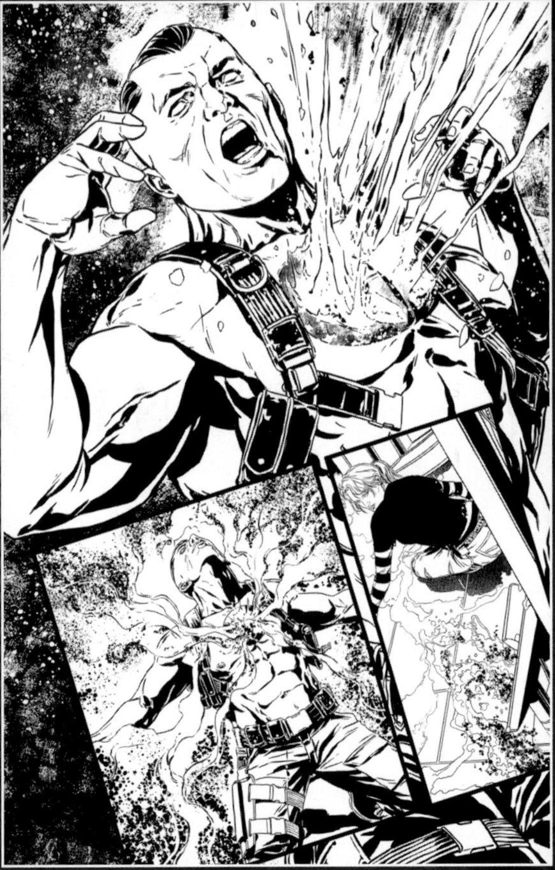

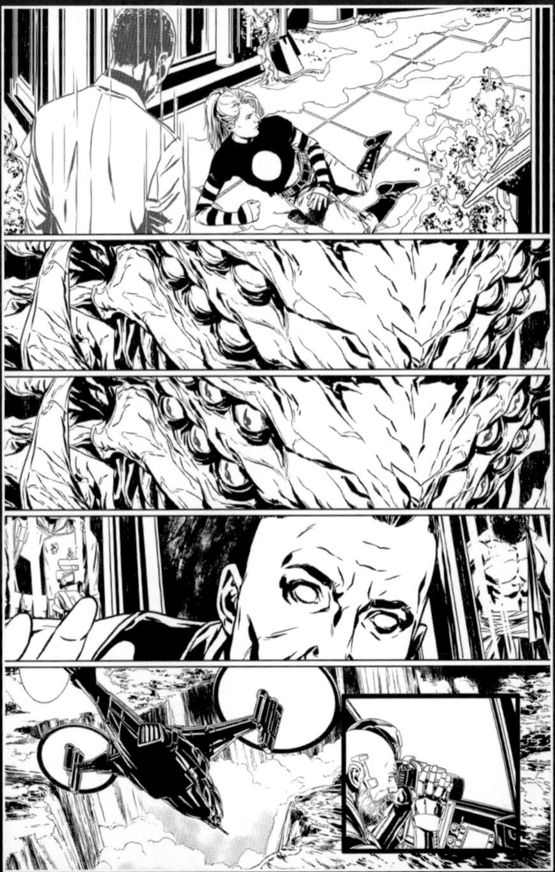

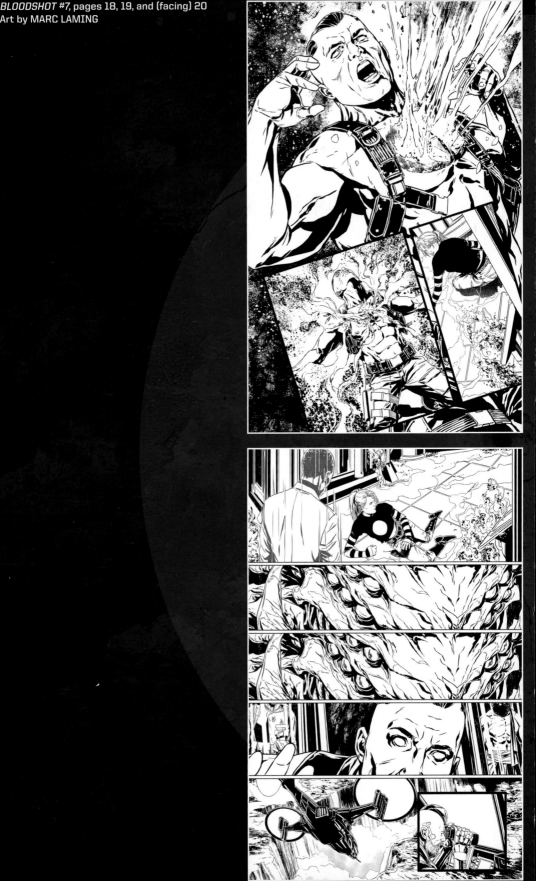

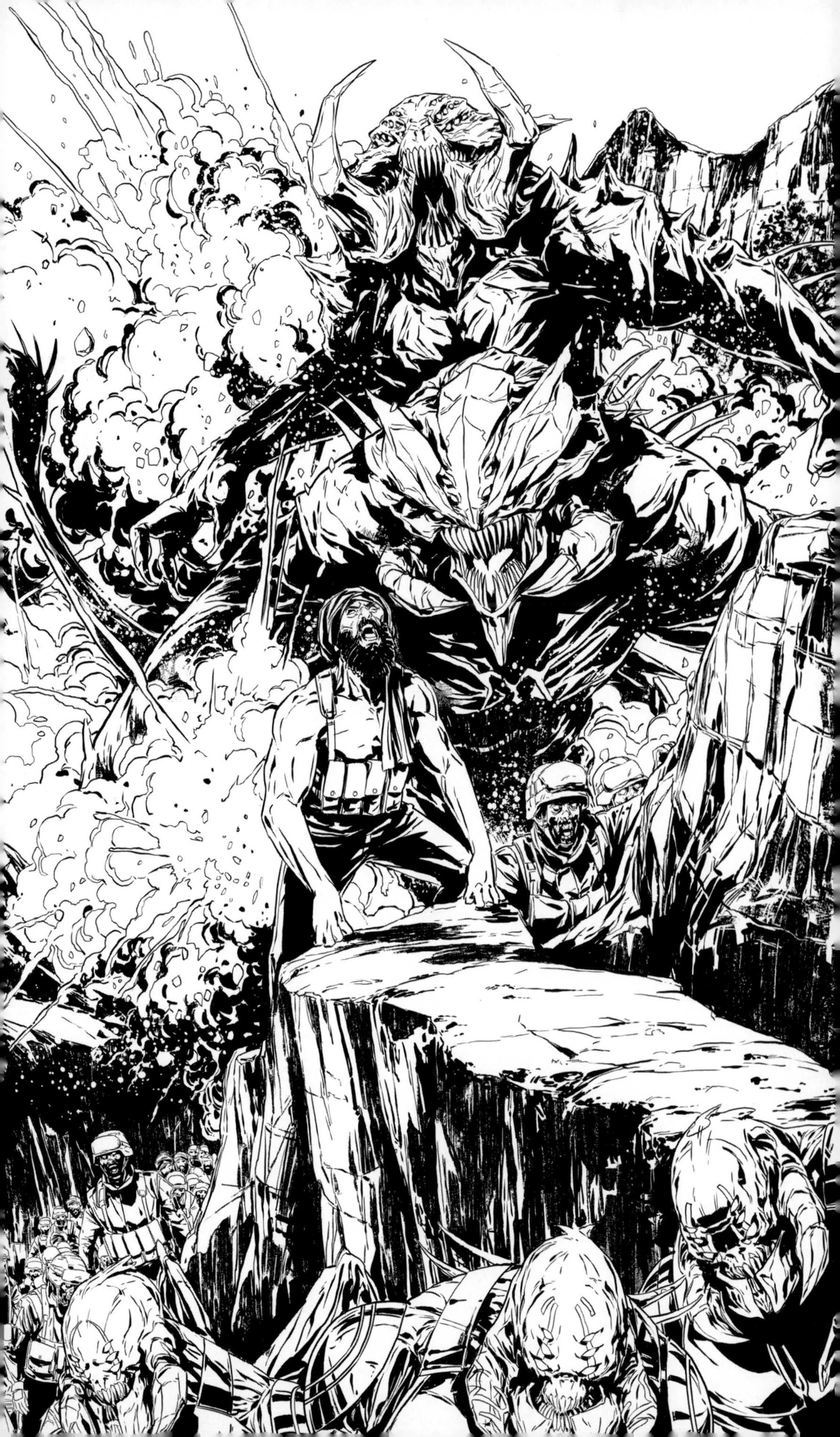

BLOODSHOT #9, pages 1, 2, and (facing) 6
Art by MARC LAMING and JASON MASTERS

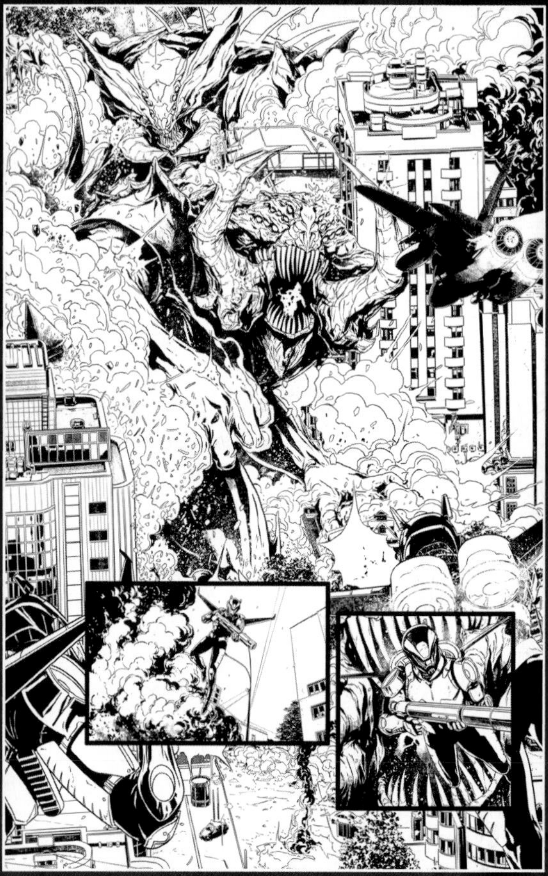

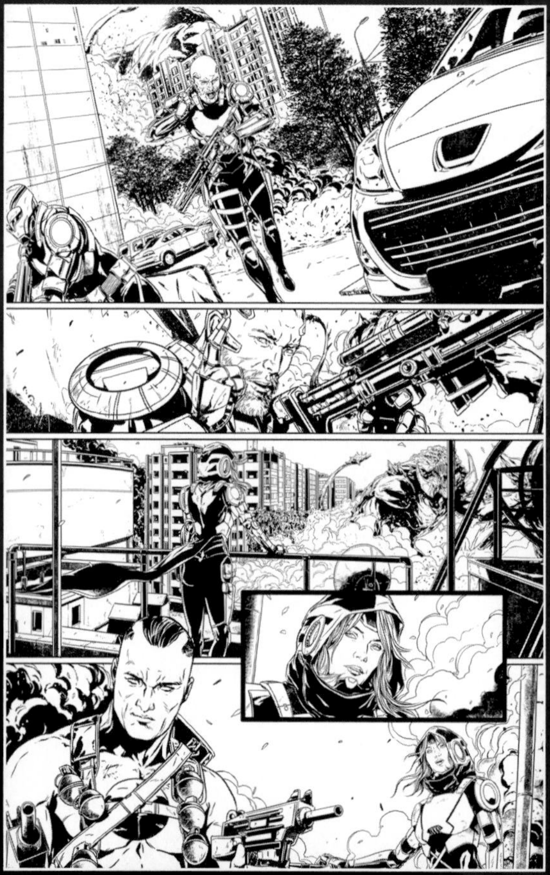

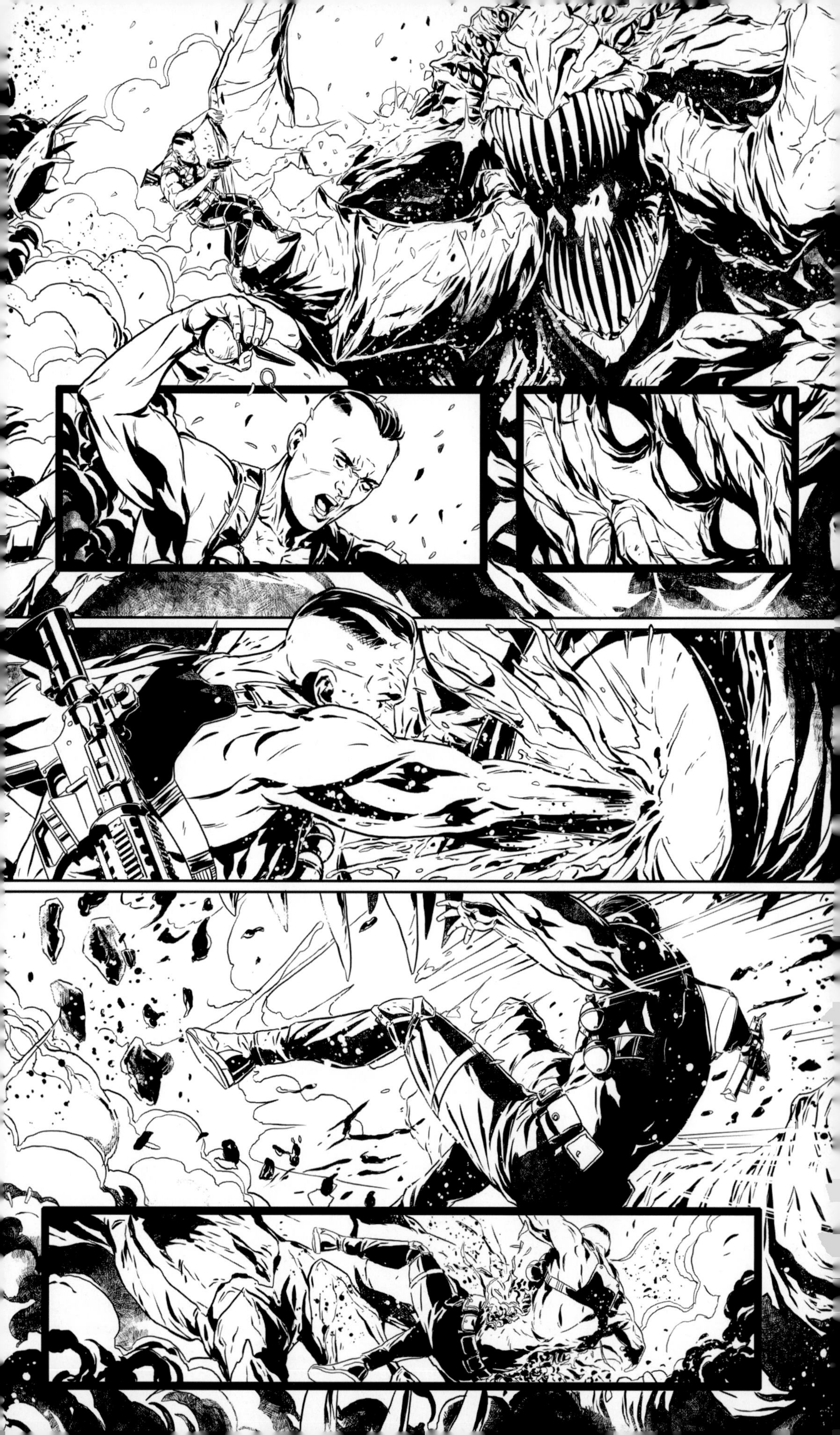

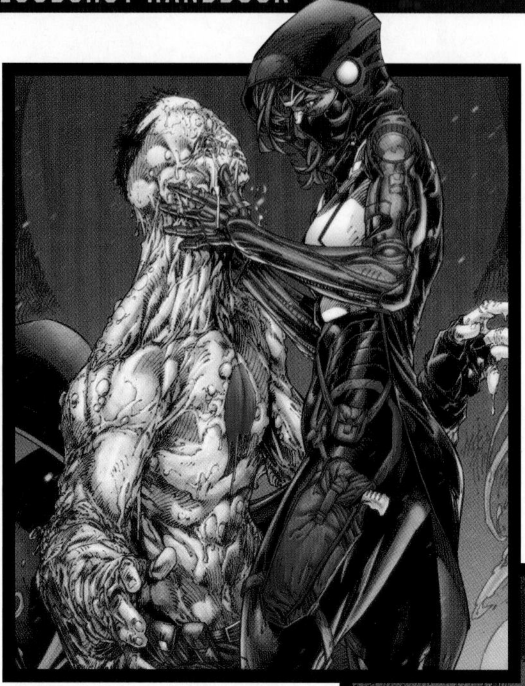

EIDOLON:

REAL NAME: Mina Nez

AFFILIATION: Black Bar, Sons of the Last Flesh (formerly)

BASE OF OPERATIONS: Black Bar Headquarters

FIRST APPEARANCE: Bloodshot (2019) #1

CAPABILITIES: The psionic ability to "communicate" with DNA, allowing her to detect and track individuals of interest, as well as to dramatically overwrite their genetic code.

HISTORY: Used for years by the scientific cult, **Sons of the Last Flesh**, Eidolon was captured by Project Rising Spirit with the aid of Bloodshot, and ultimately sold into service with **Black Bar**. Resenting her captors, Eidolon welcomed Bloodshot's rescue when he returned to liberate her from Black Bar.

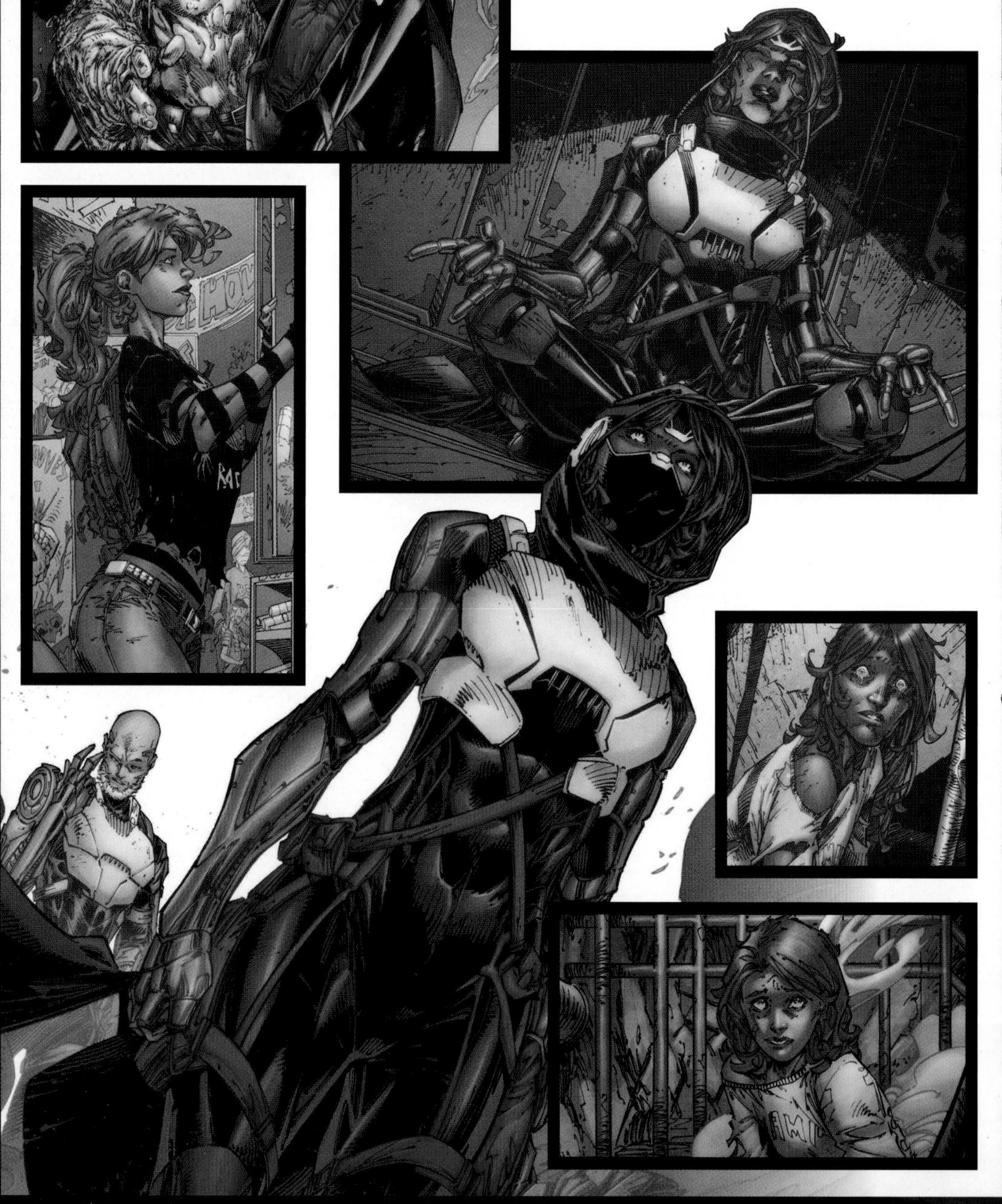

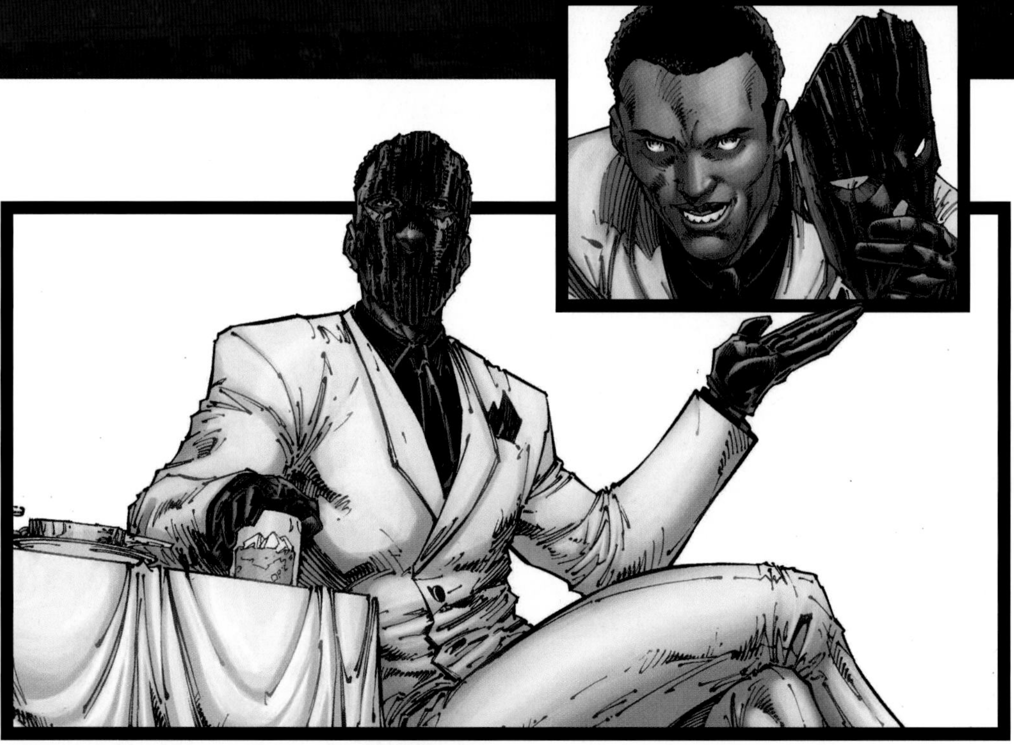

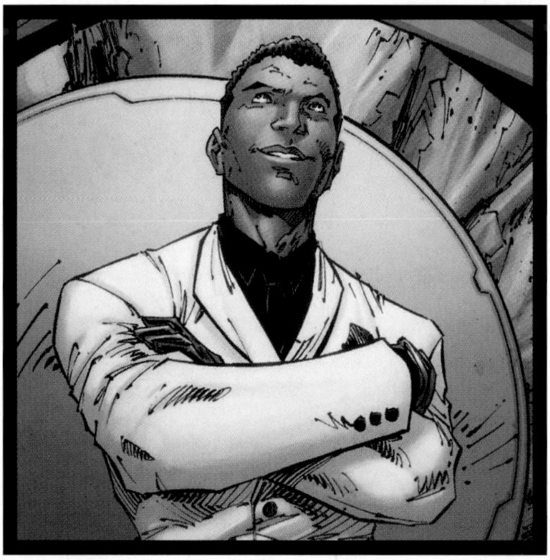

NIX:

KNOW ALIASES: Michael Heel, Jonathan Brock, Ben Pryce

AFFILIATION: The Burned, MI6 (formerly)

BASE OF OPERATIONS: The Desolate House

FIRST APPEARANCE: Bloodshot (2019) #3

CAPABILITIES: Extensive counterintelligence training, expert marksmanship and hand-to-hand combat training, access to the the Burned's advanced covert technology.

HISTORY: Feeling abused and discarded after years of service at MI6, Agent Nix founded **The Burned** as a haven for disavowed agents to pursue their own agendas. Pooling the stolen resources of the world's major intelligence agencies, Burned agents have access to advanced cloaking technology, which Nix helped install in Bloodshot.

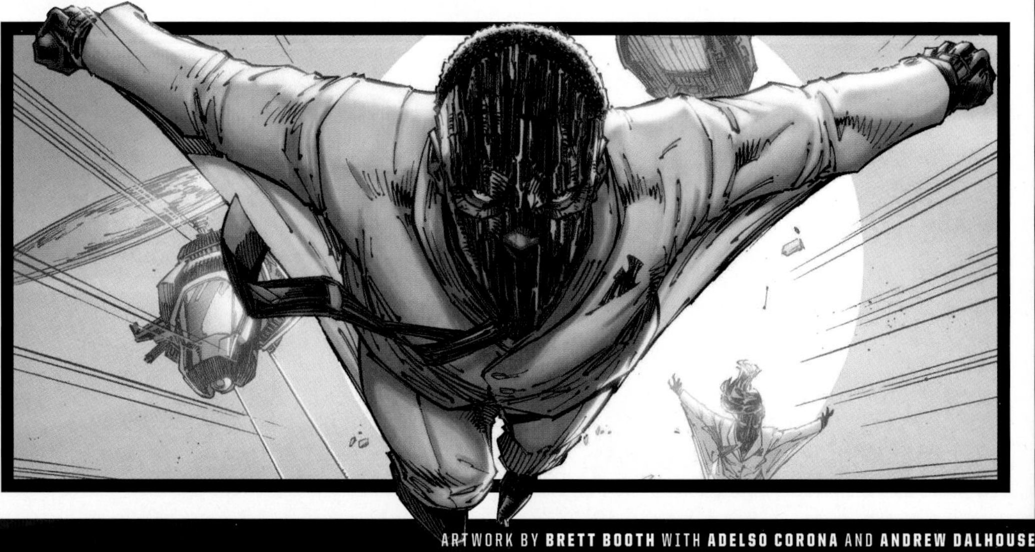

ARTWORK BY **BRETT BOOTH** WITH **ADELSO CORONA** AND **ANDREW DALHOUSE**

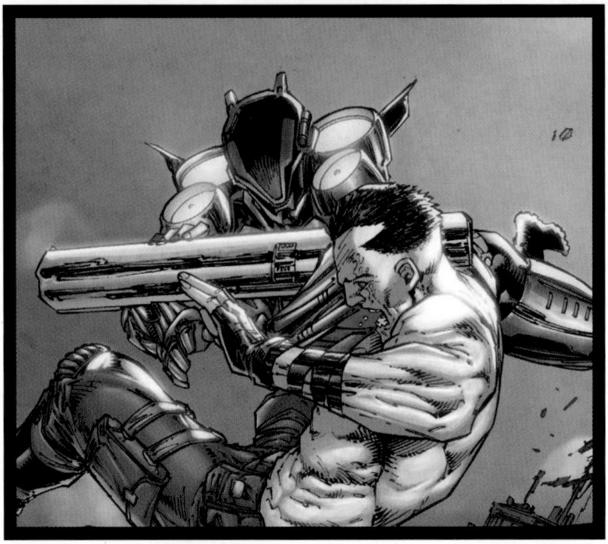

APOSTLE AIR SQUAD:

AFFILIATION: Black Bar

BASE OF OPERATIONS: Mobile

FIRST APPEARANCE: Bloodshot (2019) #2

CAPABILITIES: Advanced military technology including wareable ultralight flight suit, EMP weapons, and tracking devices.

HISTORY: Serving at the pleasure of General Grayle, the Apostle Air Squad has flown for years as Black Bar's elite air division. In their first encounter with Bloodshot, he managed to use their own weapons against them, hacking their flight computers to eliminate them from the fight. This left the survivors -- most notably squad leader, Zealot, eager for a rematch.

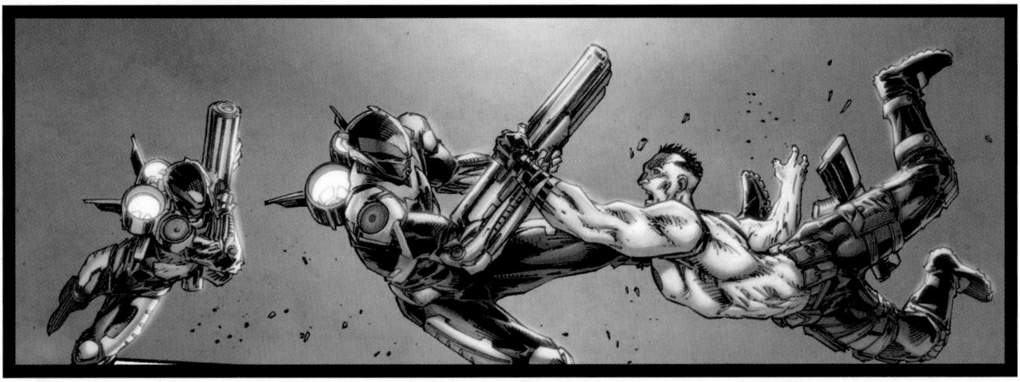

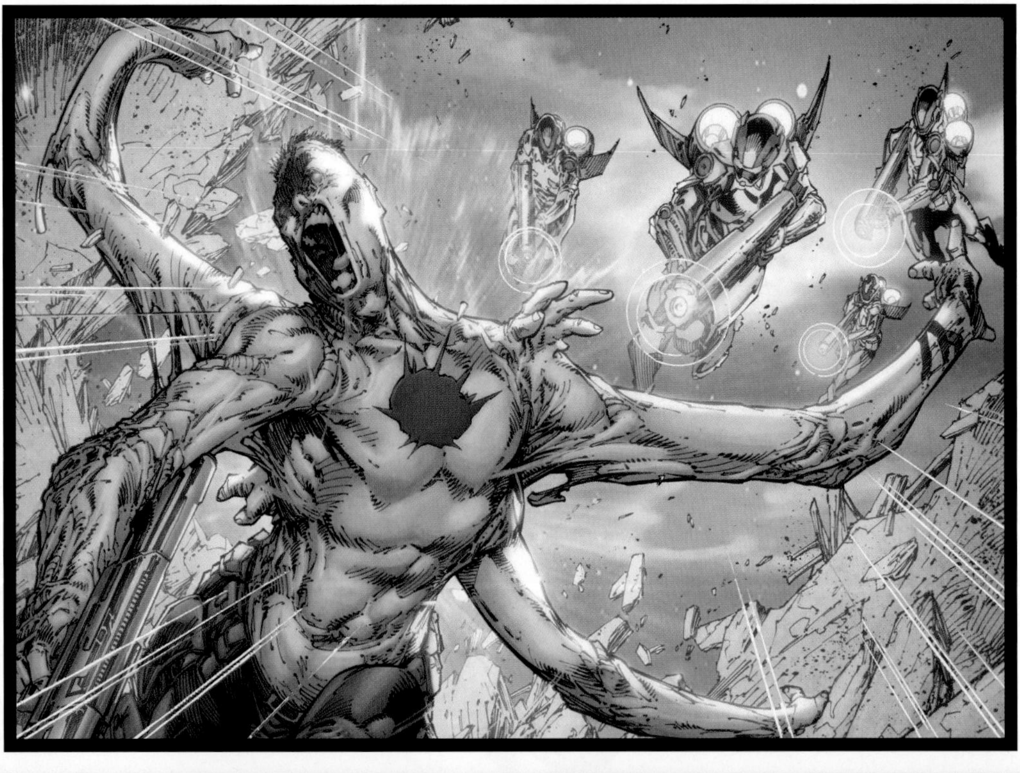

ARTWORK BY **BRETT BOOTH** WITH **ADELSO CORONA** AND **ANDREW DALHOUSE**

THE BURNED:

KNOWN ENEMIES: Black Bar, all international intelligence agencies

NOTABLE MEMBERS: Agent Nix, Ms. Mienai, Agent Zilch, Agent Brink, Agent Cant (deceased)

BASE OF OPERATIONS: The Desolate House

FIRST APPEARANCE: Bloodsho (2019) #3

HISTORY: Made up of the disavowed "burned" agents of the world's intelligence agencies, The Burned pool their resources and information to correct injustices inflicted by their former masters. Their promise of freedom from the governments and agencies that use and abuse them appealed to Bloodshot, but Agent Nix revealed his true colors, secretly manipulating Bloodshot's nanites to release biological weapons from Black Bar's custody.

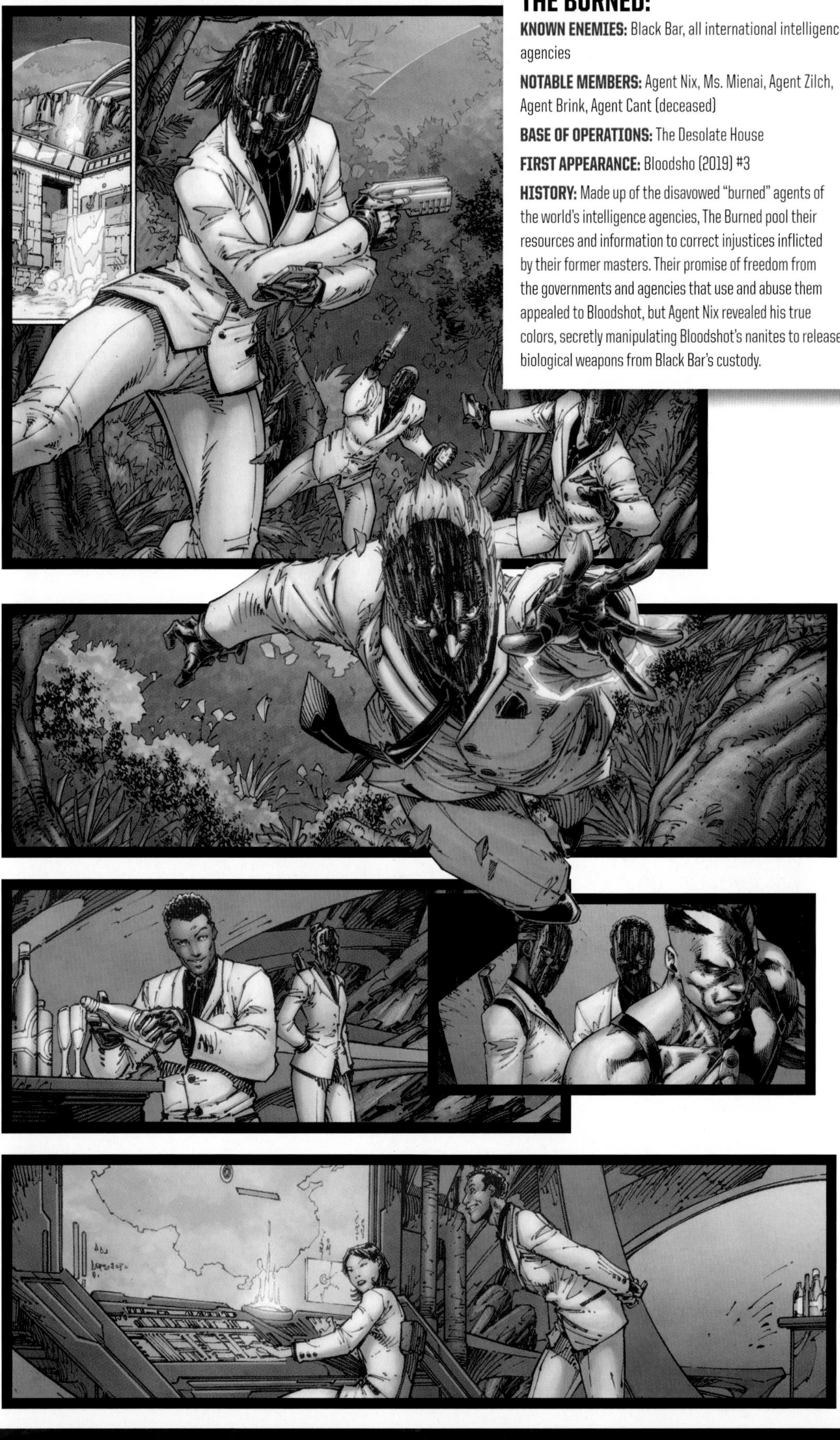

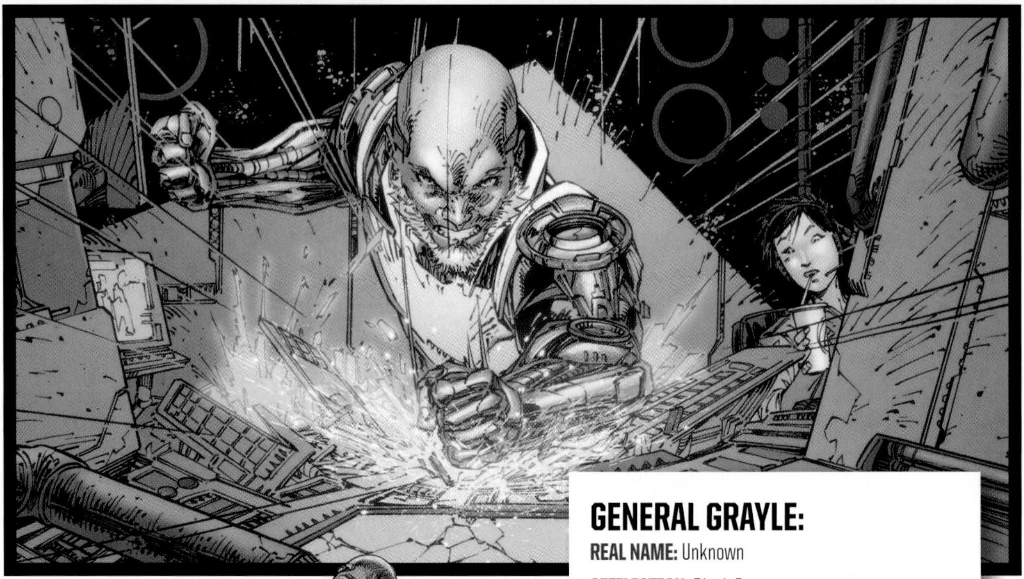

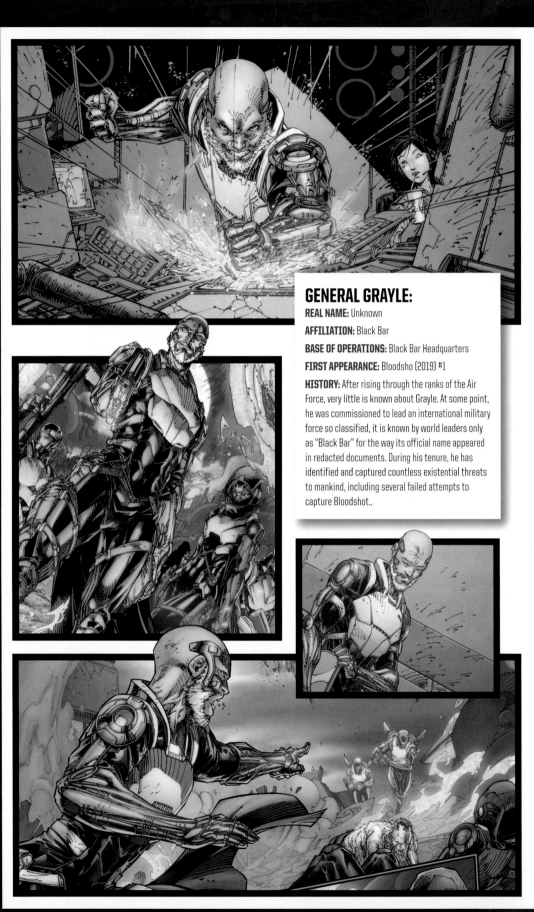

GENERAL GRAYLE:

REAL NAME: Unknown

AFFILIATION: Black Bar

BASE OF OPERATIONS: Black Bar Headquarters

FIRST APPEARANCE: Bloodsho (2019) #1

HISTORY: After rising through the ranks of the Air Force, very little is known about Grayle. At some point, he was commissioned to lead an international military force so classified, it is known by world leaders only as "Black Bar" for the way its official name appeared in redacted documents. During his tenure, he has identified and captured countless existential threats to mankind, including several failed attempts to capture Bloodshot..

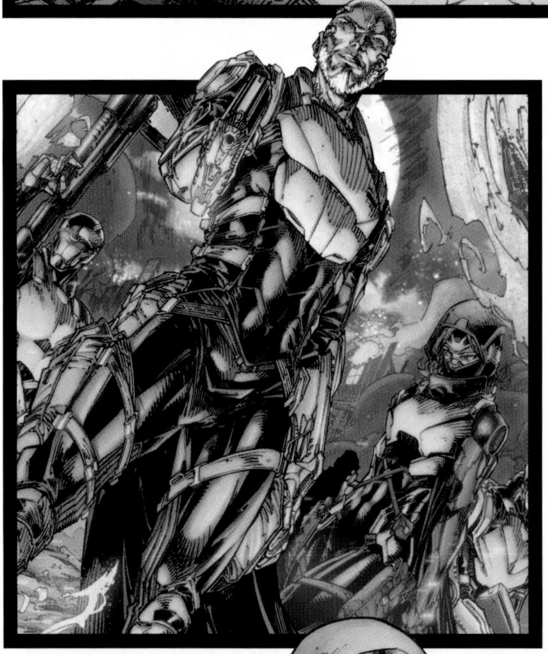

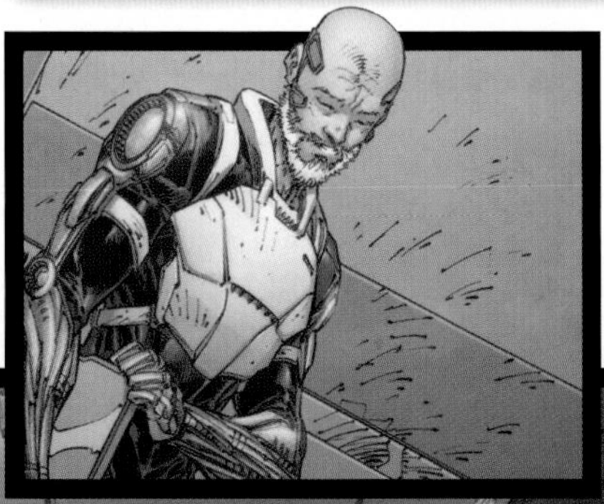

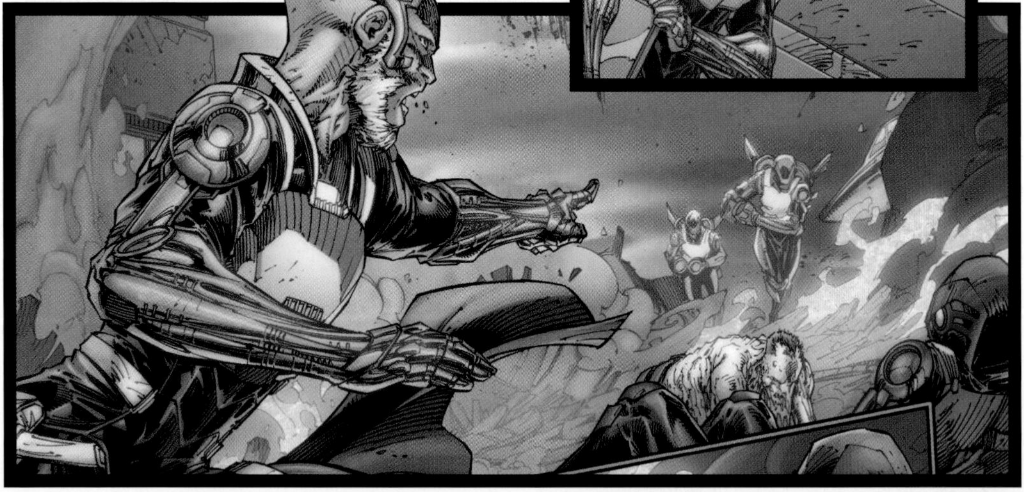

ARTWORK BY **BRETT BOOTH** WITH **ADELSO CORONA** AND **ANDREW DALHOUSE**

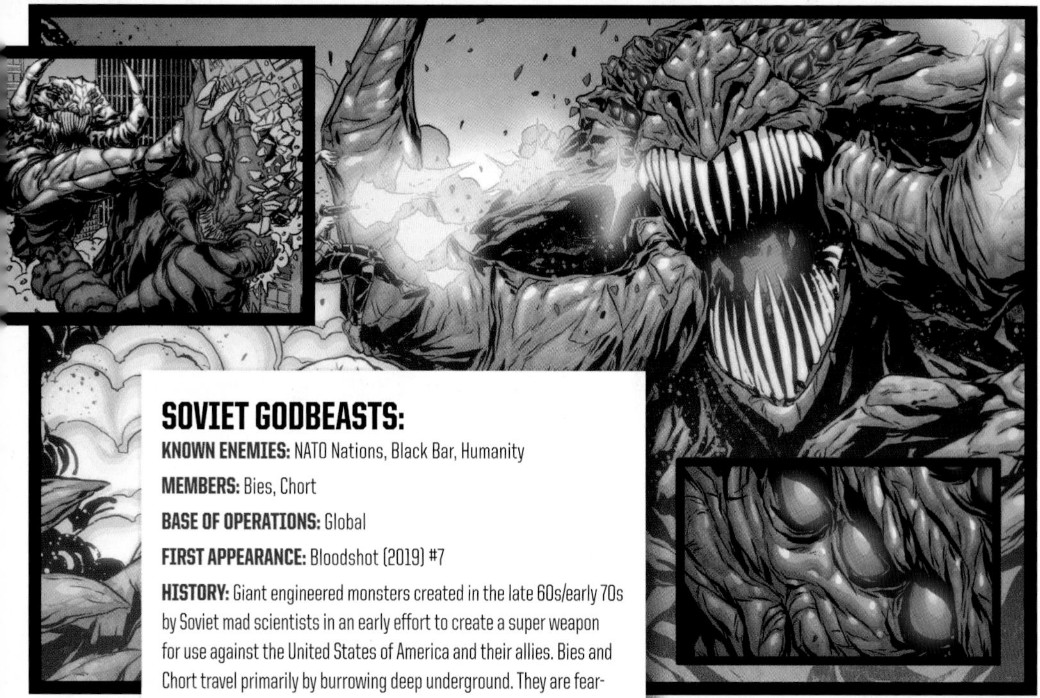

SOVIET GODBEASTS:

KNOWN ENEMIES: NATO Nations, Black Bar, Humanity

MEMBERS: Bies, Chort

BASE OF OPERATIONS: Global

FIRST APPEARANCE: Bloodshot (2019) #7

HISTORY: Giant engineered monsters created in the late 60s/early 70s by Soviet mad scientists in an early effort to create a super weapon for use against the United States of America and their allies. Bies and Chort travel primarily by burrowing deep underground. They are fearsome, vicious creatures capable of disastrous levels of destruction.

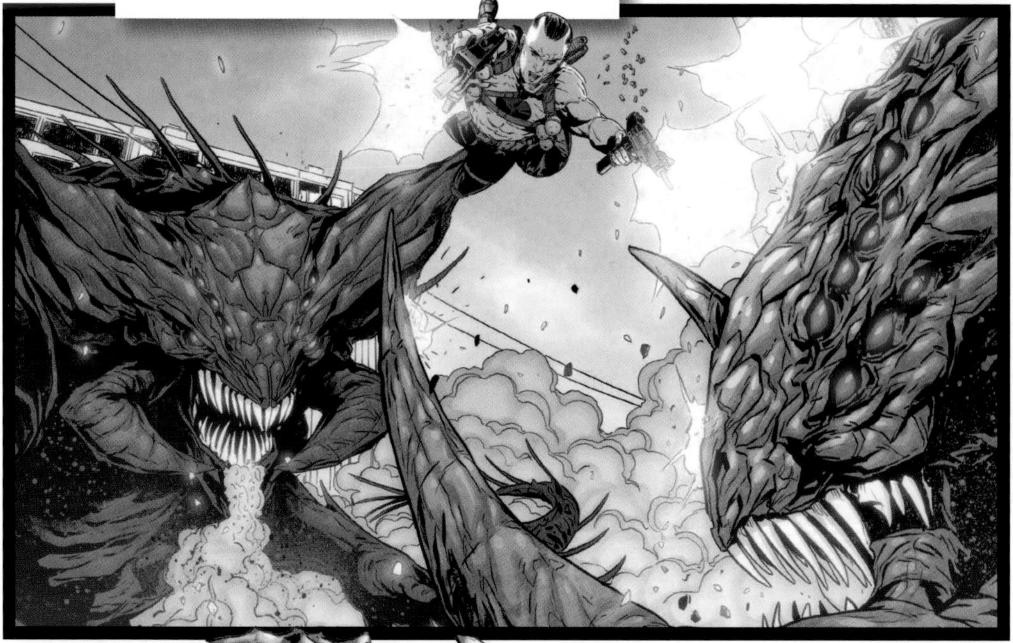

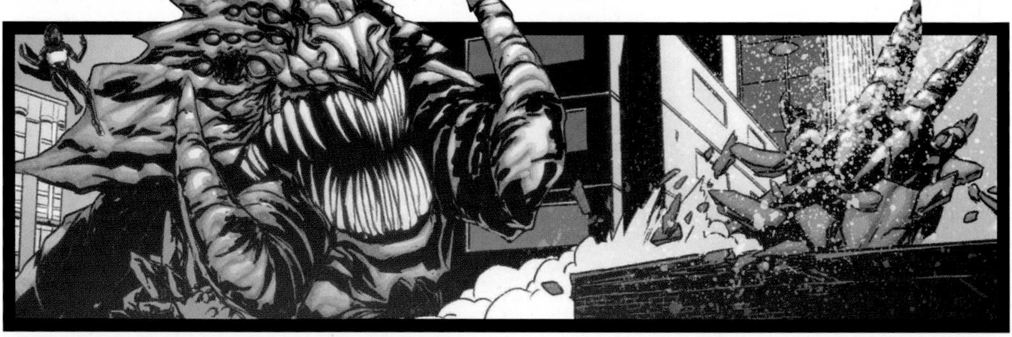

EXPLORE THE VALIANT U

ACTION & ADVENTURE

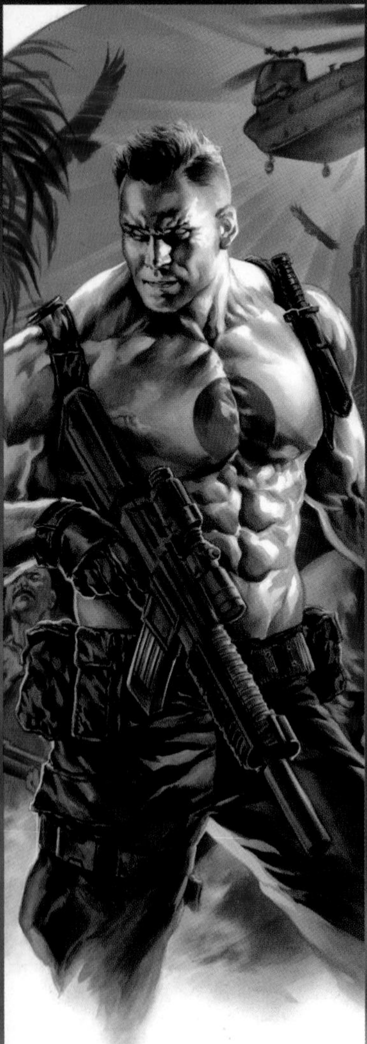

BLOODSHOT BOOK ONE
ISBN: 978-1-68215-255-3
NINJA-K VOL. 1: THE NINJA FILES
ISBN: 978-1-68215-259-1
SAVAGE
ISBN: 978-1-68215-189-1
WRATH OF THE ETERNAL WARRIOR VOL. 1: RISEN
ISBN: 978-1-68215-123-5
X-O MANOWAR (2017) VOL. 1: SOLDIER
ISBN: 978-1-68215-205-8

BLOCKBUSTER ADVENTURE

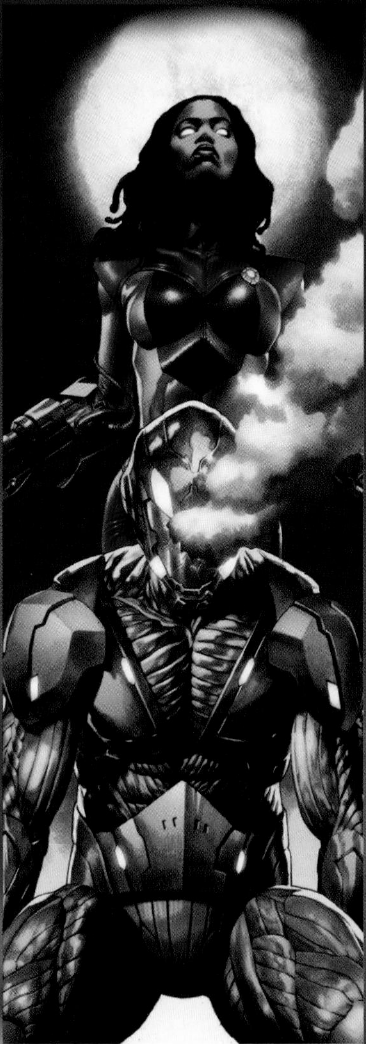

4001 A.D.
ISBN: 978-1-68215-143-3
ARMOR HUNTERS
ISBN: 978-1-939346-45-2
BOOK OF DEATH
ISBN: 978-1-939346-97-1
FALLEN WORLD
ISBN: 978-1-68215-331-4
HARBINGER WARS
ISBN: 978-1-939346-09-4
HARBINGER WARS 2
ISBN: 978-1-68215-289-8
INCURSION
ISBN: 978-1-68215-303-1
THE VALIANT
ISBN: 978-1-939346-60-5

COMEDY

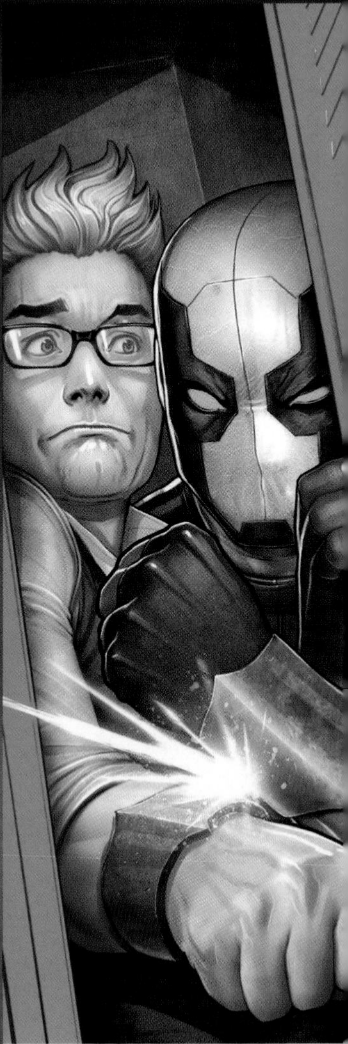

A&A: THE ADVENTURES OF ARCHER & ARMSTRONG VOL. 1: IN THE BAG
ISBN: 978-1-68215-149-5
THE DELINQUENTS
ISBN: 978-1-939346-51-3
QUANTUM AND WOODY! (2020): EARTH'S LAST CHOICE
ISBN: 978-1-68215-362-8

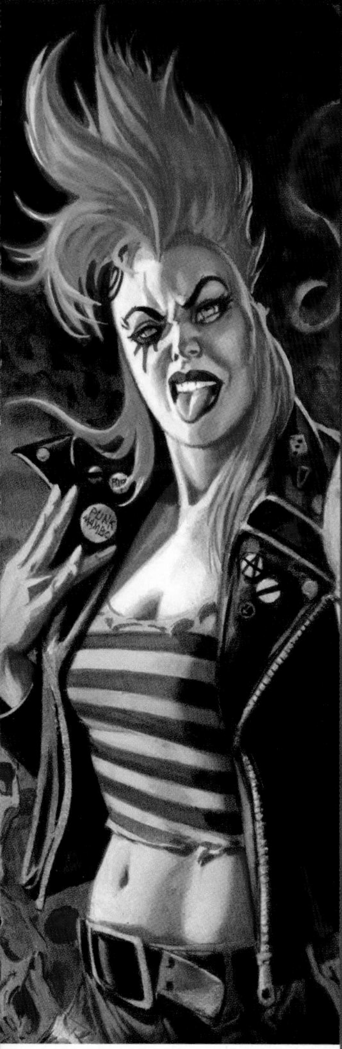

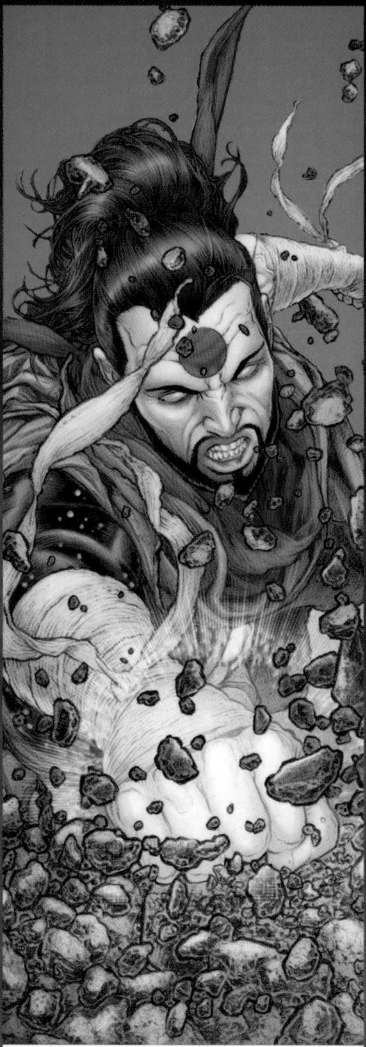

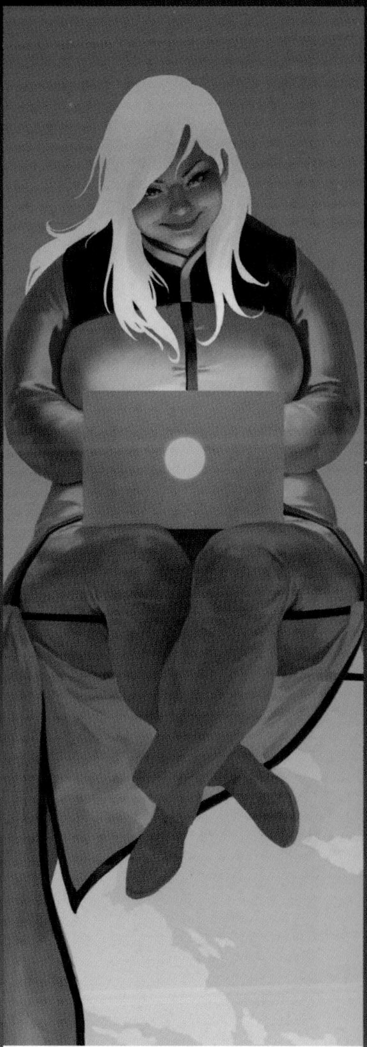

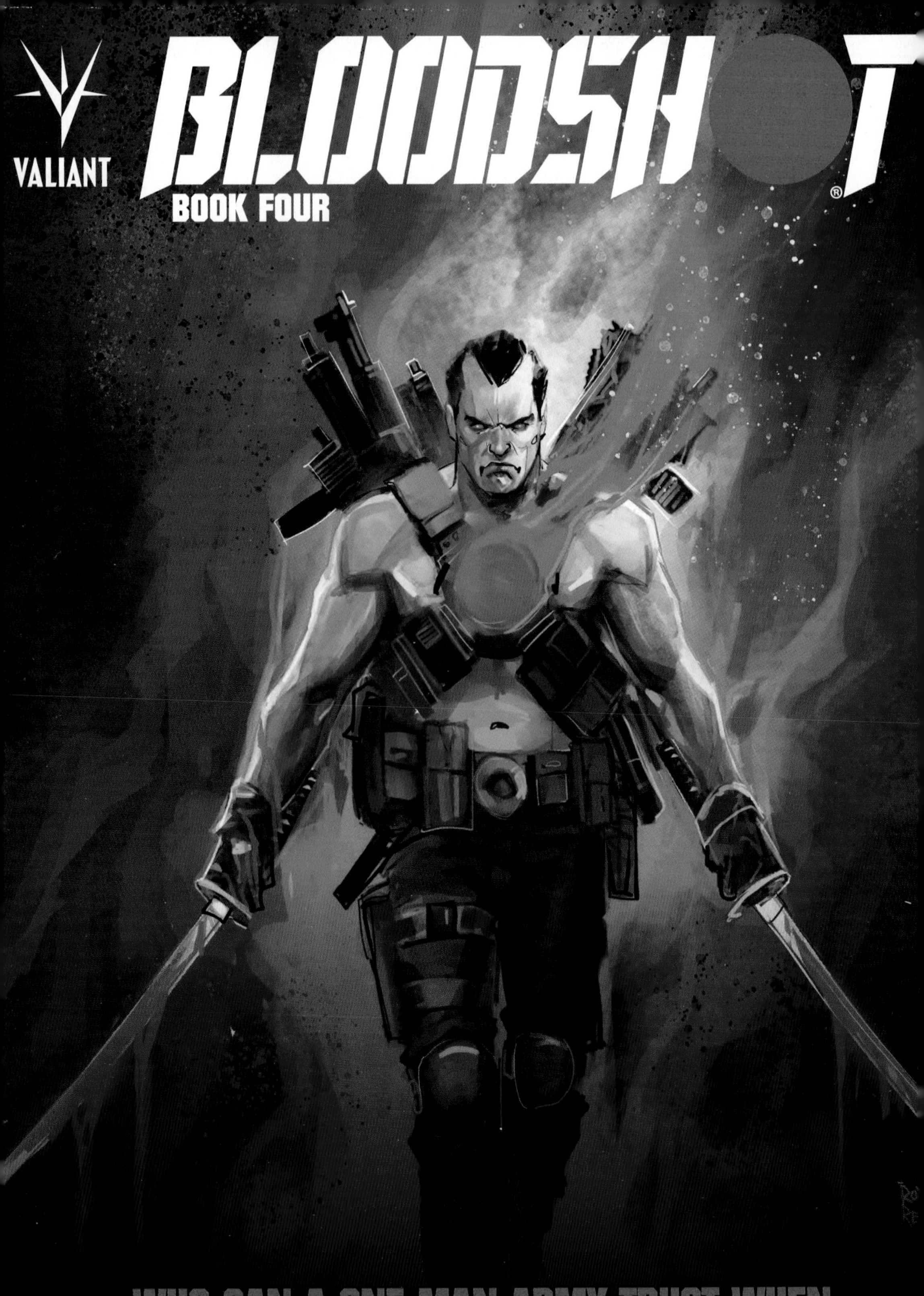
VALIANT
BLOODSHOT
BOOK FOUR

WHO CAN A ONE-MAN ARMY TRUST WHEN EVERYONE'S TRYING TO KILL HIM?

New York Times best-selling writer Tim Seeley (*Nightwing*) joins superstar artist Brett Booth (*Titans*) on Bloodshot's road to retribution in the next incendiary volume of the series CBR calls "a fast brutal return for Valiant's action hero."

Collecting BLOODSHOT #10–12, along with material from VALIANT 2020: THE YEAR OF HEROES FCBD SPECIAL.

TRADE PAPERBACK
ISBN: 978-1-68215-376-5